FROM
SOCIAL WORKER
TO CRIMEFIGHTER

FROM
SOCIAL WORKER
TO CRIMEFIGHTER

Women in United States Municipal Policing

Dorothy Moses Schulz

Westport, Connecticut
London

Library of Congress Cataloging-in-Publication Data

Schulz, Dorothy Moses.
    From social worker to crimefighter : women in United States
municipal policing / Dorothy Moses Schulz.
        p.   cm.
    Includes bibliographical references and index.
    ISBN 0–275–94996–6 (hc : alk. paper). — ISBN 0–275–95174–X (pb :
alk. paper)
    1. Policewomen—United States—History.   I. Title.
HV8023.S28   1995
363.2'082—dc20   94–42841

British Library Cataloguing in Publication Data is available.

Library of Congress Catalog Card Number: 94–42841
ISBN: 0–275–94996–6
      0–275–95174–X (pbk.)

First published in 1995

Praeger Publishers, 88 Post Road West, Westport, CT 06881
An imprint of Greenwood Publishing Group, Inc.

Printed in the United States of America

The paper used in this book complies with the
Permanent Paper Standard issued by the National
Information Standards Organization (Z39.48–1984).

10 9 8 7 6 5 4 3 2 1

Copyright Acknowledgments

The author and publisher gratefully acknowledge permission for the use of the following
material:

Portions of Chapter 1 appeared previously as "The Police Matron Movement: Paving the
Way for Policewomen," by Dorothy M. Schulz, in *Police Studies* 12, no. 3 (Fall 1989) and is
used with the permission of *Police Studies*.

Portions of Chapter 5 appeared previously as "Policewomen in the 1950s: Paving the Way
for Patrol," by Dorothy M. Schulz in *Women & Criminal Justice* 4, no. 2, 1993 and is used with
the permission of The Haworth Press.

Every reasonable effort has been made to trace the owners of copyright materials in this
book, but in some instances this has proven impossible. The author and publisher will be
glad to receive information leading to more complete acknowledgments in subsequent print-
ings of the book and in the meantime extend their apologies for any omissions.

To my parents, Henry and Marion Moses

and to my husband, David

Contents

Preface

While it is certainly true that every book is the creation of its author, few authors are able to turn ideas into a self-contained work without the advice and assistance of others. Certainly, this is so in my case. Among those whose efforts must be recognized are David Reimers and Paul Baker, friends and advisors who taught me that a historian faces quite different challenges from those of a working police officer; Susan Ware, who sharpened my portrait of policewomen within a women's history context; and Don White, who added a cultural perspective that is uncommon in writings on police. Clarice Feinman enriched comparisons with women in corrections and in the process became a friend, while Barbara Raffel Price offered not only her knowledge, but her moral support as a friend and as a mentor. I thank them all, but take full responsibility for the final product.

Each of the editors with whom I worked at the Greenwood Publishing Group helped ease the task of creating the present work.

Thanks are also due the librarians at the New York University Elmer Holmes Bobst Library and the John Jay College of Criminal Justice Lloyd George Sealy Library. It is no exaggeration that a national study of the police could not have been undertaken without the resources of John Jay's special collection, which includes untapped riches in police history. The New York Public Library, particularly "the Annex," yielded an array of early police magazines as well as publications of the International Association of Policewomen.

Among those who also aided me were colleagues in law enforcement. Many were friends at the start; many became friends in the course of this project. Special thanks to Mary Rita Ostrander (who, unfortunately, did not live to see this book in print) and Lois Lundell Higgins for early papers of—and insights into—the International Association of Women Police; Ronald C. Van Raalte for information gathered during his research for the Law Enforcement Memorial Association; Anne Findlay Patton for her entertaining master's essay on San Diego matrons and policewomen; and Felicia Shpritzer, a long-time friend who inspired me to learn more about what made her and her generation of policewomen different from those who came before them.

Inspiration of a different sort came from my family. My parents believed I was glued to my computer, for whenever they called or visited, that's where I was.

Very special thanks are due my husband, David, who somehow survived the disruption to normal living this book engendered. A writer himself, he was able to understand my obsession with the project, if not the length of time and amount of living space it took.

Abbreviations

ASHA	American Social Hygiene Association
GFWC	General Federation of Women's Clubs
IACP	International Association of Chiefs of Police
IAP	International Association of Policewomen
IAWP	International Association of Women Police
LAPD	Los Angeles Police Department
NCCC	National Conference of Charities and Correction
NCSW	National Conference of Social Workers
NYCPD	New York City Police Department
PAS	Public Administration Service
WCTU	Women's Christian Temperance Union
WPOAC	Women Peace Officer's Association of California

FROM
SOCIAL WORKER
TO CRIMEFIGHTER

Introduction

No civilian occupation in the United States (with the possible exception of firefighting) is more identified with masculine stereotypes than policing, and no facet of policing is viewed as more of a male preserve than uniform patrol. Yet, by the end of 1990, women comprised 12.8 percent of all sworn officers in municipal departments serving populations over one million, and 8.1 percent of the almost 600,000 sworn officers in all local law enforcement agencies.[1]

Despite the interest in these women, police officers, historians, and police executives have paid scant attention to pioneer policewomen, even though they are an excellent case study of how women used the concept of "women's sphere" to enter the world beyond their homes, and then to create positions for women in police departments in large and small cities. The history of women in policing represents a continuum of women's involvement in the police environment, first in their uniquely female role and today in a unisex role with male colleagues. The history also illustrates how initial demands for a limited, specialized role based on gender were replaced by demands for equality by later generations of women with totally different social histories and self-images. These demands by the late 1960s included participation in uniform patrol duty.

While gender segregation existed, and continues to exist in professions that grew out of women's maternal roles and in occupations in which women workers predominate (teaching, nursing, and social work are obvious examples), women in these fields have achieved a degree of equality without repudiating their past. Policewomen, on the other hand, were forced to reject their history to move into the mainstream of their profession. This, too, may account for the absence of any serious historical look at women in police service.

Over the past 25 years, much has been written about women's "entry" into policing, as if women had never been involved in police work earlier.

Numerous articles appeared which surveyed the attitudes of the public, male police officers, and male police executives toward women on patrol. While the women were the objects of this attention, only recently have they been the subjects of researchers. Their attitudes and beliefs were commonly subordinated to how others felt about them.

In contrast to these sociological/psychological surveys of women's role adaptation, this is a historical study. Its major theme is that the demands for creation of the position of policewoman and appointments to the position were almost always forced on an unwilling municipal and police hierarchy. The roots of the policewomen's movement can be traced to earlier demands for female jail and prison matrons and then for female police matrons. The movement was strongly dependent on temperance leaders, social purity crusaders, and women social reformers generally.

The demands for women in policing can be traced to the early decades of the nineteenth century, the jail and prison matron era. This period began in the 1820s, when volunteer Quaker women, following the example set by British Quakers, entered penal institutions to provide religious and secular training for women inmates. These volunteers were joined by other upper-middle-class women who also wanted to reform the inmates and train them for respectable lives and jobs, primarily as domestics in Christian homes. They soon blamed the poor conditions under which these inmates lived on neglect and sexual exploitation by their male keepers. Their concerns evolved into a new profession for women—prison matron. For almost 50 years, until the 1870s, this remained the only position in corrections open to women.

At the end of the Civil War, another group of women took the philosophy of women's sphere beyond jails and prisons. Their new definition of municipal housekeeping encompassed virtually all activities that placed government agencies into contact with women and children. At a time when components of what today constitute the criminal justice system were less distinct, the care of those in police custody was a special concern. Since police stations often also functioned as homeless shelters, and many of those who sought refuge were women and their children, it seemed natural to these female reformers that women should be available to assure that women seeking shelter, almost always poor and frequently intoxicated, were not vulnerable to advances by the men responsible for them.

The tactics of the women demanding an expanded role for women caring for women and children in police custody were identical to those of the women who came before them. These post-Civil War reformers were themselves virtually identical to the women in whose path they followed. They, too, were socially prominent, well-connected, upper-middle-class women of native-born families. Many were abolitionists prior to the Civil War; now they turned their attention to religious, temperance, and benevolent associations. By the 1880s they had succeeded in creating another profession for women—police matron.

Police matrons brought custodial care into police stations. They represented a second phase of women's involvement in the criminal justice system—and their first entry into police departments. It took only a few years for police matrons to fulfill more than strictly custodial functions. By the early years of the twentieth century they had ushered in the era of policewomen.

To explain why reformist women in the last two decades of the nineteenth century felt compelled to advocate roles for women in U.S. police departments—first as matrons and then as policewomen—this book provides an overview of changes within policing. Activities by and on behalf of matrons and policewomen must be viewed within the context of police history. Many cities were organizing their police forces at the same time that women sought expanded public roles. Prior to this, most cities depended on volunteers or part-time employees to provide what little public safety service was demanded by citizens. These volunteers or hourly paid employees, always men, performed primarily watchman functions, often only at night, frequently doing little more than maintaining a fire watch or guiding strangers into (or out of) town.

By the 1880s and 1890s, cities had established paid police departments and mandated that officers be available 24 hours a day. Responsibilities were diverse—including maintaining order, preventing crime, protecting life and property, fighting fires, suppressing vice, assisting in health services, supervising elections, directing traffic, inspecting buildings, and locating truants and runaways. In many cities police also cared for transients, tramps, and homeless people; maintained animal shelters, licensed pets and livestock, and returned runaway animals to their owners; cleaned the streets, and stood by until the dead and dying were removed to either the morgue or the hospital. Few of the these tasks were performed well and no one—not even the police—considered police service a profession.

It was not until the Progressive era and the first decades of the twentieth century that policing became a real career—for men or women—with regular, rather than per diem salaries; tenure that lasted longer than the next local election; and benefits such as vacation, sick pay, and pensions. Despite these improvements, policing remained a job filled by working-class, immigrant men. Requirements rarely exceeded the ability to read and write English; high school diplomas became mandatory as recently as the 1950s.

In 1910 into this environment stepped the nation's first "officially designated" policewoman—Alice Stebbins Wells. The policewomen's movement overlapped and ultimately obscured the matron movement by expanding and professionalizing women's roles within police departments. But because of their similar origins, both these movements provide insights into how prominent women were able to join together and, with the support of like-minded men, create employment for women in a field that had been previously closed to them.

Wells and the women who followed her until after the Great Depression embodied the concept of the policewoman-as-social worker. They also brought with them into policing issues pertaining not only to gender and sex but to class. Although their philosophy gave way in the 1930s to a more middle-class, female careerist outlook, it was not until the modern, women-on-patrol period (which began tentatively in 1968) that the path set by early policewomen was seriously altered.

This comprises the book's second major theme, which compares the economic and social class differences between policewomen and police-men. It then compares the differences among the generations of police-women themselves. These generational changes among the women, more than changes in policing or policemen, resulted in modern women who enter policing having, for the first time, a class orientation identical to their male colleagues.

The policewomen who served from 1910 until the post-Depression years were not working-class immigrants, but, quite the opposite, usually up-per-middle-class, native-born, college educated social workers. These early policewomen were eager to act as municipal mothers to those less fortunate or those whose lifestyles they believed needed correction and discipline. Some were actually called "city mothers." They separated themselves from the male police world and sought to bring social services and order into the lives of women and children. Their allies and peers were female (and male) social workers, Progressives, feminists, temper-ance leaders, and club women, not male police officers or chiefs.

They agreed with their supporters that many elements of the police world were contrary to their mission of serving women and juveniles in a professional, non-threatening atmosphere. They did not view themselves as female versions of policemen, a concept they derogatorily termed "little men." Nor did they view policemen as equal to them in social class, education, or professionalism. For these reasons they avoided the trap-pings of police, opposing uniforms for themselves and choosing not to carry firearms even if permitted to do so.

Their vision transcended race. African-American policewomen, hired specifically to work with women and juveniles of their race, were similar to their white sisters, often teachers, social workers, or ministers' wives. These highly specialized roles filled by early policewomen—whether white or African-American—were not forced on them by the male police estab-lishment but were the roles they sought. Despite this, women's acceptance by male peers has always been marginal. From the first day that they entered police stations, their presence was imposed on police executives by outside, reform forces. It was a rare government official or police chief who sought policewomen. Demands for them almost always came from outsiders.

When their extreme isolation within their departments ended in the post-World War II years, the first generation of policewomen had been replaced by the "Depression babies," who were middle-class careerists, not all of whom were college graduates and fewer of whom were or wanted to be social workers. As these women's duties began to expand, they became discontent with the limited roles—and limited opportunities—that hampered their career development. Still better educated and higher in class orientation than their male peers, these women were more like their male colleagues than their predecessors had been. They formed a bridge generation from early policewomen to today's female police officers.

In 1968, when the Indianapolis Police Department assigned Betty Blankenship and Elizabeth Coffal to patrol, they became the first policewomen to wear uniforms, strap gun belts to their waists, drive a marked patrol car, and answer general purpose police calls on an equal basis with policemen. Although they eventually left patrol and returned to traditional policewomen's duties, they broke the link to the mothering concept that had been the basis of women's roles in policing. Once this link was severed, the stage was set for the modern women-on-patrol era to begin.

Today's women police officers, like their male colleagues, are primarily working-class high school graduates who enter policing for its salary, benefits, and career opportunities. Their demands no longer reflect the upper-middle-class, educated roots of the past, but reflect working-class concerns about pay, promotions, and pensions. Their law enforcement concept is also similar to that of their male peers; as crimefighters they enforce the law, maintain order, and provide for the public's safety, just as men do. Thus, not only is the role of women in the police service radically different from its historical roots, the women are also radically different from their foremothers.

In documenting 100 years of women in municipal police departments as matrons, policewomen and police officers, this book does not delve into current issues surrounding whether or not equality has actually been achieved by women in policing today. Although women are slowly moving up the ranks of police departments, studies are finding that women frequently do not avail themselves of promotion opportunities both for personal reasons but also because systemic discrimination against them still exists. The personal reasons women list involve not wanting to give up positions with daylight hours due to family and child-care requirements. Systemic reasons involve lack of assignment to high-profile units, weighted seniority beyond the minimal eligibility requirements, negative supervisory evaluations, and general attitudes of male co-workers that psychologically discourage ambition. Sexual harassment and male resentment over affirmative action hiring goals and what many officers see as a dilution of physical standards are also of concern.[2] These systemic reasons belie the legal equality women have achieved and highlight issues pertaining to the subtle and not so subtle discrimination women face as they compete with men on terms defined by and for men.

Women chiefs of police are a rarity. Although Penny E. Harrington, a 20-year veteran member of the Portland, Oregon, Police Department, served as chief of the 940-member department for seventeen months from January 24, 1984 until June 2, 1986, exceedingly few women have reached the top of all but small police agencies. As of 1994, only two additional women had served as chiefs in major cities and fewer than 100 of the more than 17,000 municipal law enforcement agencies were led by women. Many of these women, though, expect their numbers to grow in the coming years and they often voice discontent with the "numbers games" and hoopla surrounding their appointments, believing instead that women will have arrived when effectiveness is more important than gender.[3]

Feminist criminologists, on the other hand, are asking whether advocates of gender-neutral policing—including female police managers—are doing themselves and other women a disservice and should, instead, be stressing their differences from, rather than their similarities to, the men who make up the overwhelming majority of the police.[4]

While these are significant issues, it will be the task of today's social scientists and tomorrow's historians to determine whether or not true equality has been—or can be—achieved. Also of interest, as the second century of women in policing overlaps discussion of community policing, is whether the police—male or female—will continue to be seen by themselves and by citizens primarily as crimefighters or whether policing will return to its more generalist, order maintenance roots.

NOTES

1. *Sourcebook of Criminal Justice Statistics—1992* (Washington, DC: Government Printing Office, 1993), 46, 61. Women also comprised 15.4 percent of sworn personnel in sheriffs departments and 4.6 percent of sworn state police personnel.

2. Comments typical of the concern over promotion are from Susan Erlich Martin, *Women on the Move? A Report on the Status of Women in Policing* (Washington, DC: Police Foundation, 1989), 1, 3-4, and Cynthia G. Sulton and Roi D. Townsey, *A Progress Report on Women in Policing* (Washington, DC: Police Foundation, 1981), 4-5.

3. The two major city chiefs serving in 1994 were Elizabeth Watson and Beverly Harvard. Watson, an 18-year veteran of the Houston Police Department was appointed chief in February 1990. A new mayor did not retain her two years later, but by the end of 1992 she had been named chief in Austin. Harvard, a 21-year veteran of the Atlanta Police Department, was appointed chief in October 1994.

She is the first African-American woman to lead a major city department. For views on gender versus effectiveness, see Dorothy M. Schulz, "California Dreaming: Leading the Way to Gender-Free Policing Management?" *Criminal Justice the Americas*, June-July 1994, pp. 1, 8-10.

4. Gender-neutral proponents include Clarice Feinman, *Women in the Criminal Justice System*, 3d ed. (Westport, CT: Praeger Publishers, 1994); Dorothy Bracey, "Women in Criminal Justice: The Decade after the Equal Employment Opportunity Legislation," in *Criminal Justice Administration: Linking Practice and Research*, ed. William A. Jones, Jr. (New York: Marcel Dekker, 1983), 57-78; Edith Linn and Barbara Raffel Price, "The Evolving Role of Women in Policing," in *The Ambivalent Force: Perspectives on the Police*, 3d ed. eds. Abraham S. Blumberg and Elaine Niederhoffer (New York: Holt, Rinehart & Winston, 1985), 69-80. Proponents of feminist criminology include Kathleen Daly and Meda Chesney-Lind, "Feminism and Criminology," *Justice Quarterly* 5, no. 4 (Dec. 1988), 497-535 and Nanci Koser Wilson, "Feminist Pedagogy in Criminology," *Journal of Criminal Justice Education* 2, no. 1 (Spring 1991), 81-93.

Chapter 1

Forerunners: The Matrons, 1820–1899

Matrons in jails and prisons were the first women to work in law enforcement or corrections in the United States. Demands for jail, prison, and later, police matrons came overwhelmingly from private women's groups, and almost never from police departments or government officials. Private groups, notably temperance, benevolent, moral reform, and women's clubs, provided either voluntary or paid personnel until municipalities could be convinced of the necessity of creating and maintaining the positions. These early developments frequently led to ill-defined and overlapping job responsibilities. Despite the recurring blurring of title and function, the term *matron* is today generally applied to women having care and supervision of women and juveniles in custody. A matron functioned solely as a keeper of the jail, guaranteeing that women were kept separate from men and assuring that their food, clothing, and shelter needs were met while in police custody, whereas a *policewoman* was engaged in more than a custodial role. She had such law enforcement functions as patrol, court case preparation, and investigation.

Women had always been viewed in their maternal roles and they used this to develop an ideology of "women's sphere," which eventually brought them out of their homes and into the public arena. Women's sphere included "a special responsibility to alleviate harsh conditions." This concept of duty led women from their homes to schools, settlement houses, hospitals, prisons, and police stations. Solutions to problems outside the home required organization, and by the 1830s women were involved in "a bewildering array of organizations, with a great deal of overlap among their members, [seeking] both to provide relief and to create a Christian nation." First through churches, then through auxiliaries to men's groups, and finally in their own associations women gathered together to solve society's problems.[1]

The women also reflected the nation's preoccupation with sexual purity.

As women sought to eradicate prostitution, campaigns against vice became the basis for attacking many social problems. Initially disdained as fallen women who were beyond redemption, prostitutes, who made up the largest number of female prison inmates, began in the 1820s to arouse the concerns of women. Out of this concern grew private benevolent groups and later, in the post-Civil War period, demands that women assume authority for other women.

These concerns place the women squarely within the women's social reform movement that developed after the Civil War.[2] Both Estelle B. Freedman and Nicole Hahn Rafter identify women prison reformers as part of this movement. "Like temperance advocates, social purity leaders, and settlement house founders," Freedman observes, the post-Civil War reformers "believed in women's separate sphere and superior morality . . . [and as] social feminists continued to argue that women had unique, feminine virtues that should be embodied in social policy." Rafter notes that the women, "armed with belief in inherent differences between the sexes," sought to establish "all-female institutions, prisons uncontaminated by male influence, in which criminal women would receive sympathetic care from members of their own sex."[3] The same precepts of women's moral superiority over men and unique ability to care for other women motivated the police matrons' and the policewomen's movements.

As early as 1823 Philadelphia Quaker women, following the lead of Quakers in England, had begun visiting women inmates in local prisons. Visitors offered "individual and systematic instruction" to female prisoners to aid their spiritual redemption. They also provided a library, as well as sewing and writing classes.[4] These women were followed in other cities by female evangelical reformers, who visited institutions to comfort and to proselytize the inmates.

In 1926, Rachel Welch, one of the small number of women in Auburn prison in New York, became pregnant while serving a punishment sentence in a solitary cell. As a result of a flogging by a prison official, Welch died after childbirth. Freedman found that a grand jury investigating the flogging seemed unconcerned about Welch's pregnancy or about the women at Auburn generally, but the subsequent scandal may have influenced the passage of an 1828 law requiring county prisons to separate male and female inmates. Auburn officials hired a matron in 1832 to oversee the women's quarters.[5]

Blake McKelvey attributes the appointment of the Auburn matron to an increasing number of female commitments in the early 1830s, which overcrowded the female facilities and prompted New York State officials to build a separate cellblock for women in a corner of the Sing Sing yard. By 1837 the first matron and her assistants were unable to maintain order and were replaced by a woman who proved no more successful. Finally, "an accomplished school mistress" was appointed and served until she ran afoul of the chaplain, which, coupled with political changes, resulted in her resignation.[6]

Despite this inauspicious beginning, other appointments followed. In 1845, responding to urging by the American Female Moral Reform Society, New York City officials hired six matrons for its two jails. The society tried to extend use of matrons to the police department, recommending they assist women lodged in police stations after their arrest. Ahead of its time, the society was not successful. Members met with ridicule and opposition that was largely supported from within the police hierarchy.[7]

Activity on behalf of female inmates was not sustained. Women's issues in the years surrounding 1850 centered on "the great seduction debate . . . agitation for women's rights, years when the last bonds of womanhood broke as the lives of women separated along deepening class lines." Among middle-class women, whose economic roles were defined by home, husband, and children, there was a decline in workplace participation.[8] When women began to question this cult of domesticity, they concentrated on "women's sexual powerlessness and the dangers to which women were subject, seeking to devise ways to protect them within this framework."[9]

The post-Civil War period brought new opportunities in the public arena for women. Women's colleges had come into existence, and women entered occupations previously closed to them. Women's clubs had moved from literary and domestic pursuits to social and moral issues outside the home, including reform of institutions caring for less fortunate women. As women once again reached out to incarcerated women, they found that the inmates had not benefited from prison reform as had male inmates between 1820 and 1870. Female prisoners faced overcrowding, harsh treatment, and sexual abuse by their male keepers.

These reformist women shared historical experiences and social characteristics: "a majority came from middle- and upper-middle-class Protestant families in the northeastern United States. A disproportionate number belonged to liberal denominations; almost a third were Quakers and many others were Unitarians."[10] The prison reformers resembled women abolitionists, feminists, and women active in expanding the responsibilities of matrons to also include police stations. Rafter posits that it was not only similar women, but the very same women who had been abolitionists and health-care workers during the Civil War, who, in the late 1860s "turned their attention to . . . campaigns against sexual immorality and delinquency, and crusades for suffrage and temperance," eventually becoming interested in improving conditions for incarcerated women.[11]

Prior to 1870 men refused to accept women in the public sphere, but "more importantly, most women were not interested in rejecting" their female identities. Since "men and women feared the demise of the female sphere and the valuable functions it performed," feminists drew on "concepts of female moral superiority and sisterhood" as they affirmed the separate nature of women. Through this affirmation of separatism, feminists hoped to reduce the limitations on women within their own sphere "as well as to gain the right of choice—of autonomy—for those women who opted for public rather than private roles."[12]

Anne Firor Scott describes the relationship between reform movements and the emergence of women in a public role. She finds that "as some women tried to change the world, they changed themselves," stating that abolitionist women were among the first to advocate women's rights. "Since men often talked about the superior moral sensitivity of women," Scott noted, "there was a certain logic to the tendency of women to become interested in the human problems of an industrialized civilization."[13]

Women prison reformers based their appeals on a combination of women's special sphere and "separate but equal" strategies that derived from the nature of the work they defined for themselves. They saw their roles in terms of the prevailing concepts of women's roles in society and they shared with their male contemporaries an acceptance of their sphere of influence as maternal and moral concerns. Just as they were housekeepers at home, women who entered public service were society's housekeepers. They were the backbone of the women's movement. Members of such groups as the Women's Christian Temperance Union and the General Federation of Women's Clubs committed themselves to a wide range of social and moral reforms—one of which was the appointment of matrons.

Demands for police matrons were spearheaded by the WCTU, probably the most powerful women's group of the era. Often seen only as a temperance group, the WCTU embraced a number of issues pertaining to women. Its efforts to reform prisons, jails, and juvenile asylums were based on rescuing the inmates through personal encounters—identical to early Quaker prison and jail visits. Ruth Bordin lists prison reform as the first non-temperance issue to attract the WCTU's attention. Underlining the link to an earlier generation of prison and jail visitors, she attributes the interest to temperance meetings held in jails as early as 1875. This personal contact with inmates led to petitions for police matrons, halfway houses for released women prisoners, and demands that women be appointed to state boards of charities and corrections. The WCTU's commitment to the concept of women's sphere in prison reform was strong. One official noted: "It is a standing rebuke to our civilization that women are arrested and given into the hands of men to be searched and cared for, tried by men, sentenced by men, committed to . . . institutions where only men have access to them."[14]

An analysis of temperance movements described WCTU members as primarily middle-class women whose "cross-class contact . . . occurred in a paternalistic (or maternalistic) context." WCTU leaders who worked outside the home were lecturers, authors, editors, teachers, professors, or full-time temperance workers and were usually native-born members of evangelical Protestant churches. Visits to jails were one of the earliest activities, and it is probable that the women visitors began to notice who ran the jails (men) versus whom they were visiting (women). Political action followed.[15]

By the time police matrons were being advocated in the 1880s, three states—New York (1839), Indiana (1873), and Massachusetts (1877)—had established separate women's prisons. Creation of these institutions resulted not only in specialized care for the inmates, but in new positions of authority, prestige, and visibility for women. Women prison administrators provided examples of women who had achieved authority and status by caring for other women, such as at the Indiana Reformatory Institution for Women and Girls, established in 1873 under the direction of a Quaker couple. Not only was it the first independent women's prison, it was the first to be run by an entirely female staff. The superintendent and her assistants were responsible for all internal administration. Prison officers had to be women "unless the superintendent were married, in which case her husband might also be an administrator."[16]

The WTCU's leadership in the matron movement was in keeping with its strength in reform circles and its importance in recruiting and training women activists in areas beyond temperance. Founded in 1874, the WCTU became active in all manner of reform activities after electing Frances Willard president in 1879. Before her death in New York City on February 17, 1898, Willard used the doctrine of women's sphere—women caring for women—to also move into such areas as suffrage and the kindergarten movement. This sphere was no longer merely the home; it now included all public facilities utilized by women. The nation had become a macrocosm of the home, where the woman cared for other women, children, and those unable to care for themselves.[17]

While the WCTU depended on women's and church groups to lobby with them, state chapters were usually the largest and most politically potent groups to involve themselves in efforts to secure police matrons. The Portland, Maine, chapter is credited with obtaining appointment of the first police matron in the United States. The chapter in 1877 paid the salary of a female jail visitor; then the city paid half and by 1878 the visitor had became a full-time employee of the city's police department.[18] At the urging of the national WCTU, other chapters increased their lobbying efforts for police matrons.

By 1890, WCTU efforts had resulted in the hiring of matrons in 36 cities. Chapters in 45 states and territories were working for additional appointments.[19] Sadie M.W. Likens, a matron in Denver, was one of those appointed through WCTU influence. As with many of these appointments, the exact date Likens became the matron is difficult to determine. Because some women served in unpaid positions prior to receiving salaries, their employment dates are often in dispute. Likens may have been among the first "actual policewomen—usually termed matrons" as early as 1884. She was responsible for supervising the home for "friendless women and children," visiting the sick and the dying at all hours of the day and night, and "going unquestioned into houses of prostitution, variety theaters, dance halls, and wherever needed."[20]

Likens also performed activities often expected of a woman in a man's world. According to the *Colorado Sun*, as part of the July 4, 1891 celebration, "Police Matron Likens, known as one of the 'most genial of women,' prepared an 'elegant cold lunch' in the police court room for officers . . . . [consisting] of cold meats, ice cream and various other delicacies." Again busy at holiday time, Likens, no longer the sole matron, on December 25, 1895, decorated the court with American flags and evergreens. At the conclusion of the Christmas assembly, the "bustling matrons, like busy bees" served "delicacies . . . for the pleasure of the boys in blue."[21]

In Buffalo the WCTU succeeded in 1885 in getting several matrons appointed. It was responsible, too, for the matrons receiving salary increases in 1909 and 1910 and becoming members of the force, enabling them to receive pensions.[22] Chicago matrons were also appointed in 1885 at WCTU urging. Ten (two per station) were appointed "after . . . the impropriety of having [female prisoners] placed in the charge of men was, on several occasions, brought prominently before the public." The matrons were viewed as a "genuine reform . . . that gave wide satisfaction [and] . . . removed all possibility of scandal from the stations." Those selected were intelligent, patient, and "above all" of "irreproachable character." In 1887 they cared for 8,000 women. By 1898, a chief matron earned $1,500 annually and 30 matrons each earned $720 (the same as blacksmiths' helpers and switchboard operators).[23]

Elsewhere similar developments occurred. A source crediting the 1885 appointment of a police matron in Philadelphia to political pressure is amplified by another who specifies that four matrons were selected specifically in response to WCTU activity.[24]

In Los Angeles the WCTU's role is unclear. In 1888, Lucy Thompson Gray, a mother of 10, who also cared for a number of homeless children, was named the city's first matron. An 1889 Los Angeles Police Department photo includes Gray, who traveled west with her family in the 1850s. By the 1880s she

had created a police department position to aid women and children—both victims and offenders—who were not receiving appropriate care. She was fearless and kind, known for her ability to calm unruly prisoners. She earned the title City Mother, and although not a policewoman, performed many of the duties associated with that position.[25]

Local efforts were reinforced in some areas by the enactment of state laws. In 1887, Massachusetts passed the first such law, directing all cities with 30,000 or more inhabitants to appoint police matrons. The law, termed one of the WCTU's "most notable" successes, was passed through the combined efforts of the WTCU and educational and moral uplift groups, "aided by prominent gentlemen."[26] By 1892 there were 22 police matrons throughout the state, including ten in Boston. Worcester, one of the affected cities, responded to the legislation immediately, appointing a matron in May 1887. Pittsfield, which was not required to follow the law because its population was below 30,000, appointed a matron anyway, while Somerville and Salem, with populations over 30,000, did not.[27]

Efforts by the New York City Women's Prison Association, a group attempting to improve conditions under which women were incarcerated, resulted in the passage in New York State in 1889 of a law similar to the one in Massachusetts.[28] Even before this, some cities had hired matrons. On November 16, 1887, Rochester appointed as matron a teacher who passed a civil service test for the position. The impetus for hiring her was the success of the matron in Buffalo. Brooklyn officials hired 15 matrons in 1887; each earned $600 annually.[29]

The nation's largest city, New York, moved slowly. Homeless women was a key issue. At the turn of the century, the New York City Police Department was one of many charged with the care of homeless persons as well as prisoners. Since no public shelters existed in cities, transients, poor travelers, and the homeless spent their nights in the vacant cells or corridors of police stations. In 1887, New York City officials termed matrons unnecessary, primarily because police and other public officials did not want to provide space or salaries for them. In the same year, the city detained 14,000 women prisoners and received 42,000 female lodgers for overnight shelter; two children were born in precincts.[30] In 1887 the Women's Prison Association described lodging rooms in stations as

filled with dirty, half-naked women, the air filled with tobacco smoke and the odor of decaying garbage which the women bring in for their breakfast. They either sit covered with their dresses or crouch together when there is not space to lie down. All ages, from 25 to 60, and in one case 96 years, are represented.[31]

The report details that the scrubwoman was required to search "the more respectable women prisoners." Concluding that "matrons should be appointed for each stationhouse where women are either prisoners or lodgers," the report notes that with only one exception, all the men in charge of stations agreed that a matron would be of "utmost service. She should have charge of each woman as soon as she is placed in a cell; . . . she should search all the women."

But the Men's Prison Association objected—based on lack of space for a matron, on the violent state of the women, and on their fear of a matron's physical inability to handle the women. The objections were dismissed by the Women's Prison Association as "silly." Conceding that a "drunken and disorderly woman is a most depraved creature," the women refused to accept that such a woman would demoralize a decent, sober matron. They described the arrested women as usually drunk and wholly irresponsible; "they freely take off all their clothing; and stand naked at the cell doors. Their language is frightful. A woman could control them far better than a man. She would see that the prisoners are not imposed upon . . . that the sexes are separated."[32]

Matrons finally entered the New York City Police Department in October 1891—after ten years of lobbying.[33] Appointments may have been hastened after an 1890 report in *Harper's Weekly* of a police officer who pleaded guilty and was sentenced to imprisonment for attempting to assault a 15-year-old girl in custody.[34] This was exactly the type of incident matrons were supposed to prevent.

The Women's Prison Association's 1887 report had noted the police establishment's lack of enthusiasm for matrons and remarked that "whenever a woman asks for a position formerly occupied by men, she is met with the ancient cry, that there is no room for her."[35] Although the association did not respond to the physical strength issue, had the women been clairvoyant, they could have predicted that the objections of the Men's Prison Association and other male police and corrections groups to matrons would follow women throughout their police careers.

During Theodore Roosevelt's 1895-1897 term as New York City police commissioner, the number and role of matrons was expanded. Although Roosevelt was technically only one of four commissioners managing the department, he ran it as if he had sole authority. In 1896, Roosevelt appointed 32 matrons, the most ever named in one year. Duties called for 24-hour coverage in most stations. Matrons searched female suspects, processed, escorted and supervised women in precinct detention facilities, and cared for lost children. By 1899, two years after Roosevelt resigned to become U.S. Secretary of the Navy, there were 59 matrons.[36]

In 1908, the president of the NYCPD Police Matrons' Endowment Association noted the difficulties in describing qualifications for matrons, since so much depended on a candidate's "temperament and her attitude toward her work and the persons over whom she has temporary charge." She listed "tact, patience and alertness" as key qualities. As to concern over filthy and abusive language by detainees, she recommended "take no notice. . . . It would be useless and a waste of time to talk back." She advised applicants that there were 70 matrons in Greater New York, each earning $1,000 annually (the same as a doorman, who fulfilled functions similar to a matron for male detainees) and each entitled to seven vacation days and a pension; yet she believed matrons to be "underpaid," since the job "is very onerous and unpleasant and the hours long."[37]

Southern cities were less pressured to appoint matrons and, therefore, were slower to add women to their police departments. In 1892 Knoxville employed a matron, although efforts for a similar appointment in Nashville failed. New Orleans opened a woman's lodging house in 1873 to remove adult women and their children from the "especially inhospitable" station lodgings, but a history of the police force from 1805 to 1899 does not mention a police matron. The sole matron appointed in 1892 served only in the jail. Elsewhere only a few matrons were employed. In Atlanta, for example, a matron was hired in 1901. Not busy her first year, by 1903 she was handling almost 300 cases annually. In 1919, after additional hiring, the city had a sufficient number of white matrons to allow them to go on 12-hour shifts, rather than work around the clock without relief. Atlanta hired its first African-American matron in 1921.[38]

Matrons in cities and towns brought social service into police stations. The 1904 NYCPD civil service examination asked: Would you discriminate in treatment of girls under 18, if so, how or why; how would you handle a drunk and disorderly woman; what would you do while awaiting a doctor to treat an epileptic having a fit; what information would you obtain from a prisoner; how would you handle unruly prisoners; under what circumstances would you administer drugs to a prisoner; and how would you assure that all premises for which you are responsible are inspected for cleanliness? Other questions tested arithmetic skills.[39]

Not only did matrons begin to define the roles that would eventually be filled by policewomen, they set the pattern of women entering police departments at the urging of outsiders, rather than in response to a perceived need by agency officials. Since the demands for matrons and then policewomen stemmed from similar concerns by women about women, it is not surprising that the movements had parallel development.

While matrons served an important custodial function, policewomen were viewed as able to prevent crime through social service intervention. Policewomen had greater professional prestige than matrons. The majority were college-educated social workers, rather than widows or good women in need of employment. Although the ages of women appointed matrons or policewomen are rarely mentioned, the police histories that contain pictures of the matrons support the belief that they were older than policewomen. This view is also supported by the fact that many matrons were widows of policemen and many lived alone, without dependents, in rooms or small apartments adjoining the cells for which they were responsible. As the number of policewomen increased, they eclipsed the less organized and usually less educated matrons.

NOTES

1. Lori D. Ginzberg, *Women and the World of Benevolence: Morality, Politics, and Class in the Nineteenth-Century United States* (New Haven, CT: Yale University Press, 1990), 17, 37.

2. William L. O'Neill, *Everyone Was Brave: The Rise and Fall of Feminism in America* (Chicago: Quadrangle Books, 1969), x, describes reformist women as social feminists who, "while believing in women's rights, generally subordinated them to broad social reforms they thought more urgent." Lois W. Banner, *Women in Modern America: A Brief History* (New York: Harcourt Brace Jovanovich, 1974), vi, using O'Neill's definition, describes social feminists as women for whom social reform took priority over strictly women's causes. Because O'Neill stretched his description by contrasting social feminists with so-called hard-core feminists (those who put suffrage before all other issues), and argued that the two groups were mutually exclusive, his distinctions have been questioned. Nancy F. Cott, "What's in a Name? The Limits of 'Social Feminism'; or, Expanding the Vocabulary of Women's History," *Journal of American History* 76, no. 5 (Dec. 1989), 828-829, feels *municipal housekeeping* or *civic maternalism* are more appropriate to describe what she calls "organized women's efforts to assure public health, sanitation, and children's welfare." Whatever nuance each term may carry, policewomen and their supporters are among the women who, during the late nineteenth and early twentieth centuries, greatly expanded women's roles in public affairs and public employment. To avoid ascribing to them roles or motives undergoing reinterpretation among women's historians, they are here termed reformist women.

3. Estelle B. Freedman, *Their Sisters' Keepers: Women Prison Reform in America, 1830-1930* (Ann Arbor: University of Michigan Press, 1981), 39; Nicole Hahn Rafter, *Partial Justice: Women in State Prisons, 1800-1935* (Boston: Northeastern University Press, 1985), 46.

4. Freedman, *Their Sisters' Keepers*, 28.

5. Ibid., 15.

6. Blake McKelvey, *American Prisons: A History of Good Intentions* (Montclair, NJ: Patterson Smith, 1977), 39.

7. Theresa M. Melchionne, "The Changing Role of Policewomen," in *The Ambivalent Force: Perspectives on the Police*, 2d ed. eds. Arthur Niederhoffer and Abraham S. Blumberg (Hinsdale, IL: Dryden Press, 1976), 371.

8. Marcia R. Carlisle, "Prostitutes and Their Reformers in Nineteenth Century Philadelphia" (Ph.D. diss., Rutgers University, 1982), 116, 119.

9. Ruth Bordin, *Frances Willard: A Biography* (Chapel Hill: University of North Carolina Press, 1986), 133.

10. Freedman, *Their Sisters' Keepers*, 15.

11. Rafter, *Partial Justice*, xx.

12. Estelle B. Freedman, "Separatism as Strategy: Female Institution Building and American Feminism, 1870-1930," *Feminist Studies* 5, no. 3 (Fall 1979), 515-516.

13. Anne Firor Scott, ed. *The American Woman: Who Was She?* (Englewood Cliffs, NJ: Prentice-Hall, 1971), 88.

14. Quoted in Ruth Bordin, *Woman and Temperance: The Quest for Power and Liberty, 1873-1900*, 1981; reprint (New Brunswick, NJ: Rutgers University Press,

1990), 99-100 (references are to reprint edition).

15. Jack S. Blocker, Jr., *American Temperance Movements: Cycles of Reform* (Boston: Twayne Publishers, 1989), 81-82.

16. Rafter, *Partial Justice*, 29-31.

17. Bordin, *Frances Willard*, 9, 10; William H. Chafe, *The American Woman: Her Changing Social, Economic, and Political Roles, 1920-1970* (New York: Oxford University Press, 1972), 13.

18. Samuel Walker, *A Critical History of Police Reform: The Emergence of Professionalism* (Lexington, MA: Lexington Books, 1977), 85; Chloe Owings, *Women Police: A Study of the Development and Status of the Women Police Movement* (New York: Frederick H. Hitchcock, 1925), 98.

19. Bordin, *Woman and Temperance*, 100.

20. Frank R. Prassell, *The Western Peace Officer: A Legacy of Law and Order* (Norman: University of Oklahoma Press, 1972), 91; Owings, *Women Police*, 98-99.

21. Eugene F. Rider, *The Denver Police Department: An Administrative, Organizational and Operational History, 1858-1905* (Ann Arbor, MI: University Microfilms International, 1987 [Ph.D. diss., University of Denver, 1971]), 320, 262, 430.

22. Ginzberg, *Women and the World of Benevolence*, 103; Karen J. Blair, *The Clubwoman as Feminist: True Womanhood Redefined, 1868-1914* (New York: Holmes & Meier, 1980), 75, 85, 90.

23. J.K. Barney, "Police Matrons," *Lend a Hand*, Aug. 1887, 472; John J. Flinn and John E. Wilkie, *History of the Chicago Police: From the Settlement of the Community to the Present Time*, 1887; reprint (New York: Arno Press, 1971), 453 (reference is to reprint edition); *Report of the General Superintendent of the City of Chicago to the City Council for the Fiscal Year Ending December 31, 1898*, 114, 52-53, 178 (for salaries).

24. David J. Pivar, *Purity Crusade: Sexual Morality and Social Control, 1868-1900* (Westport, CT: Greenwood Press, 1973), 102; Bordin, *Woman and Temperance*, 100.

25. *Two Hundred Years of American Criminal Justice* (Washington, DC: Government Printing Office, 1976), 2.

26. Barney, "Police Matrons," 473.

27. Herbert M. Sawyer, *History of the Department of Police Service of Worcester, MA, from 1674 to 1900, Historical and Biographical: Illustrating and Describing the Economy, Equipment and Effectiveness of the Police Force of Today, with Reminiscences of the Past, Containing Information from Official Sources* (Worcester, MA: Police Relief Association, 1900), 81-82, 149; Caroline A. Kennard, "Progress in Employment of Police Matrons," *Lend a Hand*, Sept. 1892, 182.

28. Barney, "Police Matrons," 474.

29. Melchionne, "The Changing Role of Policewomen," 371.

30. Ibid.

31. Women's Prison Association of the City of New York, *The Police Matron's Bill—Prisons and Station Houses* (New York: Extract from Annual Report, 1887), 4.

32. Ibid., 5, 10, 11.

33. Melchionne, "The Changing Role of Policewomen," 371. Historians agree that matrons officially entered the NYCPD in 1891, but at least one woman filled the role prior to that. See Augustine E. Costello, *Our Police Protectors: A History of the New York Police*, 1885, reprint (Montclair, NJ: Patterson Smith, 1972), 460 (reference is to reprint edition) and George W. Walling, *Recollections of a New York Chief of Police*, 1887, reprint (Montclair, NJ: Patterson Smith, 1972), 193, 506 (refer-

ences are to reprint edition). James J. Richardson, *The New York Police: Colonial Times to 1902* (New York: Oxford University Press, 1970), 171, found that "conservatism, or rather foot dragging, of the authorities made New York one of the last large cities to establish matrons." He questioned whether "this innovation was resisted because it was championed by reformers."

34. "Police Matrons," *Harper's Weekly*, Aug. 30, 1890, 675.

35. Women's Prison Association, *The Police Matron's Bill*, 12.

36. Jay S. Berman, *Police Administration and Progressive Reform: Theodore Roosevelt as Police Commissioner of New York* (Westport, CT: Greenwood Press, 1987), 77; Richardson, *The New York Police*, 171. Roosevelt created a stir by naming Minnie Gertrude Kelly clerk to the president of the Police Board. Kelly earned $1,700 annually and was the first woman in an administrative position in the NYCPD.

37. "Police Matron," *The Chief* (New York: Chief Publishing Co., 1908), 1, 2-3.

38. Kennard, "Progress in Employment of Police Matrons," 182; Dennis C. Rousey, *The New Orleans Police, 1805-1899: A Social History* (Ann Arbor, MI: University Microfilms International, 1979 [Ph.D. diss., Cornell University, 1978]), 239; William J. Mathias and Stuart Anderson, *Horse To Helicopter: First Century of the Atlanta Police Department* (Atlanta: Georgia State University, 1973), 42, 80, 89.

39. "Police Matron," *The Chief*, 3-4.

Chapter 2

The Early Policewomen, 1900–1928

In September 1910, Alice Stebbins Wells, who stood a little over five feet tall, wore no uniform, carried no weapon, and usually stuffed her star-shaped badge into her pocketbook, joined the Los Angeles Police Department as the "first policewoman" in the United States.[1]

Wells's appointment to the 350-member LAPD is recognized as the beginning of women's formal entry into U.S. law enforcement even though her status as the first woman called "policewoman," combined with her leadership in the policewomen's movement and her role as founder and first president of the International Association of Policewomen, have provided her with a distinction that is historically inaccurate.

Women had functioned as police before Wells's selection. In 1893 the Chicago Police Department gave Mary Owens, the widow of a Chicago policeman, the rank of "policeman" with the power of arrest. Her employment was part of a pattern around the nation; at a time when departments offered no pensions or death benefits, widows were often hired as matrons to provide them with an income. What was unusual about Owens is that she was given the title and pay of a policeman rather than a matron. Her duties, including visiting courts and assisting detectives on cases concerning women and children, were typical of matrons and later of policewomen. Owens, who served for 30 years before she retired, is usually credited with being the first woman with full arrest powers conferred by a municipal law enforcement agency.[2]

Another factor that may have convinced Chicago to hire a woman was that large crowds were expected for the 1893 World's Columbian Exposition, which celebrated the four hundredth anniversary of Christopher Columbus's first voyage to North America, as well as Chicago's role in American civilization. This set a pattern for policewomen's appointments. American cities have repeatedly turned to policewomen to enforce morals regulations and protect the virtue of local women when groups of men were drawn to the area by economic conditions, large-scale events such as expositions, or the establishment of military bases.

Officials in Portland, Oregon, for example, hired Lola Baldwin during the 1905 Lewis and Clark Exposition, empowering her to deal with social conditions threatening the moral safety of young girls and women. Civic leaders saw the large number of unattached lumbermen, miners, and laborers attracted by the exposition as creating undesirable influences among Portland's women. To counter these dangers, Baldwin was put in charge of a force of social workers and given police powers. A social worker who was secretary to the Travelers' Aid Society, Baldwin was considered so effective that in 1908 Portland organized a Department of Public Safety for the Protection of Young Girls and Women, naming her director. Since neither the department nor Baldwin wished the women to be known as police, they were called either operatives or workers. Baldwin worked through the incumbency of six chiefs of police and five mayors.[3]

Similar conditions involving transient men and local women in Grand Forks, North Dakota, in 1909 led the Florence Crittenden Circle to advocate giving women police powers to stem female delinquency. In May 1910—four months before Wells's appointment in Los Angeles—Grand Forks created the position of police matron, which carried duties identical to those performed in Chicago by Owens, in Portland by Baldwin, and, soon, by Wells in Los Angeles. The groups that lobbied for these appointments began lobbying for women police officers in other cities. The Travelers' Aid Society was trying to control negative influences on young women, whom they viewed as easily lured into amoral conduct and prostitution. To stem these influences, groups of women began, in the 1880s and 1890s, to greet female arrivals at seaports and railroad stations to advise and shelter them. Originally a voluntary effort, by the early years of the twentieth century the activities were institutionalized as the Travelers' Aid Society. The Crittenden Circle had similar concerns. It was started in 1892 by Charles Crittenden after he attended a Women's Christian Temperance Union convention and agreed to finance its homes for unwed mothers and fallen women.[4]

Another group supporting women police was the WCTU, which had been instrumental in the appointment of matrons. It now spearheaded efforts to create positions for policewomen in cities around the nation. The WCTU was without a doubt the group most instrumental in the spread of the policewomen's movement. Its sponsorship of Wells's speaking tour and lobbying by its local chapters provided publicity and political strength for the movement.

Women lobbying for police positions were involved in the same "female institution building" that had occurred in other public areas.[5] This overlapped the creation of what is today the criminal justice system. Samuel Walker, one of few police historians who mentions policewomen more than fleetingly, has noted that by 1900 the key institutions in the U.S. criminal justice system—the police, prisons, probation, and parole—were parts of a newly-created apparatus of social control.[6] Prior to the turn of the century, police departments were general-purpose agencies that performed whatever municipal functions politician deemed necessary to retain power. Although they began to shed some of their non-law enforcement functions by the late 1880s, police were only beginning to view themselves as part of a larger system of justice.

As the system evolved, it did not take long for women to develop roles for themselves within these agencies. Between 1840 and 1900 women had taken up the cause of women inmates. By 1910 women prison reformers had gained legitimacy as professionals in public agencies caring for female clients. In this capacity, they paved the way for policewomen to establish their own legitimacy in the criminal justice field.

Earlier successes by prison and jail matron advocates convinced women that they had a role in law enforcement. Since both the matrons' and the policewomen's movements stemmed from similar concerns about women, it is not surprising that they had parallel developments. The matrons' movement prefigured the policewomen's movement in its two most important aspects, namely, the belief that women were best suited for handling women and juveniles, and that private groups provided the impetus, personnel, and sometimes the salaries to fill positions prior to municipal funding. This was exactly how Baldwin's Portland position originated. Funds donated by a well-to-do woman enabled her to expand her efforts until public funding was provided in 1908.[7]

Wells, a graduate of Oberlin College, lobbied actively for her position in Los Angeles. Born in 1873 in Kansas of Puritan ancestry, she became a bible lecturer and ran a small church in Oklahoma Indian territory. It was here that she met her husband and that her two children were born. After the family settled in Los Angeles, Wells became convinced that police work offered an opportunity for "applied Christianity," that crime could be reduced by curing society's ills, and that women serving as police officers were best suited for dealing with women and children.[8] She believed that the protective and preventive work for women and children done by private organizations would yield better results if the agents were public officers, vested with police powers, because the police department was "the strategic point at which virtue can meet vice, strength can meet weakness, and guide [those needing help] into preventive and redemptive channels."[9]

To achieve her aims, she presented the mayor and police commissioner with a petition signed by more than 100 influential citizens requesting appointment of a policewoman to undertake protective and preventive work among women and children. It was circulated secretly so as not to arouse opposition and so that "the antifeminist press would not editorially condemn her and her concept."[10] Wells recalled the petition as a request to create a civil service title for a woman police officer "with the same standing as her brother officers, with the purpose, however, not of duplicating, but of supplementing their work as it pertained to children and women." The mayor's acceptance was followed by "three months of vigilance and explanation to every . . . councilman, ending with the passage of the desired ordinance August 12, to become effective thirty days later, September 12, 1910."

After being sworn in at City Hall, Wells received her badge ("a man's badge, for there was no other until a die could be made, and the historic 'Policewoman Badge Number One' was cast"). The chief assigned her to the patrolman who for two years had handled cases involving juveniles. In addition to her badge, Wells received a patrol box key, a book of rules, and a first aid book, "the same as the men." She did not mention receiving a gun.[11]

Wells then followed the example set by Owens, Baldwin, and agents of the private protective associations. She enforced laws concerning dance halls, skating rinks, penny arcades, movie theaters, and other places of recreation frequented by women and children. She searched for missing persons and provided social service information to women. At the arcades she discouraged the display of "suggestive or evil" pictures; at theaters she saw "that no minors are admitted without parent or guardian and that no questionable still shots are displayed outside." Writing in 1933 of her 24 years as a policewoman, Wells observed that "police duty by long tradition and habit had been considered so wholly a man's field, that the question was not raised by men until entrance by women came when sufficient pressure was brought to bear from without." Recalling her appearance at headquarters, she said, "they neither wanted me nor knew what to do with me."[12]

Her appointment was treated jocularly by Los Angeles journalists, who pictured her

in caricature as a bony, muscular, masculine person, grasping a revolver, dressed in anything but feminine apparel, hair drawn tightly into a hard little knot at the back of the head, huge unbecoming spectacles, small stiff round disfiguring hat, . . . presenting the idea in a most repellant and unlovely guise.[13]

Many, though, took her seriously. Interest was widespread and Wells lectured widely. In 1911, on a speaking tour arranged by the WCTU of Northern California, Wells spoke in 31 cities in 30 days. She also addressed the 1911 session of the General Federation of Women's Clubs, winning support that resulted in local clubs' lobbying for policewomen. Wells is credited, too, with having made 13 arrests during her first year of duty. In the period from 1912 to 1914 she gave 136 speeches in 73 cities in the United States and eastern Canada. She addressed women's and men's clubs, church, civic, school, and university associations, social workers, and, in 1914, the annual gathering of the International Association of Chiefs of Police. Wells spent so much time away from Los Angeles that she took leaves of absence totaling two years, during which she supported herself from her lecture fees.[14]

Interest in Wells stemmed not only from her unusual work, but from her speaking in public ("a very unwomanly activity"), and traveling around the country, also novel. She "caused great curiosity. . . . Photographers met the train in Philadelphia;" and in a small Pennsylvania town one movie theater owner posted a sign reading, "Mrs. Wells, First Policewoman—See Her!" In New Orleans, a man begged her to arrest him[15] just as men would in later years make similar comments to the first women on uniform patrol.

A story about Wells also indicates her pioneer status. According to the anecdote, on her first day as a policewoman, attempting to take advantage of free transportation for police officers, Wells identified herself to the streetcar conductor. He is said to have severely berated her for "stealing her husband's badge and abusing its privilege." But by 1912 she was one of three Los Angeles policewomen, and she had established a routine. She had office hours, and women came for help and advice for which they would not go to the regular police department.[16]

Wells's 1914 IACP address aroused controversy within the all-male association. August Vollmer, police chief in Berkeley, California, a leading police reformer and an advocate of policewomen, was a proponent of the social work aspects of policing, believing that police should do more than merely arrest offenders. He recalled that when Wells spoke

there was acid comment [by] the men. . . . They couldn't see why any woman should want to work around a police station; . . . they all but put Mrs. Wells out of the meeting. So forcefully, however, did she present her argument that women and children, and especially wayward girls, were best served by women officers, that many of those who arrived scoffing remained—convinced.[17]

Among Wells's appeals to the chiefs was that policewomen would protect male officers from delicate and troublesome situations. A male officer jeopardized his reputation whenever he had to handle a female offender, she observed, portraying women as "a protection to the department" and reassuring them that "the policewoman is not going to take the place of the policeman."[18] This dual protection of both women in custody and male officers forced to come in contact with them had served as one rationale for the earlier appointments of matrons.

The writer of an editorial in *The American City* in November 1913 commented on the interest in policewomen. "It was not so very long ago that the mere mention of the term *police-woman* could be depended upon to provide a smile," the magazine said, adding: "There are those who still regard the idea as inherently humorous; have they not seen . . . caricatures in magazines and newspapers of an Amazon, crowned with the old-time helmet, clad in blue uniform with a liberal supply of brass buttons, and *always* brandishing a club?" Readers were assured a policewoman "bears little resemblance to her spurious portraits." Rather, she "is usually quiet, often slight in build, filled with the seriousness of her work, and has no use for the big stick. She comes into a field that has long been waiting for her. Much of [her] work . . . has not been done by men; it has . . . been left undone because men were not fitted to do it."[19]

As Wells argued for the appointment of policewomen, several cities began to act. In 1912 officials in Denver selected Josephine A. Roche, "daughter of well-to-do parents, graduate of Vassar College, and post-graduate of Columbia University," who had done settlement house work in New York City. A year later, the chief noted "the best man" on his force was a woman—Policewoman Roche. She established control of dance halls, movies, skating rinks, and similar amusements and assured that those under sixteen were barred unless accompanied by their parents. Roche became one of the most politically prominent of the early police-women. She served as the probation officer and director of the girl's department of the Denver Juvenile Court in 1915, remaining until 1918. After a series of career changes, including managing a coal mine she inherited, she was narrowly defeated in the 1934 Democratic Party pri-mary for governor of Colorado and then served from 1934 to 1937 as assistant secretary of the treasury in the administration of President Franklin D. Roosevelt.[20]

Eva L. Corning and Elizabeth Barr-Arthur were appointed in 1913 in Topeka, after urging by the WCTU and the state's largest civic organiza-tion. Corning, who carried only a badge and a whistle, settled quarrels among women and solved neighborhood troubles through arbitration, avoiding "the unpleasant notoriety and expense of police court." She noted the power of the word *police* "has a force with the wayward and unruly; they know the penalty of resisting an officer, so they will listen to us and we can help them." A new mayor did not see these benefits. Despite the women's having been appointed under civil service, in 1915 he dismissed them.[21]

On the West Coast, officials in San Diego acted in 1913 and those in San Francisco the next year, although the women selected by the two cities were very different. San Diego selected E. Belle Robinson. Not cut from the same social worker cloth as most of the pioneer policewomen, she was "colorful and corrupt," repeatedly made local headlines, and was not reappointed in 1915. It was later determined that she ran a house of ill repute, but whether this was during her police employment has never been determined. On May 1, 1916 she was convicted of using a hotel she ran for "purposes of lewdness, assignation, and prostitution" and was ordered by the court to sell the hotel furniture and fixtures. There is no indication that she received any further punishment from the court.[22]

Kate O'Connor in 1914 was one of three policewomen appointed in San Francisco. She recalled being greeted by her male colleagues with skepticism and resentment. She and the other appointees, Kathlyn Sullivan and Kathryne Eisenhart, became known as the "Three Kates." Two had connections to law enforcement; O'Connor's late husband had been chief jailer in the sheriff's office and Sullivan's deceased father had been a San Francisco detective. Although the women were assigned to handle women and children, they worked stakeouts in Golden Gate Park and were present at numerous violent incidents. O'Connor was involved in a series of cases that left three male colleagues shot and killed; Sullivan was credited with breaking up a "white slave gang . . . preying on high school girls," and Eisenhart in 1917 was so seriously beaten and kicked when arresting two brothers that she retired on disability in 1931 after recurring physical ailments.[23]

Officials in Syracuse, New York, appointed a policewoman in 1914 after a year of lobbying by women who had heard Wells describe her duties. The women, aided by the WCTU, suffrage groups, and church leaders, buttressed their argument with the fact that earlier that year officials in San Francisco had appointed the "Three Kates."[24] That actions in San Francisco, a large West Coast city, would impact a much smaller Eastern city provides an indication of the degree to which the appointment of policewomen was a movement which women spearheaded, using each success to lobby elsewhere around the country.

The policewomen's movement was not an isolated phenomenon, but was part of women's movement into other newly created or newly professionalized fields in which they frequently replaced volunteers or employees of private charities or benevolent groups. The women entering these fields were frequently from the upper-middle-class, college educated, and native-born, while those they sought to assist were overwhelmingly poor, immigrant women and their families. Among other areas undergoing similar growth and conversion to paid, professional status were social work, nursing, and home economics. These professions, in which these college-educated women eventually predominated, were impacted by early twentieth-century social reform efforts.[25]

While sources disagree on the actual numbers, officials in many cities appointed policewomen in the years 1910 to 1915. The 1915 U.S. Census reported that 25 cities employed policewomen paid by the police department, rather than by private protective agencies. The largest number was 21 in Chicago. Most cities had only a handful. The census confirmed that despite higher education levels and broader professional orientation than male colleagues, policewomen were usually paid less than policemen. In Chicago male officers had a salary range of $900 to $1,320; policewomen earned no more than $900. The Three Kates in San Francisco earned $1,200; the 765 male officers earned $1,464. Generally, women earned between $800 and $1,200 annually, with one officer in Portland (Baldwin) earning $1,860.[26]

Cities that did not appoint policewomen increased the number and duties of matrons. An overlap in duties created confusion and arbitrary distinctions in rank and function. This is what occurred in Grand Forks, when the matron named in 1909 performed duties identical to those associated with policewomen. The confusion stymied even so dedicated a follower of the movement as Chloe Owings, who in 1925 completed *Women Police*, a book prepared in affiliation with the Bureau of Social Hygiene. The bureau, financed by John D. Rockefeller, Jr., after he served as fore-man of a New York City special grand jury investigating prostitution in the city, set out to study prostitution. Among the related issues it examined were police systems, court reform, and the need for women police.[27]

Women Police was written in conjunction with the IAP after Rockefeller decided it was crucial to document "in an impartial way a picture of . . . women police in the more important cities where they are now employed." Owings listed 34 cities that appointed policewomen, distinct from matrons (although she noted that some women served as both), in the 1910-1915 period.[28] Due to confusion over titles her list differs from census figures.

Policewomen throughout their history have tried to distance themselves from matrons. Yet Alice Stebbins Wells eschewed this distinction, as well as the one between policewomen paid from public funds and agents of protective associations. In a 1914 letter to *The Survey*, Wells, probably thinking of developing a policewoman's association, urged women in police work to write her so she could develop a census by name, location, title, and function. She also asked each to list problems in carrying out her assignment.[29] That Wells would consider *The Survey*, a journal of social service reform, as the place to reach women police says much about Wells and the early policewomen, who were first and foremost social workers and social reformers.

Speaking at the 1915 National Conference of Charities and Correction meeting, where the IAP was formed, Wells listed 28 U.S. and four Canadian cities that had "regular policewomen—those who are a regular part of the police department, appointed as men are for outside work." She added two U.S. cities in which women were doing police work with the chief's approval although their salaries were paid privately. There are in small cities, she reported,

matrons who . . . do . . . protective work of a policewoman, taking care, in addition, of the occasional woman prisoner.... I have included them in the regular list, for such they are and should be called.

There are ... police matrons who, in addition to their own arduous duty of taking full care daily of women prisoners, receive other requests because there are no policewomen.... One is Mrs. J.J. Farley, of Dallas.... The city has paid tribute to her ... by giving her the title and salary of captain, with a handsome gold badge to prove it.[30]

Wells's acceptance of matrons as sister professionals stemmed from personal experience. When she joined the LAPD all officers worked every day of the year except for their 15 days of vacation. The chief was able to give the men one day off a month by overlapping days and hours on duty, but he was unable to accommodate the three matrons. Wells was asked to spend three Sundays a month in the jail, providing a day off for each matron.

By the early 1920s most policewomen showed the same disdain for matrons that other social workers were showing for the volunteers who had preceded them in their specialties. Just as medical social workers in 1920 decried the "indiscriminate use of untrained people," which in their minds resulted in a "lack of standards" which discredited their work,[31] so did policewomen view matrons as untrained, custodial personnel standing in the way of their professional recognition. Similar developments were also occurring in nursing, where, as a way of maintaining their new status, women endorsed high entry standards to keep out those less qualified and to distinguish themselves from volunteers.

One city in which the overlap of matrons and policewomen resulted in confusion and animosity was New York City. Although matrons had served the city's jail since 1845 and its police department since 1891, it was not until 1896 that they were assigned to search subjects, process, escort, and supervise inmates in precinct detention facilities, and care for lost children. Appointed in 1911, Mary Sullivan, a young widow with two children, came from a police family. Although she was the first woman in the clan to enter policing, her younger sister soon followed her. Sullivan eventually became involved in the fight to make the matrons into policewomen. Her autobiography, *My Double Life: The Story of a New York Policewoman*, features a colorful description of her reporting for duty and provides some idea of how any woman—matron or policewoman—was perceived by male officers. As Sullivan recalled, on June 12, 1911, she

reported ... as a probationary member of the New York Police Department. Men ... on duty ... tell how I came along 47th Street bedecked with a long green gown, a picture hat trimmed with white flowers, and a fluffy green parasol. I was still in my twenties, and I hadn't had a single day's training for the duties I was about to assume. With my heart in my mouth I walked up the steps between the green lights and entered the yellow brick building.

When I fluttered in, the desk lieutenant reached for a sheet of paper, assuming, as he later remarked, that I had come in to complain about a barking dog, or a piano played too late at night. A look of utter amazement came over his face when I told him that I had come to report for duty.[32]

No longer fluttering by 1918, Sullivan became president of the Police-women's Endowment Association and battled to change the women's title from matron to policewoman. She found that matrons "were paid less than the patrolmen, had no opportunities for promotion, and were given very low pensions when they retired. Considering all that they were called upon to do, this discrimination seemed very unfair." She carried her fight to the legislature, winning a change in the women's "official designation to *policewoman* and giving women officers the same salaries and pension rights as men." Her battle was not merely for a cosmetic change; in 1921, the year New York City finally opened its ranks to women as fully sworn officers, its police officers earned $2,280 annually, a fairly high salary. An officer and his family also received health and welfare benefits and a pension after a prescribed number of years of service.[33]

Two other large cities where supporters met resistance when they lobbied for policewomen were Cleveland in 1911 and Boston in 1912. In neither city were women appointed until the 1920s. Despite this, by 1915 there were even a small number of women supervisors: Annie McCully in Dayton, Ohio; Blanche H. Mason in Seattle; Mary S. Harvey in Baltimore; and Lola Baldwin in Portland, Oregon. There might have been a female chief of police, Dolly Spenser, appointed in 1914 in Milford, Ohio, a community of 1,500 people in which gambling was a major problem. Spenser, who was

the general adjuster of . . . social problems . . ., went "after the boys and took them out of the gambling joints to her own home." Here they were joined by their parents. . . . She held her position as chief . . . for two years, or until a new mayor took office, when the appointment was not continued.[34]

Whether Spenser actually served as chief is subject to dispute. The Milford Area Historical Society lists "Aunt" Dolly Spenser as a Clermont County Juvenile Court probation officer who never held public office, although she ran unsuccessfully for mayor after 1920. About Spenser's personality though, there is little disagreement. She was "a very tough, civic minded individual said to fear only one thing, thunder storms." Yet a front page photo of Aunt Dolly braiding a rag rug appeared on February 28, 1921 in the *Columbus* (OH) *Evening Dispatch* under the headline "Made Good As Police Chief, She's To Be Promoted." It reported that Spenser had been so successful as police chief that Milford was expected to "unanimously elect her mayor. . . . She is the candidate of both parties and has no opposition." Despite this, Spenser's 1926 obituary never mentioned her being chief, but described her as a county probation officer and a 1921 Milford mayoral candidate.[35]

The appointment of African-American policewomen lagged behind that of whites. On July 26, 1916, Georgia Robinson, born in 1879 in Opelousas, Louisiana, became the first African-American female member of the LAPD. After moving to Kansas to work as a governess, she met and married her husband, with whom she moved to Los Angeles in 1912. She attracted the police department's attention through her activities with a number of civic groups. Initially appointed a matron, she became a policewoman on June 10, 1919, and is probably the first African-American female municipal policewoman in the United States. A second African-American woman was appointed in 1925, joined by a third in 1929.[36]

Officials in New York City appointed Nettie B. Harris on December 29, 1924; although she is often listed as the first African-American police-woman, records indicate that other African-American women served in the department as early as 1917 as juvenile court probation officers. But *The New York Age*, an African-American-oriented newspaper, called Lawon R. Bruce New York City's first African-American policewoman. Bruce, a graduate nurse who had been a high school teacher prior to her January 1920 appointment, had, according to *The Age*, "all the equipment of the regular patrolman," although she wore no uniform and that "only when the flashing of her badge is necessary" is there an outward sign of her position.[37]

By 1916 cities in 21 states had policewomen; the list would have prob-ably been longer had the lack of suffrage not hampered giving women police powers. Seven states had passed special legislation making pos-sible the hiring of policewomen. A year later the movement had spread to 30 cities.[38] Entry of the United States into World War I led to increases in the number of women performing police roles. By the end of the war, municipal policewomen, while not commonplace, were no longer a curi-ous experiment. Acceptance of policewomen providing social services as part of the police function had taken hold.

Part of this acceptance stemmed from work done by women under the Law Enforcement Division of the Commission on Training Camp Activi-ties set up by the federal government during the war. The commission, directed by Raymond Fosdick, was charged with keeping military camps safe and free of venereal disease. The threat of prostitutes and sexually transmitted diseases resulted in women activists' gaining responsibility for implementing policies aimed at controlling venereal disease. Also of concern were young girls who became involved with military personnel. After receiving reports from Decatur, Illinois, that more than one half of the girls in the high school senior class had become pregnant shortly after the opening of an aviation base, Fosdick developed the idea of a force of female protective officers to stem the interrelated problems of prostitution, venereal disease, and corruption of the morals of young women.[39]

Fosdick, who traced his family in the United States to the Revolutionary War, counted among his friends John D. Rockefeller, Jr., and President Woodrow Wilson, head of Princeton University when Fosdick studied there. Fosdick wrote *European Police Systems* after Rockefeller asked him to study how European police regulated prostitution. Between 1915 and 1917, after Rockefeller suggested he do a similar survey in the United States, Fosdick visited more than 100 police departments. After time out to assist in the war effort, he published his findings in 1920 in *American Police Systems*. For many years the pre-eminent work on police administration, the book was very critical of American policing. In discussing police-women, Fosdick observed that they were often appointed without a clear idea of their functions, even though the "peculiar value of women police officers as preventive agents in working with women and girls has come to be recognized" and that neither matron duties nor uniformed, ordinary patrol were appropriate for women officers.[40]

Through the commission, Fosdick was able to put his beliefs into practice. Women, the majority of whom were social workers, performed such duties as keeping prostitutes away from the camps; enforcing federal liquor sale bans; returning runaways to their homes, particularly young girls who gravitated to camp areas, and overseeing commercial amusements around the camps. Not surprisingly, these were the duties assigned to Lola Baldwin in Portland in 1905 when the Lewis and Clark Exposition attracted large numbers of unattached males.

By 1918 Fosdick's commission had established a Committee on Protective Work for Girls, which empowered protective officers to undertake enforcement duties even though they lacked police powers. There were almost 200 of these female officers. Fewer than a third were paid from federal funds; the others received salaries from private groups. The majority received police badges from local chiefs, although as much as a courtesy as a sign of recognition.

The committee's activities brought women into the state police for the first time, when Connecticut, with no large cities, decided to use women as state police officers. Six officers and unit supervisor Dr. Valeria H. Parker, chairman of the Health and Recreation Department of the State Council of Defense, on August 17, 1917, became the State Women Police Corps. With salaries paid by the Council of Defense, the corps paid particular attention to prostitution and liquor law violations. Despite—or possibly because of—the women's participation in a large number of cases, a bill sponsored by the Connecticut League of Women to make the positions permanent failed to win approval. On March 1, 1919, the unit was disbanded.[41]

The groups which paid the salaries of Connecticut's state policewomen and other protective officers were usually the same groups that were demanding policewomen in municipal departments. Women's patriotic leagues were also demanding policewomen and protective workers to safeguard the morals of local girls and soldiers far from home. These efforts were spearheaded by the Committee on Protective Work for Girls, headquartered in New York City and chaired by Maude E. Miner, secretary of the New York Probation and Protective Association, a supporter of the policewomen's movement. Of the four additional committee members, at least two—Martha P. Falconer of Philadelphia and Mrs. John D. Rockefeller, Jr., of New York City—were advocates of policewomen. Miner urged every community with a military facility to set up a girls' protective bureau. Estimating almost 300 facilities, she recommended a woman director with two or more officers "under the regular police department or under a volunteer committee."[42]

By the end of the war, there were almost 300 policewomen [actually many were protective workers], the largest numbers serving in Indianapolis and Washington, D.C. Estimates are that policewomen were employed in more than 220 cities at the end of World War I,[43] a large increase over the pre-war number of 125 and an indication of how the war had spurred the movement nationally.

Around the nation, policewomen were safeguarding moral standards. In Newark, New Jersey, women patrolled the train station, and on one evening in 1918 seized young girls and forced them to remove makeup from their faces.[44] Sometimes the morals the policewomen protected were their own. Two Buffalo, New York, policewomen investigating a tailor accused of insulting women, reported that "he got fresh with each" and had him arrested for assault. An Oklahoma City, Oklahoma, policewoman on a similar case met with judicial resistance. Bringing into court a man accused of inviting her on a joy ride, she was advised that speaking with the man at length and asking him when he was going to leave was "flirting" and would not be tolerated. The judge dismissed the case. What the judge termed flirting eventually became the legal concept of entrapment, a notion that had not yet permeated the criminal justice system. When a New York City officer was approached by a man trying to pick her up, she walked him to the front of a station, "where she displayed her badge and invited him to 'c'mon in and meet mother'." He was arrested and fined $10 for disorderly conduct.[45]

While most policewomen protected women and young girls, a few went beyond this. In 1917, Valley Center, Kansas, had a woman mayor, a woman marshal, and a woman police judge. On April 15, 1919, a woman active in state suffrage campaigns was elected police commissioner of Fargo, North Dakota, and in May 1921, a widow who had served as a policewoman "for home protection" and had been active in Red Cross work during the war was elected police and fire commissioner of Cumberland, Maryland.[46]

Not all communities were pleased with policewomen. San Diego had particular problems—after E. Belle Robinson was not reappointed in 1915, two women joined the department in mid-1918. One resigned; one was fired. A third remained less than a year and a fourth, a widow with five children, served as both policewoman and matron. In 1920 the city did not allocate funds for policewomen and she became solely a matron until her 1938 retirement.

No additional policewomen were hired until 1926; but by 1929 they, too, were gone. The impetus for recruiting women was twofold. The department was under strength and was faced with crime in a park that had become a haven for "criminals and perverts." The women hired in 1926, termed "expert marksmen," were among the few to have used their firearms. Jessica Long, before being dismissed after three months, shot and captured a would-be assailant in the park. Olga Nelson also encountered a suspect in the park. After he lunged at her, she shot him in both legs, shattering one of his heels. Rena Wright's partner was killed during an assignment that required them to portray lovers to lure a robber. Although the women behaved heroically during their violent encounters, in February 1928 the chief requested that they resign, stating he no longer needed them. They refused and were fired. Despite court rulings in their favor, neither was permitted to return. Policewomen did not enter the department again until 1936.[47]

Other policewomen also encountered opposition. In Colorado Springs, Colorado, the two policewomen took out newspaper advertisements to publicize their resignations in 1918 after a dispute with the mayor. He maintained that the town's first policewoman failed to keep records for four years and that it was impossible to get any check upon the number of hours she had worked. To rectify this, the women were ordered to report at headquarters "just as other[s] . . . do and always have done"—which resulted in their resignations. In 1925, in Jamestown, New York, Margaret Jackson resigned after a dispute with her chief, who told her "to look after outside police work only," rather than clerical work that had been taking "from four to five hours of her time every day . . . for five or six years." He felt her outside work was more important. An editorial in the local paper, though, claimed Jackson's resignation was due to the chief ordering that her work and the matron's work be combined.[48]

Despite these setbacks, World War I had done much to raise the profile of policewomen. Social welfare activities had been particularly important. Many realized for the first time that social service could not only exist within a police department, but that the police played a role in social problems even more important than the role played by the courts and private social agencies.

Another impetus to policewomen's progress after 1922 was an IACP resolution, urged by Chief August Vollmer, of Berkeley, California, who served as IACP president in 1922, terming policewomen essential members of modern police departments. The IAP also worked with social service leaders to petition for women officers. Lt. Mina C. Van Winkle, director of the Washington, D.C., Metropolitan Police Department woman's bureau and Wells's successor as IAP president, in 1920 addressed the NCSW conference. Noting that "policewomen are aiming to bring about a close relationship between social workers, the public and the police," she called for a women's bureau, directed by a woman, in every large city.[49]

The post-World War I years until the mid-1920s saw growth in the number of policewomen. In a March 1920 editorial in *The Woman Citizen* similar to the one in *The American City* in 1913, the author noted: "The policewoman is no longer an experiment—she is a fixture and she is crying out to be taken seriously, not as a joke for the comic supplements." Writing in 1921, Van Winkle was also optimistic. Stating that there were almost 300 cities with policewomen, nearly all "appointed . . . because of pressure by women's organizations," she listed what she saw as policewomen's duties.[50] Her inventory did not differ from pre-war tasks.

Salaries, though, continued to be a concern since women were almost always paid less than men. In 1921, women in Seattle and Washington, D.C., were the highest paid, earning $2,100 and $1,900 annually. The women usually worked eight hours during the day, but were on call if situations involving women or children arose. A 1921 survey of 20 large cities found that only seven paid policewomen the same as policemen. Matrons, performing some or all of policewomen's duties, were usually paid even less.[51] Conditions had not changed by the end of the decade.

The actual number of women and the cities in which they worked after World War I continued to be the subject of various reports. A 1924 survey counted 235 policewomen in 32 departments, with New York City, Detroit, Chicago, and Washington, D.C. having the largest numbers. Van Winkle estimated in 1926 that there were approximately 500 policewomen serving in some 175 cities. A 1929 IAP count listed 593 policewomen in 154 cities.[52]

By the late 1920s cities interested in establishing policewomen had done so. Reformers in cities without women officers were not as powerful and therefore not as successful as their predecessors had been. Gains were not sustained, and after 1925 activities became more limited to morals enforcement than before the war. Responsibilities centered on preventing juvenile crime, primarily through restricting the activities of youths. Policewomen personified the two overriding assumptions of Progressive reform, namely, "that the state had to take a more active role in regulating the social welfare of its citizens, and that private and public spheres of activity could not be disentangled."[53] Curfews and dance halls dominate the writings of policewomen after 1925. Assigning policewomen to dance halls was in keeping with the interests of the Progressives and the WCTU women to whom they owed their jobs and with whose reform agenda they overwhelmingly agreed.

A thread running throughout the social history of the United States has been moral reformers, usually of middle-class or higher status, trying to curtail and contain the development of saloons and dance halls, usually frequented by working-class immigrant groups. At the same time that public amusements were regulated or banned, reformers concentrated also on controlling prostitution. Although prostitution was a central concern of nineteenth century female reformers, they saw it as an individual practice rather than as an organized cartel. When Progressives adopted prostitution as a concern, it was translated into "white slavery," a metaphor that captured the dual beliefs that "all women were potential victims of sexual enslavement" and that the enslavers were "an underworld of European immigrants operating an international traffic in women's bodies."[54] Prostitution blended with prohibition. Dance halls, frequented by men and lower-class women, came to embody these twin vices. A 1927 meeting of policewomen from six Eastern cities focused on nightlife and liquor. All agreed that "protective and preventive work is the police function of their sex."[55]

The women's agreement set the tone for their activities for years to come. Although many issues pertaining to the status and powers of women officers remained to be ironed out over future decades, policewomen had created for themselves and those who would follow a gender-based, social service role in U.S. police departments. As the 1920s drew to a close, most small police departments had one or two women involved almost solely with women, juveniles, and morals issues. Most large departments had women's bureaus of varying sizes, where the women operated apart from the rest of the department. The bureaus, sought by supporters of policewomen and by most policewomen themselves, reinforced the concept of women's sphere and affected the professional lives of policewomen until the modern era.

NOTES

1. Chloe Owings, *Women Police: A Study of the Development and Status of the Women Police Movement* (New York: Frederick H. Hitchcock, 1925), 101-102; Elizabeth Simpson Smith, *Breakthrough: Women in Law Enforcement* (New York: Walker & Co., 1982), 5. Wells was the first woman in the United States to be called a policewoman; she was not the first in the world. That distinction belongs to Margherita Ditmars, appointed in Stuttgart, Germany, in 1903.

2. Constance M. Breece and Gerald R. Garrett, "Women in Policing: Changing Perspectives on the Role" in *Criminal Justice Planning*, eds. Joseph E. Scott and Simon Dinitz (New York: Praeger Publishers, 1977), 4. Also in 1893, according to Laura Kelso and Joyce McDonald, "U.S. Marshal—200th Birthday," *WomenPolice*, Winter 1989, 13, Deputy Marshal Ada Carnutt arrested two perjurers in Oklahoma

territory. In 1856 Pinkerton's National Detective Agency used female agents to catch dishonest train conductors in the Chicago area. These agents, though, had no powers of arrest. See Frank Morn, *The Eye That Never Sleeps: A History of the Pinkerton National Detective Agency* (Bloomington: Indiana University Press, 1982), 54. By the 1880s department stores used women detectives to prevent shoplifting by middle-class women. Since most clerks and shoppers were women, female detectives, who also lacked arrest powers, were used to blend in on the selling floors. See Elaine S. Abelson, *When Ladies Go A-Thieving: Middle-Class Shoplifters in the Victorian Department Store* (New York: Oxford University Press, 1989).

3. Owings, *Women Police*, 100-101; Gary R. Perlstein, *An Exploratory Analysis of Certain Characteristics of Policewomen* (Ann Arbor, MI: Xerox University Microfilms, 1975 [Ph.D. diss., Florida State University, 1971]), 52. Clarice Feinman, *Women in the Criminal Justice System*, 3d ed. (Westport, CT: Praeger Publishers, 1994), 94, observes that Baldwin was typical of the women who followed her: "She worked for a social reform organization that focused on protecting and caring for women and children. When she transferred . . . to the police department, she kept the role of a social worker for women and children. She did not see herself as a cop." Ralph O'Hara notes in "History of Portland Oregon, Law Enforcement Functions," *The Police Chief*, Oct. 1988, 137: "In 1908, Lola Baldwin was appointed . . . Superintendent of Women's Affairs, thus becoming the first civil service appointed woman police officer in the United States."

4. Owings, *Women Police*, 101; Mark T. Connelly, *The Response to Prostitution in the Progressive Era* (Chapel Hill: University of North Carolina Press, 1980), 44; David J. Pivar, *Purity Crusade: Sexual Morality and Social Control, 1868-1900* (Westport, CT: Greenwood Press, 1973), 154, 177. Ruth Rosen, *The Lost Sisterhood: Prostitution in America, 1900-1918* (Baltimore: Johns Hopkins University Press, 1982), 126, explains how women were thought lured into prostitution: "Unsuspecting girls and women were sometimes procured at railway and bus stations. . . . Women panderers, posing as . . . social workers, would offer . . . shelter and employment. Instead, the girl would find herself sold as a white slave in a local vice district." By 1915, according to Mary Ritter Beard, *Woman's Work in Municipalities*, 1915; reprint (New York: Arno Press, 1972), 118, societies existed in every large urban center and were "of the greatest value . . . in safeguarding women and girls from criminals." (reference is to reprint edition)

5. Estelle B. Freedman, "Separatism as Strategy: Female Institution Building and American Feminism, 1870-1930," *Feminist Studies* 5, no. 3 (Fall 1979), 515.

6. Samuel Walker, *Popular Justice: A History of American Criminal Justice* (New York: Oxford University Press, 1980), 55.

7. J.E. Reavis, "The Police Department of Portland, Oregon," *National Police Magazine*, Apr. 1913, 92.

8. Alice Stebbins Wells, "Twenty and Four Years a Police Woman," WPOAC, *Convention Program*, Tahoe, CA, Aug. 24-26, 1933, 7.

9. Lois Lundell Higgins, "The Policewoman," *Law and Order*, Nov. 1958, 4.

10. William J. Bopp and Donald O. Schultz, *A Short History of American Law Enforcement* (Springfield, IL: Charles C Thomas, 1972), 81.

11. Alice Stebbins Wells, "Policewoman Badge Number One." IAWP, The Policewomen's Bulletin, *Law and Order*, Jan. 1961, 75. Six months later, the chief told Wells he was sorry to offer her "so plain an insignia of office; that when he had

a squad of Amazons he would ask the police commission to design a star edged with lace ruffles"—just what she didn't want. See Bertha A. Smith, "The Police-woman," *Good Housekeeping*, Mar. 1911, 296.

12. Smith, "The Policewoman," 296; Wells, "Twenty and Four Years a Police Woman," 7.

13. Owings, *Women Police*, 103. This unflattering view of policewomen followed them throughout the early years of their existence. Women in police garb as a source of humor predated Wells. A 1909 film, billed as a comedy, concerned a woman who dons a police uniform as a joke on her lover and is "called upon to perform the duties of an officer," giving rise "to several amusing incidents" and "trying experiences," resulting in her joy at "the opportunity to change her attire and return the troublesome uniform." See "The Policewoman," *The Moving Picture World*, Mar. 27, 1909, 377.

14. Owings, *Women Police*, 103, 104; Wells, "Policewoman Badge Number One," 76; Smith, *Breakthrough*, 5.

15. June Sochen, *Movers and Shakers: American Women Thinkers and Activists 1900-1970* (New York: Quadrangle, 1973), 88 (for women and travel); Wells, "Police-woman Badge Number One," 76.

16. "Glimpses of LAPD History Reflect The Past . . .," *The Police Chief*, Aug. 1977, 16-17; Alice Stebbins Wells, "Women on the Police Force," *The American City*, Apr. 1913, 401.

17. August Vollmer, "Meet the Lady Cop," *The Survey*, Mar. 15, 1930, 702.

18. Alice Stebbins Wells, "Remarks," *Proceedings of the IACP* (1914), 129-130 quoted in Samuel Walker, "The Rise and Fall of the Policewomen's Movement, 1905-1975" in *Law and Order in American History*, ed. Joseph M. Hawes (Port Washington, NY: Kennikat Press, 1979), 108.

19. "The Police-Woman Is Marching On," *The American City*, Nov. 1913, 403. The reference may come from *Sketch*, which on May 24, 1911, n.p., described Denmark's Teilmann Idsen as "the first uniformed female police-constable in the world," pictured her in a helmet, and reported that "if the experiment proves satisfactory a regular corps of police Amazons will be formed and distributed throughout the country."

20. Darwin, *The Nineteenth Century*, June 1914, 1374; H.M. Walbrook, "Women Police and Their Work," *The Nineteenth Century*, Feb. 1919, 377; "The Police-Woman is Marching On," Nov. 1913, 403; Susan Ware, *Beyond Suffrage: Women in the New Deal* (Cambridge, MA: Harvard University Press, 1981), 151- 152; Millard Milburn Rice, "Roosevelt, Roche, and Recovery," *Literary Digest* 118 (Sept. 1, 1934), 8. Roche's career in juvenile court is mentioned in both works; her work as a policewoman is not.

21. "A Police-Woman's Record in Topeka," *The Survey*, Sept. 25, 1915, 571; Eva L. Corning, *Women Police Service. History of the Movement. Stories of Human Interest* (Topeka, KS: n.p., 1915), Introduction, 7, 13, 8, 9, 12.

22. Anne Findlay Patton, "Women Officers of the San Diego Police Department, 1912-1988," M.A. thesis, University of San Diego, 1989, 8-16.

23. WPOAC, *Convention Program*, 1937, 44; San Francisco Police Museum and Archives, miscellaneous collected material.

24. Beard, *Woman's Work in Municipalities*, 266.

25. These efforts are commonly termed the Progressive movement. Progressiv-

ism is used here in the same way Ellen Fitzpatrick, *Endless Crusade: Women Social Scientists and Progressive Reform* (New York: Oxford University Press, 1990), 218 (fn 2) defines it, namely, "individuals and organizations who came together to advance social and political reform during the late 19th and early 20th century." It is no coincidence, therefore, that three of the four women she writes about (Sophonisba Breckinridge, Edith Abbott, and Katharine Bement Davis) were advocates for policewomen.

26. U.S. Bureau of the Census, *General Statistics of Cities* (Washington, DC, 1915), 18, cited in Albert R. Roberts, "Police Social Workers: A History," *Social Work* 21, no. 4 (July 1976): 295; Owings, *Women Police*, 104; Corning, *Women Police Service*, 7; Samuel Walker, *A Critical History of Police Reform:: The Emergence of Professionalism* (Lexington, MA: Lexington Books, 1977), 92 (for salaries). Cities and numbers of policewomen: Los Angeles (5); Seattle (5); Baltimore (5); Rochester, NY (1); Syracuse, NY (1); Vancouver, BC, Can. (1); Fargo, ND (1); Grand Forks (1); Toronto, ON, Can. (2); Ottowa, ON, Can. (1); San Francisco (3); Omaha, NB (1); Chicago (36); Aurora, IL (1); San Antonio (2); Pittsburgh (4); Sioux City, IA (1); Superior, WI (1); Racine, WI (1); St. Paul (3); Minneapolis (2); Denver (1); Colorado Springs, CO (1); Fort Wayne, IN (1); Dayton, OH (2); Poughkeepsie, NY (1); Jamestown, NY (1); Ithaca, NY (1); East Chicago, IN (1); Galesburg, IL (1); Victoria, BC, Can. (1); San Diego (3); Birmingham, AL (1); Youngstown, OH (1); Boise, ID (1); Spokane (1); Phoenix (1). Corning states, 13, Witchita and Hutchison, KS, also had policewomen in 1915.

27. Mark T. Connelly, *The Response to Prostitution in the Progressive Era* (Chapel Hill: University of North Carolina Press, 1980), 16. For a discussion of the Bureau of Social Hygiene, see Willoughby Cyrus Waterman, *Prostitution and Its Repression in New York City 1900-1931* (New York: Columbia University Press, 1932), 84-87.

28. Owings, *Women Police*, xx, 285-286. Reflecting the IAP distinction between matrons and policewomen, cities where women served as matrons received no mention, even if their duties were identical to those of policewomen. Owings failed to see policewomen as an extension of matrons—possibly because IAP leaders sought to separate themselves from matrons. Cities listed by Owings: Los Angeles; Baltimore; Birmingham, AL; Decatur, IL; Fargo, ND; Galesburg, IL; Omaha, NE; Fort Wayne, IN; Hannibal, MO; Rochester, NY; Salem, MA; San Francisco; South Bend, IN; St. Paul; Wichita; Winnetka, IL; Chicago; Dayton, OH; Denver; Des Moines, IA; East Chicago, IN; Minneapolis; Pittsburgh; Racine, WI; Superior, WI; Syracuse, NY; Virginia, MN; Flint, MI; Haverhill, MA; Minot, ND; Hornell, NY; Madison, WI; Trenton, NJ; Washington, DC.

29. Alice Stebbins Wells, "Policewomen," *The Survey*, May 16, 1914, 207-208.

30. Alice Stebbins Wells, "Policewomen," *Proceedings*, NCCC, 42nd Annual Session, Baltimore, MD, May 12-19, 1915, 414. Cities, in Wells's order of appointment and with numbers in each: Los Angeles (5); Baltimore (5); Seattle (5); Vancouver, BC, Can. (1); Fargo, ND (1); Topeka, KS (2); Toronto, ON, Can. (2); Grand Forks, ND (1); San Francisco (3); Rochester, NY (1); Chicago (36); Ottawa, ON, Can. (1); Aurora, IL (1); San Antonio, TX (2); Syracuse, NY (1); Pittsburgh (4); St. Paul (3); Minneapolis (2); Denver (1); Muncie, IN (1); Colorado Springs, CO (1); Superior, WI (1); Dayton (2); Jamestown, NY (1); Racine, WI (1); South Bend, IN (1); Phoenix (1); Victoria, BC, Can. (1); Ithaca, NY (1); Sioux City, IA (1); Beatrice, NE (1), and Omaha, NE (1). Those with privately paid policewomen were Poughkeepsie,

NY, and Des Moines, IA.

31. Mary C. Jarrett, "Remarks," Conference on Foundation and Proper Training of Hospital Social Workers, NYC, Feb. 21, 1921, quoted in Roy Lubove, *The Professional Altruist: The Emergence of Social Work as a Career, 1880-1930* (New York: Antheneum, 1975), 33. Disdain for volunteers by professional women is noted by Robert H. Wiebe, *The Search for Order: 1870-1920* (New York: Hill & Wang, 1967), 120-121 and Anthony M. Platt, *The Child Savers: The Invention of Delinquency*, 2d ed. (Chicago: University of Chicago Press, 1977), 98. Policewomen fit the pattern identified by Nancy F. Cott, *The Grounding of Modern Feminism* (New Haven, CT: Yale University Press, 1987), 222, 237-238, as "protection of prestige" that other professions practiced. What differed is that in the others it was men who sought to uphold their prestige by keeping women out, while policewomen sought to keep out other women they believed lacked proper credentials.

Police departments had shed volunteerism some 50 years earlier. Prior to the Civil War, many cities relied for police services on watch and ward societies made up of male citizens who took turns patrolling the streets. The change to salaried, formal agencies was slow until after the Civil War. In the mid-1860s only eight U.S. cities had a uniformed police force headed by a chief; by 1880, 57 cities had uniformed police forces, and the era of male volunteerism in law enforcement ended. See Blake McKelvey, *The Urbanization of America: 1860-1915* (New Brunswick, NJ: Rutgers University Press, 1963), 92 and Eric H. Monkkonen, *Police in Urban America: 1860-1920* (Cambridge, England: Cambridge University Press, 1981), 54.

32. Mary Sullivan, *My Double Life: The Story of a New York Policewoman* (New York: Farrar & Rinehart, 1938), 17.

33. Ibid., 143, 280; James I. Alexander, *Blue Coats: Black Skin: The Black Experience in the New York City Police Department Since 1891* (Hicksville, NY: Exposition Press, 1978), 29.

34. Owings, *Women Police*, 105.

35. Letter to Ronald C. Van Raalte from Barbara K. Carlson, Feb. 27, 1991; "Made Good As Police Chief, She's To Be Promoted," *Columbus* (OH) *Evening Dispatch*, Feb. 28, 1921, 1:2-3; *The Clermont* (Batavia, OH) *Sun*, Dec. 23, 1926, 1:1.

Lorain, Ohio, had a woman safety director some years later. "Mother Made Police Boss," *The Cincinnati Post*, Mar. 16, 1926, n.p., notes that Florence Grall, mother of six, was appointed by her husband, William, the mayor. She replaced a director who was fired for "lack of cooperation" and she was appointed specifically to hear charges against a lieutenant whose removal Grall sought. "An active worker among women's clubs [who] has given considerably attention to . . . public service," Mrs. Grall said she would give her new position "only two hours a day. I have seven reasons [her husband and children] for spending the rest of the time at home."

Ruth Bordin, *Woman and Temperance: The Quest for Power and Liberty, 1873-1900*, 1981; reprint (New Brunswick, NJ: Rutgers University Press, 1990), 100, 199, refers to an earlier woman chief. Citing scrapbooks (1898-1942) of Miriam E. Rains, San Diego Historical Society Library, Serra Museum, Presidio Park, San Diego, Bordin describes a WCTU member [presumably Rains, who] "served as police chief of El Cajon in San Diego County at the turn of the century." (reference is to reprint edition)

36. Homer F. Broome, Jr., *LAPD's Black History 1886-1976* (Norwalk, CA: Stockton Trade Press, 1977), 213.

37. Alexander, *Blue Coats: Black Skin*, 36; *The New York Age*, May 29, 1920, in W. Richelen Hendrik Smit and Roger Abel, Curators, *A Tribute to Lloyd G. Sealy. Reflection in Black. New York City Police Department.* Exhibit at John Jay College of Criminal Justice, CUNY, Library. *The Woman Citizen*, Apr. 23, 1921, 1197, incorrectly called Lizzie Forbes the "first colored woman to be a member of a police force" when she was appointed in Petersburg, Virginia. She probably was the first in the South.

38. Alice Stebbins Wells, "The Policewomen Movement, Present Status and Future Needs," *Proceedings* of the NCCC, 43rd Annual Session, Indianapolis, IN, May 10-17, 1916, 547- 548. States were Maryland, California, Colorado, Texas, Pennsylvania, Washington, New York, Arizona, Ohio, Wisconsin, Illinois, Alabama, Indiana, North Dakota, Massachusetts, Nebraska, Louisiana, New Jersey, Missouri, Minnesota, and Montana. Gary R. Perlstein, *An Exploratory Analysis of Certain Characteristics of Policewomen* (Ann Arbor, MI: Xerox University Microfilms, 1975 [Ph.D. diss., Florida State University, 1971]), 57.

39. Barbara Meil Hobson, *Uneasy Virtue: The Politics of Prostitution in the American Reform Tradition* (New York: Basic Books, 1987), 166, 175.

40. Raymond B. Fosdick, *Chronicle of a Generation: An Autobiography* (New York: Harper & Brothers, 1958), 3, 53, 124, 125, 132; Raymond B. Fosdick, *American Police Systems*, 1920; reprint (Montclair, NJ: Patterson Smith, 1969), 376-377 (references are to reprint edition).

41. Owings, *Women Police*, 113-114, 185-190; Maude E. Miner, "The Policewoman and the Girl Problem," *Proceedings* of the NCSW, 46th Annual Session, Atlantic City, NJ, June 1-8, 1919, 140. Women did not enter state police service again until April 1930, when Mary S. Ramsdell and Lotta Caldwell joined the Massachusetts State Police to handle "any crimes that dealt with females." According to her obituary in *The New York Times*, Aug. 16, 1986, 28:4, Ramsdell was a native New Englander who graduated from the Katherine Gibbs School and worked as a missionary with the Ute Indians before joining the State Police at age 40. She retired in 1950.

42. Winthrop D. Lane, "Girls and Khaki: Some Practical Measures of Protection for Young Women in Time of War," *The Survey*, Dec. 1, 1917, 236, 237. For a review of the effect protective workers had on the policewomen's movement, see Owings, *Women Police*, 107-117.

43. *The Woman Citizen*, May 3, 1919, 1055; Peter Horne, *Women in Law Enforcement*, 2d ed. (Springfield, IL: Charles C Thomas, 1980), 29.

44. *The National Police Journal*, Jan. 1919, 13. Makeup was new and women and girls were experimenting with it, though by mid-1919 products were advertised in women's magazines. On makeup as a fashion statement, see Sochen, *Movers and Shakers*, 101.

45. *The National Police Journal*, July 1919, 22 (for Buffalo); *The National Police Journal*, Feb. 1920, 17 (for Oklahoma City); *The National Police Journal*, Sept. 1920, 24 (for New York).

46. *The Woman Citizen*, Aug. 4, 1917, 168 (for Valley Center); *The Woman Citizen*, Apr. 26, 1919, 1015 (for Fargo); *The National Police Journal*, May 1921, 30 (for

Cumberland). In Rock Island, IL, *The National Police Journal*, Oct. 1919, 3, the matron received an unusual promotion when, due to a shortage of men, she was named night desk sergeant.

47. Patton, "Women Officers of the San Diego Police Department," 2, 3, 4, 12-16, 17, 37-50.

48. *The National Police Journal*, Oct.-Nov. 1920, 51 (for Colorado Springs); IAP *Bulletin*, July 31, 1925, 12 (for Jamestown).

49. Mina Van Winkle, "Standardization of the Aims and Methods of the Work of Policewomen," *Proceedings*, NCSW, 47th Annual Session, New Orleans, LA, Apr. 14-20, 1920, 152.

50. "Humanity on the March. Will You March With It?" *The Woman Citizen*, Mar. 27, 1920, 1047; Mina C. Van Winkle, "Policewomen—Their Duties and Opportunities," *The National Police Journal*, Aug. 1921, 14.

51. "International Association of Policewomen Meets in Milwaukee," *The National Police Journal*, June 1921, 26; Lucius H. Cannon, "A Survey of the Salaries of Police and Police Department," *The American City*, Dec. 1921, 459-462

52. Cynthia G. Sulton and Roi D. Townsey, *A Progress Report on Women in Policing* (Washington, DC: Police Foundation, 1981), 11; Mina Van Winkle, "Policewomen's Place in the Service," *Proceedings* of the IACP, 33rd Convention, Chicago, IL, July 19-23, 1926, 241; Edith Rockwood and Augusta J. Street, *Social Protective Work of Public Agencies: With Special Emphasis on the Policewoman* (Washington, DC: Committee on Social Hygiene-National League of Women Voters, 1932), 10.

53. Barbara Meil Hobson, *Uneasy Virtue: The Politics of Prostitution in the American Reform Tradition* (New York: Basic Books, 1987), 139.

54. Ibid., 139, 142. The term *white slavery* was not limited to white women but included all prostitution, regardless of the race of the prostitute.

55. *Policewoman's International Bulletin*, Aug.-Sept. 1927, 5.

Chapter 3

The International Association of Policewomen, 1915–1932

When Alice Stebbins Wells addressed police chiefs at the 1914 International Association of Chiefs of Police conference she convinced a number of them of the value of policewomen. Yet it was not to the IACP that Wells turned when she and other policewomen decided to form their own association, but to the National Conference of Charities and Correction.

The NCCC (later the National Conference of Social Work) was one of the groups through which women prison reformers and social service professionals had increased their prestige and their influence on social policy. The NCCC was, therefore, a natural forum for policewomen to unveil their own professional organization—the International Association of Policewomen.

At the 1914 NCCC meeting there was no mention of policewomen. Yet, by 1915, the corrections committee chairman noted that while "the old-time penologist and the practical police officer raise their eyes and their hands in holy horror," police jobs would allow women to "take an important part in the salvation of the world, a practical sort of salvation." Part of this interest was generated by Wells, who had contacted the NCCC to request a place on the 1915 program to discuss policewomen and their relationship to other social service fields represented at NCCC meetings.[1] Her request was granted.

On May 18, 1915, Wells and other policewomen at the NCCC conference formed the IAP. In putting forth the need for policewomen, Wells based her case on the twin concepts of women as professionals and women professionals caring for other women. These were arguments to which NCCC members could easily relate. Many of them a few years earlier had based their own demands for professional recognition on the same concepts. Combining ambitious professionalism with feminine altruism to secure recognition was not unique to women in the social services. Even women physicians and lawyers achieved advancement primarily through separation, rather than through equality. Not only the few women who became doctors, but also those who became lawyers, typically undertook tasks related to feminine roles. Wells declared in 1915:

The need for policewomen is one angle of the very general need for women in lines of activity once wholly occupied, and without dispute, by men. . . . With [today's] social complexity has come a corresponding social responsibility, as playground workers, associated charities, juvenile courts, truant officers, and a score of other forms of service attest. Always, women have cared for and protected the young; yet the police department, which has charge of these strategic places where the young gather, has been composed of men dependent upon the voluntary or collateral help of women, if any were given.[3]

Inspired by Wells's address, policewomen formed the IAP. Selected as officers were Wells, president; Mary S. Harvey, Baltimore, vice president; Georgiana Sherrott, Minneapolis, secretary; and Annie R. McCully, Dayton, Ohio, treasurer.[4] Margaret Damer Dawson, the first commandant of London's Women Police Volunteers, was the sole non-North American member.[5]

The IAP held its second meeting at the 1916 NCCC conference. Women from 14 states (nine from cities which had paid all expenses for the participants) attended. Membership included policewomen from 22 states and Canada. Throughout its existence the IAP scheduled its conferences to coincide with the NCCC and later the NCSW, providing another link to social service professionals. Police chiefs, who comprised the vast majority of IACP members, regarded the IAP with mixed feelings. Although the IACP did not oppose policewomen, it never provided the same support as the NCCC, the American Social Hygiene Association, the Women's Christian Temperance Union, and social welfare and women's groups. Underlining the social worker roots of its members, little in IAP records indicate that IACP support was sought. The exception is an address by President Mina C. Van Winkle in 1926 seeking affiliate status with the IACP.

Among the objectives set for the association in 1916 were to act as a clearinghouse for the collection and dissemination of information on the work of women police, to aim for high work standards, and to promote preventive and protective services by police departments. The policies adopted illustrate the social work, crime prevention, and educational aspirations of the attendees, who claimed to speak for about 150 policewomen in 30 cities. The education committee defined the IAP's professional orientation. It was to prepare a course of reading; set education and professional standards; devise strategies to publicize the work of policewomen at regional, state, or national conferences in related fields (particularly women's club gatherings), and issue bulletins to members and interested professionals in other social service fields.[6]

The IAP's interest in professionalism and in setting high entry standards contrasted sharply with the views of male police and with the existing standards for male police officers. Wells was aware of this disparity. In 1916 she called "women trained for [police] work" the movement's greatest need. Yet, she noted, "schools . . . to equip women for police work must be extremely practical . . . [for] there is no set of workers . . . which esteems book learning so little as a preparation for its work as do police officers." Wells's suggestion for filling the training void was that cities with policewomen train other women, who would become eligible for appointment elsewhere.[7]

At this time, the vast majority of male officers lacked a high school diploma. In 1922, when the IACP endorsed IAP recommendations that policewomen "have minimum educational qualifications equivalent to high school graduates, together with experience in social service or educational work of two years, or graduate trained nurses," another committee stated that every patrolman "should be equipped educationally so that he can use the English language in reading, writing, and speaking intelligently" and "be able to write reports which may be understood . . . without any difficulty whatsoever."[8]

Many departments followed the IAP's advice and required policewomen to have college degrees or social work or related training or experience. This double standard persisted until 1972 when Congress amended Title VII of the 1964 Civil Rights Act to bring state and local agencies—including police departments—under its anti-discrimination provisions. This forced the equalization of requirements for male and female police personnel. Overwhelmingly, standards for women were lowered, rather than standards for men raised. The pre-Civil Rights Act differences were not imposed by men seeking to segregate policewomen, but were a direct response to IAP recommendations.

In an attempt to attract social service professionals like themselves, IAP leaders fought for high entry standards and tried to segregate themselves from all non-social service aspects of policing. Wells noted in 1915 that although a policewoman is an integral part of her department and stands for law enforcement, "her largest and best work is to prevent, for the securing of obedience to law is the very best form of law enforcement." The next year, describing the evolution of policewomen, she observed that their work stemmed from

woman's desire to care for children and young people amid modern conditions, just as she has always done . . . . Policewomen began by concerning themselves with the places of amusements where the young gather—the dance halls, the skating rinks, the picture shows, the parks and the streets—through the curfew and other minor laws, and will continue to do so. Also from the beginning women have come to them for help. The power of the policewomen to counsel and protect fills a real need in the lives of many troubled women.[9]

Policewomen were in the mainstream of the newly developing helping services, the majority of which revolved around protecting children. In the years just prior to World War I, when relationships became impersonal and temporary, social agencies, the police, and corrections became more visible in the lives of city dwellers. Where once family, friends, and neighbors looked out for the well-being of women and children, now "agencies, based upon explicit, impersonal rules, with powers of enforcement, took over" functions previously fulfilled through personal, non-governmental relationships.[10]

The historian Anthony M. Platt has noted that the child-saving movement was heavily influenced by the maternal values of middle-class women who extended their housewifely role of child and family care into public service careers. By moving from volunteerism to government-supported reform, the women created career opportunities which neither threatened men nor challenged society's view of the female sphere. Thus, rather than reject the Jacksonian period's creation of women's sphere centered on home, domesticity, good works, charity, and motherliness of the unfortunate, educated, middle-class women of the early twentieth century accepted this definition and used it to move into public, paying positions.[11]

Van Winkle, director of the Washington, D.C., woman's bureau and president of the IAP after Wells, made clear that policewomen stood squarely within these helping services and the child-saving movement. "*We social workers*," she told the NCCC in 1920, approach the police from a critical rather than a sympathetic standpoint, but "unless we serve as policewomen . . . the police remain . . . a mystery." Calling police work "the greatest opportunity for service in the world," Van Winkle stressed that policewomen should be organized into a bureau under the supervision of a woman director. Van Winkle listed as qualifications for a director "college training, or training and experience in social work, school teaching, nursing, a knowledge of sociology and economics, and experience in dealing with human beings." Other recommended traits were the power of observation and insight, knowledge of municipal laws and police rules and regulations, understanding of criminal law and the rules of evidence, tact, good judgment, good physical condition, good moral character, and good personal appearance.[12]

This description fit the majority of policewomen, especially the IAP leaders. Both Wells and Van Winkle came from religious homes, were well educated, and saw the social service aspects of policing as a viable career for women such as themselves. Wells, a graduate of Oberlin College, had served as a bible reader in Indian territory before joining the Los Angeles Police Department. Van Winkle, raised by her grandparents, was a teacher and social worker. Prior to her police career she was active in charity work and the suffrage movement, moving to Washington, D.C., during World War I to organize the Food Administration's speakers bureau. When the Police Department in Washington, D.C., organized a woman's bureau, Van Winkle volunteered to do office work, taking over when the first director (Marion O. Spingarn, also a social worker) resigned.[13]

When the IACP acknowledged in 1922 that policewomen were essential to a modern police department and endorsed the IAP definitions, standards, qualifications, and training recommendations, IAP leaders considered it a great triumph. They were further encouraged by the IACP resolution supporting women's bureaus supervised by a female officer above the rank of policewoman who would report directly to the chief.

The women were struggling to establish crime prevention as a legitimate police activity at a time when this concept was new and untested. A small group of reform-minded chiefs supported them and saw their efforts as part of a larger movement toward police professionalism that developed during the Progressive era. Police thinking was fragmented in these areas; the chiefs themselves were unsure how to handle vice, prostitution, and juvenile offenders. The impetus for the IACP discussion of policewomen came in 1922 from IACP president, Chief August Vollmer, of Berkeley, California. An advocate of crime prevention, he was unsuccessful in persuading fellow chiefs that higher entry standards were required for male officers, and he appreciated the policewomen's interest in education and training.[14]

As the number of women officers and the number of cities with policewomen increased after World War I, IAP leaders, many of them managers of women's bureaus, made the establishment of additional bureaus their highest priority. After the IACP's endorsement, the IAP adopted a resolution affirming that policewomen should work within a segregated unit led by a woman director who would report directly to the chief and who would also be equal in rank to men reporting directly to the chief. Echoing the IACP resolution, the IAP outlined the responsibilities the director should oversee, stating that "policewomen shall carry out a preventive and protection program which will include social protection of women and children" and that "policewomen shall deal with all cases in which women and children are involved, either as offenders or as victims."[15]

It is likely that this resolution was based not only on philosophical beliefs, but also on the professional goals of the women to increase their numbers and to enhance their positions within their departments. By severing themselves from male officers, the women did not threaten men's jobs or environment. Thus, male officers did not actively protest the appointment of policewomen. But because the women had separated themselves from all facets of the police function not concerned with social service, there was now a need to assure that men did not enter this specialty and eliminate the need for policewomen. Also, since women in many cities were not eligible for civil service promotion, it was only through a separate chain of command that they could rise above the entry-level rank of policewoman. Unless male police executives were convinced of the need for women's bureaus, women could not increase their responsibilities, their prestige, or their salaries.

Even where bureaus were established, directors served at the pleasure of the chief and could fall victim to internal or external political shifts. This is what happened late in the 1920s to Mary Sullivan, director of the New York City Police Department women's bureau. After her handling of a raid on a birth control clinic received wide media attention, she was "punished" by having a male captain placed in charge of the bureau. Her demotion did not last long only because the captain asked to be reassigned and Sullivan again was given "titular as well as active command."[16]

The IAP achieved its highest profile in the years 1924 to 1928. An arrangement with the American Social Hygiene Association provided financial support to open a Washington, D.C., office in January 1925 and undertake a public education campaign on the role of and need for police-women. The American Social Hygiene Association gave a $5,000 matching-grant for office space and an executive secretary. Instrumental in this funding was Dr. Valeria H. Parker (the wartime director of the Connecticut State Police women's unit), who was ASHA director of protective measures. In January 1926, primarily through gifts from five contributors, the IAP met its half of the effort.[17]

The headquarters provided an operational base for the IAP educational effort, which was primarily involved with counteracting "the prejudice against policewomen—a prejudice found even within police departments themselves where it is thought that women aspire to take men's places on the force." These efforts involved writing magazine articles, supplying speakers to colleges and organizations, and offering field work and technical data to public officials interested in hiring policewomen.[18]

In 1924 ASHA also assisted the IAP in meeting another goal. It agreed to cooperate with the New York School of Social Work in developing "a program of instruction and field work intended to prepare properly women to direct the work of policewomen." Not only did ASHA provide lecturers and organize and supervise the field work component of the course, it underwrote scholarships for women with "special qualifications for this work." The first program, from March 24 to June 14, 1924, provided college credits for courses in family case work, public health, mental hygiene, criminology, police systems, and policewomen. Chloe Owings, author of *Women Police*, was field work supervisor, overseeing two days weekly in the courts, the study of public amusements, detective work, and time with the NYCPD. Many of the instructors were active in the policewomen's movement.[19]

Despite such views as those expressed by Louis Brownlow, city manager of Knoxville, that, in light of their education and training, "one of the greatest contributions that policewomen will make . . . is to raise the standard of qualifications for all police officers," this did not happen. Policewomen were finding it difficult to receive training within their departments. In 1929, Portland, Oregon, and Pasadena, California, were among the few cities that admitted policewomen to their police schools. Since there was no school of social work giving specific training for police-women, IAP leaders believed this "inability to find trained women, more than by any other one factor" limited the number of cities able to employ policewomen.[20]

In addition to expanding its influence in training, the IAP started its own publication in April 1924, and in 1925 was given a "Policewoman's Page" in *The Woman Citizen* and in *The Police Journal*. *The Woman Citizen* appealed to a reformist feminist readership; *The Police Journal* was written for police officers. A similar page had appeared in the *Journal*, but in August the IAP took over its direction. In September 1925, an editor's note described IAP members as "among . . . the world's best-known policewomen," and the *Journal* indicated its wish that "policewomen as well as policemen" would regard it "as their magazine." Early in 1926, the *Journal* listed the IAP on its masthead along with other police organizations. Van Winkle's name remained as associate editor for policewomen's activities until June 1932. In 1926, Van Winkle, who had advanced the IAP her own funds for costs associated with *The Woman Citizen* page, maintained that it was reaching 23,000 readers, the vast majority of whom were women.[21] The pages, often similar since there was little overlapping readership, reviewed activities at IAP conferences and supported the association's positions on crime pre-vention, women's bureaus, education, and training. Pages in *The Woman Citizen* were sometimes written by non-policewomen and had a more obvious feminist appeal, stressing crime prevention, pre-delinquency in-tervention, and the importance of policewomen in working with women and children.

The first IAP *Bulletin* lasted from April 1924 to February 1926. Sixteen issues were published; the first circulated free, the second carried a sub-scription blank for $1.50 per year. Members who did not wish to subscribe were asked to send 15 cents to cover the cost of the first issue; none did and few subscriptions were received. It was not until February 1925 that there were 60 subscriptions and publication began on a regular basis. A second newsletter, more ambitious in content and appearance, was published until December 1930. Titled *Policewoman's International Bulletin*, it bore the phrase "Preventive Justice" below its name. Both publications provide details of the IAP's internal workings, its constant financial difficulties despite outside support, its preoccupation with the creation of women's bureaus, and its advocacy of women's complete separation from other facets of police work and from male colleagues.

Bulletins listed an advisory committee in addition to IAP officers. In keeping with the increasing reliance on support from outside the police field, only one of the six advisers was a policewoman. Eleonore L. Hutzel, director of the women's bureau in Detroit, was joined by five social service professionals. In 1927, Vollmer from Berkeley joined the committee, which continued to be made up primarily of social service, rather than police, practitioners.

The importance of support from women's groups to IAP leaders is another sign of their link to the Progressive, child-saver philosophy dominated by college educated, middle-class women. A number of women's historians have noted the role of women's clubs in the Progressive era. Estimating that the General Federation of Women's Clubs had one million members by 1920, two authors saw the clubs as "providing the institutional voice through which middle-class women played an increasingly important role in political and social issues" and as forming powerful interlocking directorates that supported one another's pet causes while applying their resources toward suffrage.[22] One such pet cause was the appointment of policewomen.

In 1925 IAP dues were $1.00 annually. The constitution called for annual meetings, preferably in conjunction with the NCSW. An editorial in the May 1925 *Bulletin* promised that the next two years "should take the movement out of the sphere of controversy." It reminded readers that they must "make it clear that policewomen do not wish to be policemen nor do policemen's work, but . . . work which women are better fitted for, . . . with and for women and children," thus releasing men to meet the "increasing demand for traffic regulation and other types of police work that are peculiarly men's work." The editorial criticized policewomen in Great Britain and Europe, seen by American women as disregarding education and training and giving "prominence to the old jiu-jitsu conception of policewomen"—the very thing the IAP was trying to get away from and counteract.[23]

This negative view of physical training may have reflected the IAP view that women should avoid any actions that appeared to place them in competition with male officers. This may also account for virtually no mention of firearms by early policewomen or by IAP leaders. An exception occurred when Van Winkle, addressing the IACP in 1922, listed as appropriate equipment for policewomen: "badge, patrol-box key, whistle, flashlight, small flat-handled revolver easily disposed of on her person, preferably attached to a leather belt."[24]

The IAP's busiest year was 1925. All members of the St. Louis and Baltimore women's bureaus joined. Constitutional changes opened membership to "policewomen, police matrons and all others interested in the purposes of this Association," although officers of private protective associations were denied membership even if they had police powers. The superintendent of police in Houston became the first chief to become a member, followed in July 1925, by the chiefs of Oak Park, Illinois, Colorado Springs, Colorado, and Port Arthur, Texas.[25]

After specifying that meetings be held in conjunction with the annual NCSW meeting, IAP leaders in 1925 attempted a reorganization that would result in a closer affiliation, although no action was taken on the proposal. The IAP meeting in Colorado that year was arranged by Jessie Binford, director of the Chicago Juvenile Protective Association, a group that had lobbied for policewomen more than a decade earlier. Topics of papers delivered included the relation of police to the juvenile court, police and commercialized vice and amusement, women's bureaus, training schools for policewomen, and the lone policewoman (referring to cities with only one woman). One seminar dealt with the cooperation of the police in preventive work with delinquents. A probation officer, a school attendance officer, a teacher, and a policewoman formed the panel. Colorado women's organizations were very visible. The presidents of the state Federation of Women's Clubs and the state WCTU, and the superintendent of schools attended a luncheon sponsored by the Women's Clubs of Denver. The gathering was a prime example of "career women and society philanthropists, women's clubs and settlement [workers], and political and apolitical groups" working together on the problems of child care.[26]

Two affiliate organizations were also created in 1925: the Policewomen's Association of Los Angeles and the Policewomen's Association of Minnesota. In 1928, the Los Angeles group changed its name to the Women Peace Officer's Association of California and elected Wells its first president. Policewomen also became active in state social service associations, with Massachusetts women meeting in conjunction with that state's Conference of Social Work.[27]

The *Bulletin* ended 1925 by reminding readers to sign up members. Rather than concentrate only on policewomen, members were urged to "talk about us to police and court officials, to social workers, to club women. . . . Bring our announcement of group membership to the . . . clubs to which you belong or before which you speak." Members were also urged to contact businesswomen's clubs for $100 donations and to send headquarters lists of people "who are interested in this work and in a position to contribute."[28] These exhortations to enroll an increasing number of non-police members continued until the publication ceased in 1930.

The IAP formally incorporated in 1926, stating its purpose substantially as it had in 1915. New was a reference to international service. Goals were "to fix standards" for policewomen, "to secure proper training, to inspire the appointment of qualified policewomen, to encourage . . . Women's Bureaus, to work for the general improvement of the service, and to promote such service internationally."[29]

In 1926, President Van Winkle for the only time in the existence of the

IAP sought an affiliation with the IACP, asking that the IAP be permitted to meet as an auxiliary to it. This was a year after attempts at closer affiliation with the NCSW had failed. Perhaps, she suggested to the IACP, members might set aside one day to consider with the IAP problems that policewomen could solve. She urged the IACP to find some way of "taking us in, if not as individuals at least as an organization, because, after all, we do belong to you." She asked the chiefs to join the IAP "collectively . . . or singly."[30] Nothing indicates that either plea was acted on by the IACP or followed up on by the IAP. The idea of loosening the affiliation with the NCSW and replacing it with a similar relationship with the IACP was never raised in IAP bulletins, which repeatedly stressed the benefits of the IAP/NCSW association. No other reference to this request was found in any other IAP literature nor in the writings of any of its leaders.

Using funds from another ASHA grant, the IAP hired two full-time staff members in 1926. Neither A. Madorah Donahue nor Helen D. Pigeon, the appointees, were policewomen; both had social work experience. Donahue, who remained only a few months, was a National Conference of Catholic Charities field representative. Pigeon, who remained a number of years, was a graduate of Radcliffe College and the Simmons College of Social Work. Her social class and professional orientation were identical to the policewomen with whom she would work. She was a graduate of the Boston School of Social Work and had been associated in Boston with the Women's Educational and Industrial Union and the Society for the Care of Girls. During World War I she was a Massachusetts protective agent under the auspices of the Committee on Training Camp Activities. She had also served as an executive of the Girls Welfare Society of Worcester and director of the Boston School of Social Work Training School for Public Service.[31] In addition to her extensive travel and speaking schedule, Pigeon wrote many of the articles that appeared in *The Woman Citizen* and *The Police Journal*.

In 1927, at Pigeon's urging, the IAP tried to raise a three-year budget of $100,000 by including 1,000 women sponsors and 1,000 men advisers to assure its permanence. An editorial asked members to "enlist . . . lay friends who will become interested in this progressive journal of world-wide activity on behalf of women and children." The "One Thousand Sponsors" was a fund-raising and awareness campaign, calling for sponsors to meet with policewomen to learn about their work and to assist in convincing city officials to hire more of them. Sponsors were to pledge $25 yearly for three years so the IAP could continue to "educate public opinion, to give technical advice and field service to public officials, to collect data and by all other means to secure high standards of service." There were also plans to organize a similar group of men.[32]

The campaign, which was Progressive, feminist, and reformist in its approach, won the support of a few prominent and wealthy women, including suffrage leader Carrie Chapman Catt.[33] Lady Astor of Great Britain, whose previous gifts had allowed the IAP to match its first ASHA grant, served as chair and major financial benefactor. In 1919, Lady Astor had been the first woman seated as a member of Parliament in Great Britain, and she was a vocal supporter of British policewomen. When Great Britain tried to eliminate policewomen at the end of World War I, Lady Astor invited Van Winkle to England to speak on their behalf.

The trip initiated the IAP's increasingly international outlook. Contacts were cemented in 1924, when Mary S. Allen, head of the British Women Police Service, visited the United States as a guest of the League of Women Voters, speaking frequently and meeting with policewomen and with ASHA officials.[34]

Despite the affinity with international policewomen, particularly the British, one issue over which there was no agreement was uniforms. British policewomen had been wearing uniforms since their creation in 1914; U.S. and Canadian women were opposed to this. Allen called the uniform in the United States and Canada one of the "burning questions continuously argued." She felt her own "simple but well-cut uniform was . . . the most forcible argument in favour of its adoption, especially when I had emphasised its undoubted force as a deterrent to misdemeanour and immorality." She ended her visit hopeful that she would soon find U.S. and Canadian policewomen in uniform.[35]

IAP leaders did not share her hope. In an interview in the April 1924, *Police Journal*—the same month Allen arrived in New York from London—Van Winkle described the uniform of the London policewomen as "so ugly that it looks as though it had been designed by their enemies. Their shoes are so heavy that I do not know any woman in America, in any class of life, who would wear them." Although neither Mary E. Hamilton nor Mary Sullivan of the New York City Police Department were active in the IAP, the uniform issue was one on which they agreed with its leaders. Hamilton believed that when policewomen put on uniforms and carried guns and clubs "they became little men." Sullivan recalled that during a visit to London in 1927 she found the women's uniforms "unattractive, mannish suits, topped by a helmet that looked like a soup tureen . . . held in place by a broad chin strap."[36]

The U.S. position was summed up by Vollmer, who in 1930 recalled that he had never met a policewoman who wore a uniform or carried a gun, since "the right kind of woman does not need a uniform any more than other social workers do."[37] And so the issue remained until after World War II, when most policewomen were issued uniforms for ceremonial events at about the same time city officials hired and uniformed meter maids and female school crossing guards.

The 1927 IAP conference brought together women from more than 30 cities, including heads of seven women's bureaus. Attending were women from small communities, "where they are combining the duties of police officer and matron with those of relief agent, welfare worker, school attendance, and health officer, or any other role which circumstances demand." At year's end, the IAP reported that 213 jurisdictions (including states, cities or counties) had policewomen; 51 employed more than one woman, and 20 had women's bureaus.[38]

By 1929 the lack of funds was apparent. In 1931 and 1932 the IAP did not hold its own meeting at the NCSW conference. The only police speaker either year was Henrietta Additon, director of the NYCPD Crime Prevention Bureau, a social worker who had taught at Bryn Mawr College and had been affiliated with the Philadelphia Big Sister Association.[39] She was not a policewoman and, although employed by the NYCPD, was a non-sworn manager.

The IAP is frequently viewed as a casualty of the Great Depression. While the Depression did lead to a loss of non-police financial backing, the direct cause of the IAP's inability to continue operating was the death in 1932 of Van Winkle, who had not only served as president since 1920, but who had provided considerable financial support from personal and family resources.[40] Yet even before Van Winkle's death, the decline of the policewomen's movement was catching up with the IAP.

It is ironic that the IAP achieved its greatest visibility between 1924 and 1928, when interest in and activity on behalf of policewomen had peaked. The loss of momentum conforms to changes in feminism after 1925, when women's groups became more conservative and more concerned with special interests rather than with overall social justice issues. Stanley J. Lemons points to the large number of associations formed between 1912 and 1925 in which women predominated, noting that only two were formed between 1926 and 1928. He sees this as indicative of women's need for affiliation in the early period of their professional development. Lemon's view is challenged by Nancy F. Cott, however, who views this period as one in which feminism had not ceased, but had merely become more fractured. As women—and their associations—became less monolithic due to battles for or against the Equal Rights Amendment (introduced in Congress on December 10, 1923), Prohibition, international pacifism, and a variety of class-based issues ceased to be unifying factors.[41]

Regardless of interpretation, policewomen—and the IAP—suffered from these changes within the women's movement. Although an infusion of funds after 1924 brought greater stability to the IAP, the movement itself was stagnating. Ideas expressed in 1915 had undergone no expansion and no new leaders emerged. Leaders turned increasingly to social workers and clubwomen for support, rather than to police managers, many of whom were viewed as impediments to women's goals. That financial and philosophical support continued to come from these groups, rather than from the law enforcement community, was ultimately a factor in the IAP's demise.

Although IAP leaders felt they had received a major boost from the IACP in 1922, the opposite may have been more accurate. Despite numerical increases in policewomen immediately after World War I, by the mid-1920s virtually all large cities had policewomen. Many smaller cities no longer saw a need for more than one or two women officers; some saw no need for policewomen as long as matrons continued to perform a variety of duties. Although 41 cities hired policewomen between 1922 and 1925, the fact that 19 made the appointments in 1922 is further evidence of erosion. Also, all the cities (with the exception of Cleveland) were small, and none had more than five policewomen by 1925.[42]

Another reason for the decline of the movement, and the IAP itself, was the decline of the temperance and reformist groups that had been the major advocates for policewomen. The disadvantages of association with these groups, rather than with the police hierarchy, never occurred to IAP leaders. After being rebuffed in their sole attempt to join with the IACP, IAP leaders failed to pursue the matter. Policewomen owed their existence to groups outside the police establishment. Their ability to succeed was based on forces outside their departments. A 1926 IAP survey of 56 U.S. cities with women officers found that only 13 had hired them at the suggestion of the chief. Of the remaining cities, 32 hired them at the urging of women's clubs, 3 attributed hiring to the efforts of private social agencies, and 6 cited requests by other city agencies, usually health or welfare.[43]

Additionally, women were increasingly on the periphery of police activity, stagnating intellectually as police professionalism became synonymous with crimefighting and managerial efficiency, rather than with crime prevention and social intervention.

This "militarization of the police" was "one of the disturbing consequences of professionalization." The Progressives, who had influenced police thinking in the 1920s, were convinced that the "military model," stressing uniformed police officers with a well-defined rank structure based on the military, would bring to municipal policing much-needed discipline and would also eliminate patronage and inefficiency. Standards did improve through these changes, but by the 1930s the police were highly militaristic in character and outlook.[44]

Sixty years after the demise of the IAP and more than 80 years after Wells's appointment, it is easy to ask how IAP leaders failed to anticipate any of these societal shifts. But such a question fails to recognize that even though the early policewomen were greatly expanding women's sphere by entering the police environment, they continued to accept the view of different roles for men and women. Their place, they believed, was women's bureaus, which were to remain the domain of the majority of policewomen until the 1970s. Modern women police officers, with different attitudes, supported a unisex approach to policing, and they eventually demanded to enter police departments on the same basis as their male colleagues. These demands would have been inconceivable to early policewomen and to IAP leaders.

NOTES

1. *Proceedings* of the NCCC, 41st Annual Session, Memphis, TN, May 8-15, 1914, 514; Demarchus C. Brown, "Corrections—Introductory Remarks," *Proceedings* of the NCCC, 42nd Annual Session, Baltimore, MD, May 12-19, 1915, 371; Lois Lundell Higgins, "Historical Background of Policewomen's Service," *Journal of Criminal Law and Criminology* 41, no. 6 (Mar.-Apr. 1951), 831.

2. Ellen S. More, "'A Certain Restless Ambition': Women Physicians and World War I," *American Quarterly* 41, no. 4 (Dec. 1989), 639; Lois W. Banner, *Women in Modern America: A Brief History* (New York: Harcourt Brace Jovanovich, 1974), 9.

3. Alice Stebbins Wells, "Policewomen," *Proceedings* of the NCCC, 42nd Annual Session, Baltimore, MD, May 12-19, 1915, 411, 412.

4. Information on the IAP is based on Chloe Owings, *Women Police: A Study of the Development and Status of the Women Police Movement* (New York: Frederick H. Hitchcock, 1925), and on papers presented by members and supporters at IACP, IAP, NCCC, and NCSW conferences, on IAP bulletins from 1925 to 1930; and on policewomen's writings. All reinforce the social work orientation of members and supporters from 1915 to 1932.

5. Mary S. Allen, *The Pioneer Policewoman*; 1925; reprint (New York: AMS Press, 1973), 213 (reference is to reprint edition).

6. Owings, *Women Police*, 191. The IAP's concern with recognition and credentialization in 1916 places it ahead of many groups—male or female—that would, in the 1920s, see this as vital to professionalization. See Nancy F. Cott, *The Grounding of Modern Feminism* (New Haven, CT: Yale University Press, 1987), 215-224, for how men used professionalization to keep women out of certain fields and how educated women used it to distinguish themselves from volunteers.

7. Alice Stebbins Wells, "The Policewomen Movement, Present Status and Future Needs," *Proceedings* of the NCCC, 43rd Annual Session, Indianapolis, IN, May 10-17, 1916, 549, 550, 551.

8. "Report of Section on 'Police Organization and Administration'," *Proceedings* of the IACP, 29th Convention, San Francisco, CA, June 19-22, 1922, vol. 1, 35. Paul G. Shane, *Police and People: A Comparison of Five Countries* (St. Louis, MO: C.V. Mosby, 1980), 154, observed that qualifications for police were that they be "burly . . . big, strong, healthy, white, and male until well into the 20 century. . . . Other qualifications were minimal." When, in the 1960s, the National Commission on the Causes and Prevention of Violence endorsed a college degree for recruits, Jerry V. Wilson, chief in Washington, D.C., insisted that anyone with a tenth grade education should have no trouble assimilating police training and understanding department regulations. See Robert M. Fogelson, *Big-City Police* (Cambridge, MA:

Harvard University Press, 1977), 272.

9. Wells, "Policewomen," 413; Wells, "The Policewomen Movement, Present Status and Future Needs," 548.

10. Murray Levine and Adeline Levine, *A Social History of Helping Services: Clinic, Court, School, and Community* (New York: Appleton-Century-Crofts, 1970), 28.

11. Anthony M. Platt, *The Child Savers: The Invention of Delinquency*, 2d ed. (Chicago: University of Chicago Press, 1977), 14, 75, 79; Donald Meyer, *Sex and Power: The Rise of Women in America, Russia, Sweden, and Italy* (Middletown, CT: Wesleyan University Press, 1987), 430; Robert H. Wiebe, *The Search for Order: 1870-1920* (New York: Hill & Wang, 1967), 123.

12. Mina C. Van Winkle, "Standardization of the Aims and Methods of the Work of Policewomen," *Proceedings* of the NCSW, 47th Annual Session, New Orleans, LA, Apr. 14-20, 1920, 151, 152. [my emphasis]

13. Alice Ames Winter, "The Policewoman of Policewomen," *Ladies Home Journal*, July, 1927, 27, 62.

14. Vollmer established what is often termed the first formal training program for policemen in Berkeley in 1908. According to William J. Bopp and Donald O. Schultz, *A Short History of American Law Enforcement* (Springfield, IL: Charles C Thomas, 1972), 84, New York City followed in 1909, Detroit in 1911, and Philadelphia in 1913. Thomas J. Deakin, *Police Professionalism: The Renaissance of American Law Enforcement* (Springfield, IL: Charles C Thomas, 1988), 25-26, states that St. Louis established a police school in 1870, followed a few years later by Cincinnati. Sidney Lee Harring, *The Buffalo Police—1872-1915: Industrialization, Social Unrest, and the Development of the Police Institution* (Ann Arbor, MI: University Microfilms International, 1979 [Ph.D. diss., University of Wisconsin-Madison, 1976]), 108, notes that the Buffalo, New York, police had a school as early as 1895 but describes it as more concerned with teaching strike duty methods than police practices. Vollmer is recognized as the first major advocate of police training and education in the United States, but it was not until the late 1920s that recruits regularly received training before being sent on patrol.

15. IACP resolution quoted in Owings, *Women Police*, 197.

16. Mary Sullivan, *My Double Life: The Story of a New York Policewoman* (New York: Farrar & Rinehart, 1938), 281-282. Eleonore L. Hutzel, deputy commissioner, Detroit Police Department, observed in "The Policewoman," *The Annals of the American Academy of Police and Social Science* 146, (Nov. 1929): 111, that no promotion exams existed for women. In the few departments that used ranks between the director and the policewomen (usually a senior policewoman or a sergeant), promotions were on the recommendation of the director.

17. IAP *Bulletin*, Jan. 1926, 4.

18. Mary B. Harris, "The Policewoman's Organization," *The Police Journal*, Sept. 1925, 14; Helen D. Pigeon, "Woman's Era in the Police Department," *The Annals of the American Academy of Political and Social Science* 143 (May 1929), 254.

19. "Courses for Policewomen Executives," *Journal of Social Hygiene* 10, no. 2 (Feb. 1924), 108. For courses and instructors, see "A Program of Vocational Training for Directors of Policewomen Units," *Journal of Social Hygiene* 10, no. 3 (Mar. 1924), 178-184. Other schools had attempted similar courses. According to Owings, *Women Police*, 272-275, in 1918, the University of California, Southern

Division (later UCLA), offered a course on women police and their work. Organized and directed by Wells, it included lectures by criminal justice and social service practitioners and visits to public and private social agencies. The Boston School for Public Service started a five-month course in 1921. Requirements were high school training and social service experience. Academic areas included community organization, casework methods, criminology and psychiatry, criminal law and procedure, history, organization and function of police work, preventive and protective measures, combined with three days weekly of field work. About the time the New York program started, George Washington University in Washington, D.C., in cooperation with Van Winkle, offered social service and police organization and administration classes in the evenings. The majority of the first 55 enrollees were social service professionals.

20. Louis Brownlow, "The Effectiveness of the Policewoman," *The Police Journal*, Dec. 1928, 19; *Policewoman's International Bulletin*, June 1929, 4.

21. Editor's note in text of Harris, "Policewoman's Organization," 15; *The Police Journal*, Aug. 1925, 23; Feb. 1926, 24; June 1932, 1; IAP *Bulletin*, Jan. 1926, 4.

22. William H. Chafe, *Women and Equality: Changing Patterns in American Culture* (New York: Oxford University Press, 1977), 27; Mary P. Ryan, *Womanhood in America: From Colonial Times to the Present*, 2d ed. (New York: New Viewpoints, 1979), 140. Karen J. Blair, *The Clubwoman as Feminist: True Womanhood Redefined, 1868-1914* (New York: Holmes & Meier, 1980), 142, estimates that in 1914, there were 1,600,000 GFWC members.

23. IAP *Bulletin*, Jan. 1925, 3; IAP *Bulletin*, Apr. 1925, 4; IAP *Bulletin*, May 15, 1925, 7.

24. Mina C. Van Winkle, "Purpose and Scope of a Woman's Bureau," *Proceedings* of the IACP, 29th Convention, San Francisco, CA, June 19-22, 1922, vol. 2, 13.

25. *Policewoman's International Bulletin*, Apr. 1929, 3; Lent D. Upson, "The International Association of Chiefs of Police and Other American Police Organizations," *The Annals of the American Academy of Political and Social Science*, 146 (Nov. 1929), 125; IAP *Bulletin*, May 15, 1925, 9; IAP *Bulletin*, July 31, 1925, 7.

26. *Policewoman's International Bulletin*, June 30, 1925, 6; *The Police Journal*, Aug. 1925, 23; Mina C. Van Winkle, "Policewomen in Conference," *The Woman Citizen*, Aug. 8, 1925, 15;. Platt, *The Child Savers*, 77.

27. IAP *Bulletin*, Sept. 30, 1925, 4; WPOAC, *Yearbook and Official Program*, Santa Monica, CA, Oct. 15-17, 1936, 3; IAP *Bulletin*, Oct. 31, 1925, 3 (for Massachusetts).

28. IAP *Bulletin*, Dec. 1925, 3.

29. Certificate of Incorporation of IAP. Recorded July 28, 1926 at 10:46 A.M. as Instrument #18503 in Incorporation Liber 42 at Folio 255, Washington, D.C. Dated Aug. 1, 1967.

30. Mina C. Van Winkle, "Policewomen's Place in the Service," *Proceedings* of the IACP, 33rd Convention, Chicago, IL, July 19-23, 1926, 246.

31. IAP *Bulletin*, Feb. 1926, 2-3; "Helen D. Pigeon Dies Suddenly; Prominent in Correctional Work," *Federal Probation*, Oct.-Dec. 1945, 46. According to Barbara Meil Hobson, *Uneasy Virtue: The Politics of Prostitution in the American Reform Tradition* (New York: Basic Books, 1987), 177, as a protective agent Pigeon had hidden in the bushes of the Boston Common, waiting for women who came with servicemen late at night.

32. *Policewoman's International Bulletin*, Aug.-Sept. 1927, 8; Helen Pigeon, "The

Policewomen Meet in Conference," *The Police Journal*, June 1927, 15.

33. Carrie Chapman Catt was not the first suffrage leader interested in police-women. On December 14, 1918, Dr. Anna Howard Shaw, honorary president of the National American Woman Suffrage Association and chairman of the Woman's Committee of the National Council of Defense, fulfilled a 40-year-long desire to serve as a policewoman when she was sworn in as a special member of the Washington, D.C., Metropolitan Police. *The Woman Citizen*, Dec. 21, 1918, 611.

34. John Carrier, *The Campaign for the Employment of Women as Police Officers* (Aldershot, England: Avebury/Gower, 1988), xiii, xxi; Allen, *The Pioneer Police-woman*, 213-225.

35. Allen, *The Pioneer Policewoman*, 221, 225.

36. Lillian Madden, "The Modern Policewoman's Work," *The Police Journal*, Apr. 1924, 15; Mary E. Hamilton, "Woman's Place in the Police Department," *The American City*, Feb. 1925, 196; Sullivan, *My Double Life*, 283, 284.

37. August Vollmer, "Meet the Lady Cop," *The Survey*, Mar. 15, 1930, 702.

38. Pigeon, "The Policewomen Meet in Conference," 14; *Policewoman's International Bulletin*, Nov.-Dec. 1927, 9.

39. *Proceedings* of the NCSW, Minneapolis, MN, June 14- 20, 1931, 649, 651; *Proceedings* of the NCSW, 59th Annual Session, Philadelphia, PA, May 15-21, 1932, 644.

40. Rhoda Milliken, Director, Woman's Bureau, Washington, D.C., quoted in Higgins, "Historical Background of Policewomen's Service," *Journal of Criminal Law And Criminology* 41, no. 6 (Mar.-Apr. 1951), 832.

41. Stanley J. Lemons, *The Woman Citizen: Social Feminism in the 1920s* (Urbana: University of Illinois Press, 1973), vii, 58-59; Cott, *The Grounding of Modern Feminism*, 263, 264, 266.

42. Owings, *Women Police*, 287. Cities were Appleton, WI; Atlantic City, NJ; Charleston, SC; Cleveland; Elizabeth, NJ; Fall River, MA; Herkimer, NY; Huntington, IN; Kenosha, WI; Long Beach, CA; Michigan City, MI; Milwaukee; New Haven, CT; Pontiac, MI; Richmond, VA; Saginaw, MI; Sault Ste. Marie, MI; Wausau, WI; York, PA; Alliance, OH; East Cleveland, OH; Gloucester, MA; Greensboro, NC; Lancaster, PA; Oshkosh, WI; Savannah; Topeka; Trinidad, CO; Belfast, ME; Benton Harbor, MI; Davenport, IA; Hamtramck, MI; Hattiesburgh, MS; Hutchinson, KS; Ithaca, NY; Knoxville; New London, CT; Port Arthur, TX; Pueblo, CO; Wilmington, NC; Berkeley, CA. Of the 41 cities, four (Appleton, Michigan City, Milwaukee, and Alliance) no longer had policewomen in 1925 and three (East Cleveland, Trinidad, and Hutchinson) combined policewoman and matron duties for the sole woman officer in each department.

43. *Policewoman's International Bulletin*, Aug. 1928, 8.

44. Samuel Walker, "The Rise and Fall of the Policewomen's Movement, 1905-1975," in *Law and Order in American History*, ed. Joseph Hawes. (Port Washington, NY: Kennikat Press, 1979) 109-110; Samuel Walker, *Popular Justice: A History of American Criminal Justice* (New York: Oxford University Press, 1980), 136. Janis Appier, "Preventive Justice: The Campaign for Women Police, 1910- 1940," *Women & Criminal Justice* 4, no. 1, 1992, 3-36, theorizes that militarization was a way for police managers to maintain hegemony over the better educated policewomen. This theory, though, ignores developments in policing in the 1930s unrelated to gender.

Chapter 4

Establishing Women's Bureaus, 1918–1928

To accommodate policewomen, urban police departments created special women's bureaus. Women played a key role in the development of these bureaus, many of which were modeled on the Washington, D.C., bureau, created in 1918. The Washington Metropolitan Police Department appointed two policewomen in 1915 at the urging of Superintendent Raymond W. Pullman. Pullman, a journalist without police experience when named chief in April 1915, heard Alice Stebbins Wells speak at the National Conference of Charities and Correction meeting where the International Association of Policewomen was formed. When he returned to Washington, he put Wells's ideas into practice.

By 1917 Washington had four policewomen, all earning less than policemen. That year, a reinterpretation of 1906 legislation led to the appointment of policewomen as regular entry-level police officers earning the same salary as men. In September 1918, Marian O. Spingarn, a social worker, was selected to organize a woman's bureau. Spingarn, the wife of an Army captain, had previously investigated conditions around military bases during World War I. Prior to that, she was on the staff of the New York Probation and Protective Association, serving for five years as director, following positions in settlement house work. On October 15, 1918, the woman's bureau, with four policewomen, became a reality.[1]

The Washington, D.C., bureau set the tone for bureaus throughout the nation. Its functions were preventive, corrective, and general police work. Preventive work meant supervising theaters, dance halls, skating rinks, parks, railway stations, and all large public gatherings; finding jobs for girls; advising them about associates and amusements; and meeting with families of delinquent girls under a voluntary probation system. Corrective duties involved "voluntary commitments of first offenders over 17 to public institutions,. . . psychopathic and physical exams,. . . [finding]

missing girls, [and returning] fugitive children to parents, guardians and institutions." General police work was "detecting crime and apprehending offenders, interviewing and searching female offenders," and being present with "girl criminals at their trials and escorting them to the institutions." These varied duties were summed up as working "in the capacity of the wise mother who brings her child to justice, but protects and comforts it through the process."[2]

When Spingarn resigned, Mina C. Van Winkle became director. She stressed case work over all other activities. Van Winkle, IAP president after Wells stepped down in 1920, emphasized advanced training and a social work background for policewomen. She also stressed the need for highly trained women organized into a women's bureau, denigrating selection of "ordinary" women "with no training or ambition to measure up to the social needs of a police department, their chief aim being to imitate the worst traditions of policemen as closely as possible." Equally damaging was assignment not to a self-contained bureau, but to a male captain or detective who usually "places her in some clerical position and nine times out of ten concludes before he sees the woman that she is unable to render any service in the police department."[3]

This was not the case in Washington, D.C., where Van Winkle's woman's bureau was located away from the police department, operating out of and in conjunction with the House of Detention. The four-story facility housed the bureau, interview rooms, a clinic, emergency rooms for stranded women and girls, recreation, occupation, and sleeping rooms for court-committed boys and girls, as well as for the staff supervising them. The policewomen were as much part of the juvenile justice system as they were of the police department. Prevention, apprehension, and correction had become merged in the policewoman's view of herself as a social worker, rather than as a police officer concerned solely with law violation. This intertwining of roles was so complete that a history of police social workers found it "almost exclusively one of policewomen providing social work services" within women's bureaus.[4]

Policewomen fought to create women's bureaus, which became the acceptable place within the police environment for them to extend their housekeeping functions without violating beliefs pertaining to women's domestic sphere. These women's view of their "place" meshed with those opposing their entry into the larger work world—opponents willing to allow women to segregate themselves and to concentrate on working with women and children.

Since sex segregation in the workplace was common in fields women had entered since the beginning of the twentieth century, the idea of a bureau staffed by women handling the problems of women and children fit comfortably within prevailing norms. At a time when upward mobility for women was limited in all professions, policewomen were not concerned that they were limiting their careers by creating women's bureaus. In fact, they were creating opportunities for advancement within the bureaus that would not have been available to them elsewhere within their departments.

In most cities where policewomen were appointed in large enough numbers to be organized into a bureau, demands for their hiring almost always came from outside the police establishment. Although a few police executives such as Raymond W. Pullman in Washington, D.C., August Vollmer in Berkeley, California, and Fred M. Valz in Jacksonville, Florida, appointed women on the basis of their own beliefs, this was unusual. Pullman and Valz were not part of the police establishment at the time of their being named chiefs; and Vollmer, although a career police officer, was the leading police reformer of his generation. Women were usually appointed only after intense effort by the Women's Christian Temperance Union, local women's groups, vice commissions, or similar groups acting together to exert political pressure on mayors and police chiefs.

Although they are rarely mentioned in the writings of early policewomen, women in Portland, Oregon, played a key role in crime prevention. Portland maintained its preventive unit as a division equal to other units and assigned to it all the tasks normally associated with a women's bureau, even though it contained two male officers who performed similar services for male juveniles. Lola Baldwin, appointed in 1905, in 1913 held the rank of captain, identical to the other division supervisors who reported directly to the chief. A 1913 article on the city's police termed her "a serious-minded, public-spirited woman trying to help her sex" and devoted two of eight pages to Baldwin, her three women and two men. It was very unusual for a woman to supervise men, and it was equally rare for men to be assigned to do strictly preventive work.

Baldwin's unit's activities tell us much about what preventive work entailed. In 1912 officers opened cases on 648 girls under 21, interviewed ("not briefly . . . [but] diagnosed and a remedy proposed") 2,753 persons, conducted 431 special investigations, aided 60 sick girls, apprehended and returned home another 74, counseled and prevented 38 more from leaving home, served 490 meals, and provided 228 nights' lodgings. Staff was also active in efforts to prohibit girls from working in pool rooms, bowling alleys, and shooting galleries and in the unsuccessful fight to regulate dance halls, all seen as places where careers of wayward girls began.

The provision for feeding and lodging runaways probably provided the model for the self-contained bureau in Washington, D.C., as well as for the short-lived women's precinct in New York City. Both were conceived as full-service social centers run by policewomen for women and children. Baldwin's social and religious orientation, also typical of policewomen of the period, is obvious in her summary of the causes of delinquency in girls. "We are forced to believe," she said in 1912, the fault lies primarily with the home and parents. Too much liberty . . ., a lack of reverence for parental authority, girls unchaperoned, homes disrupted by divorce, parents allowing girls to dress . . . in costumes bordering on vulgarity, economic conditions that force the girl into the world at her most susceptible age, where she is overworked and underpaid, but above and beyond all is the increasing disregard of definite religious home training.[5]

"Operatives" in Portland (the women, by their choice, were not called policewomen until 1927) reviewed the court docket, interviewed all arrested women, and wrote reports of conditions at home that judges relied on when deciding these cases. They investigated matrimonial bureaus, introduction agencies, fortune tellers, palmists, theatrical companies, and dance halls. The staffing of the division with women and men was copied throughout the Pacific Northwest and in parts of California, although it was rare elsewhere in the United States.

In 1919 the juvenile and women's protective division in Seattle included an equal number of women and men. By 1923 three men continued to serve under Superintendent Blanche H. Mason, who on March 19, 1912, had been appointed the first policewoman. The men handled cases involving boys under the age of 18; the policewomen, cases involving female juveniles. Mason's unit eventually included three men, five policewomen, and two matrons. The women investigated cases for the juvenile court, searched for runaways, and assisted male officers in matters involving women and children.[6]

In 1927 Los Angeles policewomen served in a crime prevention bureau with male officers. The bureau, which included 20 policewomen (one of whom was Wells) and 10 matrons, was led by a man. The Los Angeles Police Department had placed its women in a separate unit in 1913, when Wells, two other policewomen, and a number of matrons were part of the department. That year, Wells spent most of her time traveling among the Eastern cities telling departments "how she and her associates help the men do the work at the police station," while the other policewomen oversaw the juvenile unit and maintained the lost and found, which helped relatives and friends locate the many runaways and missing persons among the young, transient population of Los Angeles.[7]

In 1923 the Los Angeles Crime Commission had invited August Vollmer to reorganize the LAPD. He accepted a one-year appointment as chief. Despite his early and vocal support for policewomen, Vollmer's 1924 report to the commission did not advocate continuation of the women's bureau. His plan called for joining the city mother's and juvenile bureaus, the male and female parole boards, and the female probation unit into a bureau whose main purpose would be "to correct shortcomings early in the hope of preventing adult tragedies" by forming "friendly relationships with school and welfare agencies, to cooperate for the public good." At the time, five of the 20 women were doing policewomen's duties; the others performed matron functions.[8]

None of Vollmer's reforms mentioned policewomen. Noted in passing, the city mother's bureau had been reinforcing policewomen's maternal roles since the 1880s, when Lucy Thompson Gray had been appointed the first matron in Los Angeles and began using the title city mother to publicize her duties. At the time of Vollmer's study, the position was held by Aletha Gilbert, Gray's daughter. By 1922 Gilbert, her two assistants, and her community advisory board had established a day nursery for children of working mothers, where four nurses cared for an average of 50 children daily. She noted that while the officers had police authority, they refrained from using it except when necessary and that they tried "through love, sympathy, encouragement, and personal interest to teach children their duty to parents and to society, and by this same method to awaken parents to their responsibility."[9]

Vollmer's view of crime prevention as a principal police function was accepted by many California departments during the 1920s.[10] But many older, larger cities were not as receptive to the introduction of policewomen as Pacific Coast cities were. Generally, these cities and their police chiefs were less sympathetic to reform sentiments. Despite this, smaller cities, many affected by either WCTU or Progressive influence, did appoint policewomen.

It was through such combined efforts that in 1918 Indianapolis officials assembled the largest number of policewomen appointed up to that time. The majority of them had been appointed during World War I to protect the morals of young girls in areas with large numbers of young soldiers. Eleven policewomen served under Clara Burnside, who had previously worked in the juvenile court. By 1921 there were 24 women, Burnside had been promoted to captain, and a female sergeant was appointed her next in command. Indianapolis proclaimed its policewomen's unit "the largest in the world," followed by the 21-member bureau in Washington, D.C. The women achieved quite a reputation for their work, which included frequent assignment to the streets and inside stores to deter purse-snatching and shoplifting. They were the most active policewomen in this type of work, often neglected by other bureaus despite the importance of women in detecting shoplifting, a crime frequently committed by women.[11]

Even with her successes in more traditional areas of police work, Burnside had difficulty winning cooperation from area law enforcement agencies, whose male officers "looked on the policewoman idea as just another fad, ... for the reckless squandering of the taxpayers' good money." Eventually the women did command respect "both from the standpoint of personality and from their high efficiency," but only after statistics doubled between 1919 and 1920, despite the addition of only three officers. The bureau became a prime example of the politics surrounding policewomen. Although IAP President Van Winkle in 1924 called it "the best example of good work of any police department" in the United States, that year a new mayor abolished it. When it was re-created in 1926 it was less independent and limited to morals enforcement.[12]

The post-World War I period is characterized not by cities appointing policewomen, but by their creating women's bureaus and naming women with social service backgrounds as directors. These actions were in keeping with policies formulated by IAP leaders, many of whom were bureau directors and who viewed the creation of these units as vital to their own and other policewomen's professional development.

Actions in St. Louis leading to a women's bureau were typical of medium-sized Midwestern cities. In 1915 Wells addressed a social service conference, followed by lobbying for and passage of legislation to permit hiring policewomen, and selection of four women in 1916. The women, termed matrons, initially lacked police powers, as well as objectives beyond the mandate "to do social uplift work." Catherine Fertig, a settlement house director, was appointed a sergeant in 1918 and placed in charge of the four incumbents and ten new women. Selection of Fertig for this position was the result of lobbying by suffrage and social service activists. The bureau lasted only several months, though, after which the women were transferred to the detective bureau under the command of a male supervisor.[13]

Typical also was Youngstown, Ohio, whose women officers in 1923 were supervised by Francis Vaughn, or "'Fanny,' as she is known to ... the department and 'Mother' to the derelict girls and women who come under her care." Officials in Des Moines, Iowa, set up a bureau in 1926. Minneapolis officials formed one at the end of 1927, naming a woman with "long experience in social service work" lieutenant in charge. By late 1927, officials in Flint, Michigan, and Wichita, Kansas, had organized their women into bureaus.[14]

Separate women's bureaus also existed in Southern cities, although they were formed later than in other areas of the country as part of a wide range of social legislation advocated by Southern women.[15]

In 1918, Dorall Vance and Lore E. Davis became the first policewomen in Atlanta. They were hired specifically to arrest prostitutes and inspect buildings and rooms where male officers might encounter embarrassing situations. Two more women were added within the next two years. In January 1924, a women's bureau was created and Davis was named captain. Activity increased rapidly, although the majority of cases were "dealt with without arrest entirely away from the police station." Every girl arrested received a medical examination, including a pregnancy test, attended by a policewoman. The unit secured custodial care and treatment for the "mentally diseased and defective," and referred to juvenile court for foster care children whose parents had been arrested. Echoing sentiments of sister officers, Davis saw policewomen as "the social agency . . . for the police department, and the community, . . . fighting the forces of evil, for the salvation of souls and the redemption of life."[16]

Among the other Southern cities with women's bureau were Petersburg, Virginia, where City Manager Louis Brownlow, before taking a similar post in Knoxville, created a bureau with Sgt. Minnie Rowland in command. Among those working in Petersburg in 1921 was Lizzie Forbes, probably the first African-American policewoman in the South. Knoxville organized its four policewomen (three of whom had spent a month training with women in Washington, D.C.) into a bureau in late 1924. Sometime later, Annette Steele was appointed captain and placed in charge.[17] The Knoxville women, just as those in Petersburg, owed their existence to Brownlow, a supporter of policewomen who often wrote on the need for cities to employ women in their police departments.[18] Brownlow had been commissioner of Washington, D.C., when Pullman established it woman's bureau.

Thus, three women's bureaus—Washington, D.C., Petersburg, and Knoxville—came into being through Brownlow's efforts. This is another indication of the relatively small circle of reformers who were responsible for maintaining the momentum of the policewomen's movement through the mid-1920s. It also points up how these individuals, many of whom knew each other, continued to support policewomen—and one another—without backing from non-reform elements within the police establishment.

Charleston, South Carolina, had a very active women's bureau. A 1925 department history called it "essentially a police agency, but its work extends beyond. . . . Much of its service is of a social nature." In addition to director Gracie A. McCown, who joined the department in 1922, there were two policewomen and two matrons, a large staff in an agency of 126 men, but one that reflected Charleston's importance as a port city with a large transient population. The only women's bureau in the state, McCown and her staff handled an average of 150 cases each month, with men falling under its jurisdiction "in cases when women are involved." Again reflecting Charleston's port city milieu, one of the bureau's main functions was locating lost women and girls.[19]

Jacksonville Police Commissioner Fred M. Valz added women to his department in 1927, noting that this addition highlighted the city's role as "a progressive city." By employing women, Valz hoped to use social case work methods to treat women and children, offenders or victims, as maladjusted individuals and to reduce both the number of recidivists as well as those making their first appearance in police court. An attorney who had been a state legislator before becoming commissioner, Valz was instrumental in the passage of a legislative amendment that allowed Jacksonville to borrow policewomen from Washington, D.C., until two women had been hired. He based the need for the bureau in part on his city's role as a seaport and rail center that attracted many workers "as a huge playground brings many women and girls within its gates."[20]

Valz's interest in hiring policewomen and creating a women's bureau in 1927 came at a time when the movement was losing momentum. Virtually all large cities (with the exception of Philadelphia) by then employed policewomen. The majority had placed them into women's bureaus. The battles over women's bureaus in five large cities—Chicago, Detroit, Cleveland, Boston, and New York—presaged in different ways the problems facing policewomen after 1925.

Although the particulars of the battles women faced in these cities differed, a common theme is the diminishing importance of reformers and women's groups. Chicago and Boston dispersed policewomen throughout the department. Detroit and Cleveland were reluctant to hire women at all, although they eventually did. Philadelphia resisted and did not appoint women until 1936. New York City underwent a different battle, with matrons fighting against yielding positions and prestige to newer women with greater police authority.

Generally these older, larger cities and their police chiefs were less in agreement with reformist sentiments. The chiefs were typical of Robert M. Fogelson's description of big-city police: immigrants—frequently Irish or German—recruited mainly from the lower and lower-middle classes, with "little or no inclination to impose the morality of the upper-middle and upper classes on the ethnic ghettos."[21]

Chicago appointed policewomen by 1913, but did not organize them into either a women's or a crime prevention bureau. Women had been part of the Chicago Police Department even before 1913. In addition to "Patrolman" Mary Owens appointed in 1893, in 1911 Chicago had assigned a social worker who was not a member of the department to one of its stations in an attempt to "do away with petty, degrading litigation and adjust the less serious complaints" that citizens brought in. She succeeded in reducing complaints and was favorably received by the courts.[22]

A number of social agencies undertook lobbying for policewomen, including inviting speakers such as Wells from the LAPD. The campaign, led by anti-vice groups, resulted in the Women Police Ordinance being passed on December 30, 1912, and amended on January 27, 1913, with funds provided for one year for 13 policewomen. Ten "feminine guardians of law and order" were appointed for 60 days, after which the Civil Service Commission was to hold an exam for the job. Of the 10 appointees, eight were widows, whose ages ranged from 25 to 50. On September 7, 1914, Anne Loucks, who received the highest civil service rating among the women and had been serving since 1913, became Chicago's first civil service policewoman.[23] Still a member of the department was Mary Owens, who did not retire until 1923. Since Owens was always listed as a patrolman, Loucks, who retired in 1937, was officially the city's first policewoman.

In 1915 the city increased the number of women to 30 and assigned to matrons a number of investigative functions pertaining to detainees that in other cities were performed by policewomen. In 1920 there were 28 policewomen and 35 matrons. By 1926 there were 59 women doing "regular police work" and an additional 29 who worked for the park system during the summer. Contrary to the views of IAP leaders, Chicago policewomen did not want a bureau. Chicago, which viewed itself as comprised of cities within a city, assigned its policewomen "to work in the different police districts . . . under the orders of the [district] commanding officer just as the men" were.[24] Chicago formed a crime prevention unit in 1935, but a women's division was not created until 1947.

In Detroit, the WCTU and a local protective league had begun efforts—with little success—to have policewomen appointed in 1914. Wells spoke in 1917, resulting in renewed lobbying. In March 1919, Josephine David, a graduate of the University of Michigan and a staff member of the local protective league, was appointed specifically to interview women and girls in police detention. After recommendations from other women's bureau directors and local social service leaders, in January 1921, Virginia M. Murray became director of the new women's division. She was paid $3,000 annually; the 14 policewomen received $1,600. In May 1922, Murray was succeeded by Eleonore L. Hutzel, director of social services at the Detroit Women's Hospital and Infant's Home. A year later Hutzel was given the rank of deputy commissioner. She carried out Murray's vision of a women's division as "an additional social organization" for the "treatment of the girl who has fallen into anti-social habits."[25]

Addressing the IACP in 1927, Hutzel reported that there were 39 women in her division (including three sergeants). It was the largest number of women officers in a women's division in any U.S. city. Half of the women were doing work previously done by men, since "women officers who are trained and experienced in work with girls can accomplish much more than men officers" can.[26] Despite the prolonged battle that brought policewomen to Detroit, Hutzel achieved prominence within the movement. Throughout the 1930s and until her retirement in 1948 she remained one of the few spokeswomen on behalf of women officers and women's bureaus.

Waning enthusiasm for policewomen was presaged in two cities where the battles over initial appointment were particularly bitter—Cleveland and Boston. The Cleveland campaign began in 1910 as part of anti-vice efforts, just as it had in so many other cities. A year later, reformers began inspecting dance halls. These clean-up campaigns, combined with the brutal murder of a 16-year-old girl in 1916, led to the formation of a Women's Protective Association. The association hired Sabina Marshall as a "special investigator" to do protective work, deliberately avoiding the title "policewoman" for fear it would arouse opposition. Marshall, who became executive secretary of the Women's Protective Association, was given a police badge but was denied arrest powers.

In 1917 the city council rejected a bill to create a women's bureau with 29 policewomen. Lobbying resumed after World War I. The Cleveland mayor expressed interest in hiring women in 1921, but, due do opposition from the public safety director, nothing was done until the mayor appointed four women late in 1923.[27] A 1922 study of criminal justice in Cleveland, directed by Roscoe Pound and Felix Frankfurter for the Cleveland Foundation, had noted that Cleveland was the only city of over a half million people that did not employ women police. The study called for the establishment of a women's bureau of "not less than 10" policewomen, advocating they perform most of the duties carried out by the Women's Protective Association. In April 1924, efforts that had begun in 1910 resulted in a women's bureau. In their attempt to assist, IAP leaders visited Cleveland three times; twice at the association's expense and once with a subsidy from the Women's City Club. Dorothy D. Henry, a college graduate with experience in case work and community agency service, who had been "strongly recommended by the parties most interested," was placed in charge of the unit.[28]

The four women who had been appointed in 1923 received the pay of patrolmen, and Henry received a salary at least equal to captain's pay. On January 1, 1925, 11 more were hired; a civil service exam was given a month later. An advocate of the case method of handling women and girls coming in contact with the police department, Henry reported in 1926 that Polish, German, Hungarian, Lithuanian, and Hebrew were spoken by her officers to serve Cleveland's major ethnic groups.[29] The protracted battle to form a bureau would never have been detected by comments in 1930 made by a new police chief upon Henry's retirement. George J. Matowitz noted that there had been changes in "two important executive positions." One change was his own appointment. The second was the selection of Alpha Larsen to replace Henry, who had resigned. Although the reason for Henry's departure is not stated, by year's end only 8 of 14 policewomen positions were filled.[30]

Efforts in Boston took almost as long as in Cleveland. Six women were appointed in Boston in early 1921, ending a battle that began in 1912, when the White Slave Traffic Commission recommended policewomen to prevent young women from entering prostitution. State legislation in 1914 authorized women to serve as special police officers; in a number of cities, officials appointed women between 1915 and 1918, but Boston did not. A second round of lobbying in 1919 centered on Boston. A coalition of state and city women's, civic, and social service groups endorsed a plan for a women's bureau after an address by Van Winkle, president of the IAP.

The coalition in 1920 won legislation permitting women to serve as regular members of the department. Of the six women appointed in 1921, one had been a police officer in another city, two were stenographers, one was a nurse, and two were housewives.[31]

Demands for a women's bureau were not met. A 1934 study observed that although pressure from social service agencies had never been relaxed, except for the first success, "those who have agitated for the expansion of the policewoman's role have made no headway." Noting that the women were unwanted by the department when appointed and continued to be unwelcome, the report found that calls for a bureau were of little value in this inhospitable environment.[32]

Philadelphia was another large Eastern city that was not receptive to either policewomen or a women's bureau. After Marguerite Walz became an unpaid dance censor in 1921, no women were involved in Philadelphia law enforcement until 1927, when seven were appointed to serve on the grounds of the Sesquicentennial Exposition. Trained by IAP executive secretary A. Madorah Donahue, who had no police (but much social work) experience, the "Sesqui" special policewomen performed functions identical to those Lola Baldwin had performed at the Lewis and Clark Exposition in 1905. Despite the hope of social service and women's groups that the officers would be retained, as Baldwin had been, this did not occur. Women did not enter the police department until March 1, 1936, when a bureau of a senior policewoman and four policewomen was created by the mayor.[33] Philadelphia was the last of the large cities in the United States to appoint policewomen, although not the last to form a women's bureau.

The battle over policewomen in New York City was of a different sort. Matrons saw policewomen as a diminution of their role and lobbied for expanded powers rather than for the creation of the new, more prestigious position. In 1911 Matron Isabella Goodwin, on loan to the detective division to assist with complaints against fortune tellers, helped solve a much-publicized bank robbery. On March 1, 1912, she was promoted to first grade detective, which raised her salary from $1,000 to $2,250 annually and made her the first woman above the rank of matron. Foreseeing the calls for policewomen that would soon arise, Goodwin used the press coverage given her promotion to advocate that matrons be used more extensively in police work, especially in preventive and protection work among young girls.[34]

Her advocacy fell on deaf ears. New York was not in the forefront of utilization of women—whether as matrons or as policewomen. In 1917, when the Mayor's Committee of Women on National Defense, comprised primarily of social workers and civic leaders, proposed that six women protective officers be appointed at salaries considerably higher than those earned by matrons, Goodwin and other matrons were among those who fought the proposal. The protective officers were to be appointed as a war measure to work among girls "who loiter about armories and soldiers' camps." Theresa M. Melchionne, commanding officer of the women's bureau from 1952 to 1963, stated in her richly detailed history of New York City policewomen that this measure was defeated. Despite this, two women were appointed in 1917; but, although given police powers, they were not members of the department.[35] This was in keeping with practices in many cities, where departments recognized wartime protective officers, but neither made them members of the department nor paid their salaries.

Pressure for policewomen continued. On January 28, 1918, Ellen A. O'Grady, a probation officer in Magistrates Court, was named Fifth Deputy Police Commissioner and placed in charge of a newly created welfare bureau, which contained three matrons, Detective Goodwin, and 55 male officers. In 1918 Commissioner Richard E. Enright named 10 women to the uniformed force. Exempt from civil service since they were "an experiment," the women were permitted to carry the same equipment as men, including a firearm, and had the same police authority as men. This confused terminology and responsibilities in the department; matrons were now called policewomen while policewomen were termed patrolwomen. The confusion existed until the titles were merged in 1937 and resulted in the NYCPD's having a woman detective and a woman deputy commissioner (the first woman in U.S. policing to supervise a substantial number of male officers) before it appointed its first sworn policewoman.[36]

On May 13, 1921, New York officials gave the first civil service test for patrolwoman—the title that had been created in 1918 exempt from civil service regulation. The test was given a month after the department established a women's police precinct. Directed by Mary E. Hamilton, assisted by Goodwin, the precinct contained 20 patrolwomen and 6 policewomen. In her autobiography, *The Policewoman: Her Service and Ideals*—also a history of the policewomen's movement and a treatise on its benefits to society—Hamilton wrote:

In removing from the Women's Precinct all the earmarks of a regular police station it at once became a center where a woman could seek information, advice or aid from . . . her own sex without fear of . . . the grim atmosphere of the average police desk. The red geraniums in the window boxes would attract . . . a woman. . . . The worried mother or weary, runaway girl could find the help, understanding and protection that only a motherly policewoman can give.[37]

The precinct was an outgrowth of the combined initiative of Enright and a committee of women "prominent in civic and welfare work," who felt an important function of the precinct was addressing "the detention of girls and women who have committed no crime, and are not immoral, nor delinquent, but who, for some reason or other, must be temporarily detained." The precinct opened on April 4, 1921, with much press attention and ceremonies attended by the mayor, city officials, and social service leaders. Descriptions of it are similar to those of settlement houses. The upper two floors, which Hamilton called a "hostess house," had accommodations for runaways and girls not charged with any crime. She also planned a clinic, a temporary hospital, a workroom, and classrooms.[38]

Legal questions surrounding the hostess house were soon raised. Enright explained that it was not a detention facility for wayward girls, but only for runaways who would remain until returned home. Yet what Hamilton had conceived of as a visionary, voluntary shelter was perceived by legal authorities as illegal, involuntary detention. Mrs. George W. Loft, a civic leader who on May 21, 1921, succeeded O'Grady, did not agree with Hamilton and immediately transferred her to headquarters. By September 1923—two and one half years after its heralded opening—the women's precinct was disbanded; its welfare functions were absorbed into a unit that in March 1924 was placed under Hamilton's supervision and in November 1924 was designated the women's bureau.

The women's bureau, staffed by 16 policewomen and 13 patrolwomen, patrolled dance halls, movie theaters, piers, parks, railway terminals, subways, elevated train stations, and ferries. In 1924 staff received 25,000 telephone calls and 10,000 pieces of mail; distributed 60,000 crime prevention pamphlets; made 3,378 visits to homes, schools, or jobs; and handled 1,730 various criminal or morals matters. Hamilton remained in command until 1926, when Mary Sullivan, who began her career in 1911 as a matron, succeeded her.[39]

The protracted battles to create women's bureaus in these large cities brought to an end the influence of outside reform groups on the police establishment. The pressure from reformers and women's groups, including the IAP, to make crime prevention the pre-eminent function of the police was also at an end. The policewomen's movement was losing momentum. Although estimates vary, by 1930 there were no more than 600 women in approximately 200 departments. This decline continued; IAP figures for January 1931, reported 523 policewomen in 148 cities in 38 states.[40] Between 1929 and 1931, the number of departments employing policewomen had actually decreased. Policewomen working in fewer cities meant that there were fewer opportunities to create new women's bureaus.

Women's bureaus, in so many instances formed in response to demands outside the police establishment, suffered from the loss of influence of the groups that had fostered their creation, resulting in numerical losses followed by the loss of power, prestige, and momentum. The end of the

1920s signaled the end of reformist pressure-group politics. American women had entered the decade as one of the best-organized interest groups in the country; they emerged from it "battered and divided . . . disorganized, fragmented, and unable to agree on the best way to change their status in society."[41]

Women's bureau directors did not suffer from this fragmentation, but Hamilton in New York City may have sensed the impending crisis as early as 1924. Despite an optimistic assessment of the future of policewomen, she reluctantly admitted that prior to its being disbanded, the women's precinct had "become more or less of a routine complaint bureau, to which men and women alike were assigned."[42] This was a major disappointment. There was no room in her vision for a time when women would fight to be assigned to just such a routine complaint precinct and would enter the courtroom to win the right to respond to requests for police service on the same basis as their male colleagues.

While women's bureaus did enable a few women to achieve rank in their departments and prestige in their communities, the bureaus at the same time narrowed career development for women. Rank for women's bureau directors and supervisors was virtually always at the pleasure of the chief, rather than attained through civil service. Additionally, the percentage of supervisory positions in the bureaus was below those in the rest of the department. Yet women saw the bureaus as the most efficient way to accomplish the preventive and protective tasks they had carved out for themselves. Since sex segregation in the workplace was common in the 1920s, there was no reason for bureau directors to view their separation from male colleagues as unusual.

The decline in interest in the policewomen's movement by the late 1920s was symbolized by the demise of the IAP in 1932. The Depression also resulted in drastically reduced city budgets. Policewomen were viewed more and more on the periphery of policing, a costly frill at a time when law enforcement was shifting from a crime prevention to a crimefighter philosophy that pushed policewomen farther out of the mainstream.

Because policewomen were so closely intertwined with morality enforcement, crime prevention, and police commitment to juvenile work, the end of interest in these areas within the police hierarchy brought to an end the first era of policewomen. The Depression curtailed even lukewarm commitment to these goals, and policewomen, whether they were segregated into bureaus or scattered within their agencies, declined in numbers and importance.

NOTES

1. *The Woman Citizen*, Dec. 14, 1918, 598. This book calls bureaus of women officers women's bureaus, but since the unit in Washington, D.C., was called the *woman's bureau*, that is how it is described here. The use of *woman* may hark back to the nineteenth-century terminology of *woman's movement* (rather than *women's movement*) to denote unity of the female sex. See Nancy F. Cott, *The Grounding of Modern Feminism* (New Haven, CT: Yale University Press, 1987), 3-5, on how *woman movement* began to sound archaic in the 1910s and was replaced with the word *feminism*.

2. *The Woman Citizen*, Sept. 6, 1919, 336.

3. *The National Police Journal*, Aug. 1921, 14, 15.

4. Albert R. Roberts, "Police Social Workers: A History," *Social Work* 21, no. 4 (July 1974), 294.

5. J.E. Reavis, "The Police Department of Portland, Oregon," *The National Police Magazine*, Apr. 1913, 92, 93.

6. G.G. Evans, "The Police Force of Seattle, Queen City of the Northwest," *The National Police Journal*, Dec. 1919, 4; *History of the Seattle Police Department* (Seattle: Grettner-Diers Print Co., 1923), 36, 71, 81-82. According to Irma Buwalda, "Policewomen on the Pacific Coast," *The Police Journal*, Apr. 1927, 5, cities that followed Portland and Seattle in hiring policewomen were Eugene, Salem, Astoria, Bend, and Oregon City, Oregon, and Tacoma, Bellingham, Spokane, and Yakima, Washington.

7. Howard C. Kegley, "The Police Department of Los Angeles," *National Police Magazine*, Jan. 1913, 40-41.

8. Joseph J. Woods, *The Progressives and the Police: Urban Reform and the Professionalism of the Los Angeles Police* (Ann Arbor, MI: University Microfilms International, 1979 [Ph.D. diss., University of California at Los Angeles, 1973]), 173-175, 197.

9. Los Angeles Police Department, *Law Enforcement in Los Angeles*, 1924; reprint (New York: Arno Press, 1974), 12-14 (references are to reprint edition); Kegley, "The Police Department of Los Angeles," 41; Aletha Gilbert, "The Duties of a 'City Mother'," *The American City*, Mar. 1922, 239, 240- 241.

10. According to Buwalda, "Policewomen on the Pacific Coast," 5, in 1927 San Francisco had three policewomen (the Three Kates), and Berkeley, Santa Barbara, San Diego, Santa Monica, Pasadena, Alhambra, Monrovia, and Venice all had at least one woman.

11. Elizabeth Simpson Smith, *Breakthrough: Women in Law Enforcement* (New York: Walker & Co., 1982), 6; "The Policewomen of Indianapolis and Their New Methods," *Literary Digest* 69 (Apr. 23, 1921), 41; "Police Functions Best Performed by Men and by Women Police Officers," *The Police Journal*, Apr. 1929, 20.

12. "The Policewomen of Indianapolis and Their New Methods," 41, 43; Lillian Madden, "The Modern Policewoman's Work," *The Police Journal*, Apr. 1924, 14; IAP *Bulletin*, Feb. 1926, 9; Mabel Bray Schweir, "Supervising Public Dances," *The Police Journal*, Dec. 1926, 9.

13. *The Survey*, Jan. 26, 1918, 474; Chloe Owings, *Women Police: A Study of the Development and Status of the Women Police Movement* (New York: Frederick H. Hitchcock, 1925), 169; "Work Performed by Policewomen's Division Shows an

Increase in Every Line of Activity," *Police Journal* (St. Louis), Jan. 7, 1925, 12.

14. George M. DePetit, "Policing Youngstown, Ohio," *The National Police Journal*, Feb. 1923, 5 (for Youngstown); Helen D. Pigeon, "The Policewomen Meet in Conference," *The Police Journal*, Aug. 1926, 17-18 (for Des Moines); *The National Police Journal*, Aug. 1921, 8, 55 (for Minneapolis); *Policewomen's International Bulletin*, Oct. 1927, 10 (for Flint and Wichita).

15. Anne Firor Scott, *Southern Lady: From Pedestal to Politics, 1830-1930* (Chicago: University of Chicago Press, 1970), 191.

16. William J. Mathias and Stuart Anderson, *Horse to Helicopter: First Century of the Atlanta Police Department* (Atlanta: Georgia State University, 1973), 80-81; J.C. Davis, "Woman's Work in a Police Department," *Policewoman's International Bulletin*, June 1929, 9.

17. Louis Brownlow, "The City Manager and the Policewoman," *The Woman Citizen*, Nov. 1925, 30; IAP *Bulletin*, Dec. 1925, 12; IAP *Bulletin*, Oct. 31, 1925, 3.

18. Brownlow, "The City Manager and the Policewoman," 30.

19. *Official History. Police Department of Charleston, South Carolina. Review of the Business Activities of the Port of Charleston, SC* (Charleston, SC: Walker, Evans & Cogswell, 1925), 19, 25, 27.

20. Fred M. Valz, "Policewomen Fill Long Felt Need in Jacksonville, Fla.," *The Police Journal*, Aug. 1927, 14; Fred M. Valz, "Jacksonville Women's Bureau Latest in Field Reports Progress," *Policewoman's International Bulletin*, Aug.-Sept. 1927, 3.

21. Robert M. Fogelson, *Big-City Police* (Cambridge, MA: Harvard University Press, 1977), 38.

22. Roberts, "Police Social Workers: A History," 295.

23. "Policewomen in Chicago," *The Literary Digest* 47 (Aug. 23, 1919), 271; "Anne Loucks Dies: First Policewoman," *Chicago Tribune*, Feb. 20, 1957, sec. 3, 10:1.

24. Mabel Rockwell, "Work of Policewomen," *Proceedings* of the IACP, 33rd Convention, Chicago, IL, July 19-22, 1926, 239, 240, 241. According to *The National Police Journal*, June 1921, 28, beach attire was closely monitored; Chicago policewomen, "with tapemeasure, needle and thread" had been "surveying and reconstructing Chicago's one-piece feminine bathing suits, to conform with beach rules."

25. Virginia M. Murray, "Policewomen in Detroit," *The American City*, Sept. 1921, 209-210; Owings, *Women Police*, 144-149. Again indicating the problems with determining key dates pertaining to policewomen, although documents between 1922 and 1927 identify Hutzel as women's bureau director and Fourth Deputy Police Commissioner, a December 16, 1994 letter to the author from Sgt. Christopher Buck, Public Information Office, Detroit Police Department, states that department records show Hutzel serving in these positions from June 1928 to October 1, 1948.

26. Eleonore L. Hutzel, "A Woman's Division in a Police Department," *Proceedings* of the IACP, 34th Conference, Windsor, ON, Canada, June 6-9, 1927, 223; *Policewoman's International Bulletin*, Oct. 1927, 9.

27. Sabina Marshall, "Development of the Policewomen's Movement in Cleveland," *Journal of Social Hygiene* 11, no. 4 (Apr. 1925), 199-200, 201-209.

28. Cleveland Foundation, *Criminal Justice in Cleveland*, 1922; reprint (Montclair, NJ: Patterson Smith, 1968), 777-779 (references are to reprint edition); Mina C. Van Winkle, "Policewomen's Place in the Service," *Proceedings* of the IACP, 33rd

Convention, Chicago, IL, July 19-23, 1926, 242; Brownlow, "The City Manager and the Policewoman," 30.

29. Owings, *Women Police*, 143. Marshall, "Development of the Policewomen's Movement in Cleveland," 208; *Policewoman's International Bulletin*, May 1929, 8. Standards were a high school diploma and at least two years of experience in social service or education, or graduation from nursing school, or two years of responsible commercial work involving public contact. Dorothy D. Henry, "Woman's Bureau of Cleveland Department Gives Encouraging Report," *The Police Journal*, Jan. 1926, 5.

30. *Police Annual Report. Cleveland, Ohio, 1930*, 5, 25.

31. Owings, *Women Police*, 124-127.

32. Leonard V. Harrison, *Police Administration in Boston*, vol. 3 (Cambridge, MA: Harvard University Press, 1934), 140-141.

33. "The 'Sesqui' Policewomen," *The Woman Citizen*, Feb. 1927, 34; Geraldine A. Kelley, "Policewomen Play Important Role in Philadelphia, Pa.," *FBI Law Enforcement Bulletin*, Oct. 1957, 3.

34. Theresa M. Melchionne, "Policewomen: Their Introduction into the New York City Police Department (A Study of Organizational Response to Innovation)," M.P.A. thesis, Bernard M. Baruch College, CUNY, 1962, 67, 68.

35. Ibid., 85-87; *The Woman Citizen*, Sept. 22, 1917, 306.

36. New York City Police Department, *Annual Report*, 1918, 85-86, quoted in Melchionne, "Policewomen: Their Introduction into the New York City Police Department," 86, 89-119; *The National Police Journal*, Sept. 1918, 12.

37. Mary E. Hamilton, *The Policewoman: Her Service and Ideals*, 1924; reprint (New York: Arno Press, 1971), 18, 20, 59 (references are to reprint edition); Melchionne, "Policewomen: Their Introduction into the New York City Police Department," 120.

38. *Annual Report of the Police Department, City of New York, For the Year 1921*, 92; Melchionne, "Policewomen: Their Introduction into the New York City Police Department," 120-121. The classrooms were used immediately when 25 women officers received first aid and police practices instruction.

39. *Annual Report of the Police Department, City of New York, For the Year 1921*, 92; *For the Year 1923*, 177, 180-183; *For the Year 1924*, 142-144; Melchionne, "Policewomen: Their Introduction into the New York City Police Department," 120- 124.

40. Lois Lundell Higgins, "The Feminine Arm of the Law: Women in Crime," paper presented at the 1st Biennial IAWP Conference, Lafayette, IN, Sept. 30-Oct. 2, 1958, 2; Roberts, "Police Social Workers," 295 (for 1930); Sophonisba P. Breckinridge, *Women in the Twentieth Century: A Study of Their Political, Social and Economic Activities* (New York: McGraw-Hill, 1933), 205-206 (for 1931).

41. Joan M. Jensen, "All Pink Sisters: The War Department and the Feminist Movement in the 1920s," in *Decades of Discontent: The Women's Movement, 1920-1940*, eds. Lois Scharf and Joan M. Jensen (Westport, CT: Greenwood Press, 1983), 199.

42. Hamilton, *The Policewoman*, 64.

Chapter 5

Depression Losses, 1929–1941

The 1930s brought major changes to U.S. policing. This decade of foment, revolving around three leaders—August Vollmer, O.W. Wilson, and J. Edgar Hoover—is the dividing line between early and modern law enforcement. These men advocated changes that placed policewomen further from the police mainstream, which now stressed crimefighting above all else. Even Vollmer, the reform-minded chief in Berkeley, California, and a supporter of policewomen, seemed to have abandoned them. More damaging, though, than Vollmer's changing orientation were the views of his protégé, O.W. Wilson, who, by the 1940s, had become the leading spokesman on efficiency, deployment, manpower, and tasks that should be assigned to police departments.

Wilson, a Berkeley police officer who later served as chief in Wichita, as a consultant and dean of the School of Criminology at the Berkeley campus of the University of California, and then as Chicago police superintendent, owed his professional success to Vollmer, but his views on policewomen reflected his, rather than Vollmer's, generation. Less concerned with the social service aspects of policing than Vollmer had been, Wilson did not advocate expanded roles for policewomen. To the contrary, he believed that women were ill-equipped emotionally for leadership positions.

Loss of momentum by the women's movement cannot itself explain the decline of the policewomen's movement, although certainly policewomen suffered from the loss of public interest in feminism and reform activities associated with the Progressive era. As the nation struggled through a Depression, women's entry into the job market was viewed differently than in more prosperous times. The Depression reinforced traditional roles. The historian Susan Ware has observed: "Women were strongly encouraged to limit their aspirations to husband, family, and domesticity; work outside the home, especially for married women, was discouraged."[1]

Many official policies did more than discourage women's employment; they discriminated, if not against all women, certainly against married women. By 1932, Section 232 of the National Recovery Act specified that if both husband and wife worked for the federal government and one was in an agency where staff reductions were being made, either would be the first dismissed as long as the other remained on the payroll. While the law did not state specifically that wives were to be dismissed and husbands retained, the reality was that husbands were usually in higher-paying positions, so they remained while their wives left. More than three-quarters of those dismissed under the act were women. A number of states also passed laws that discriminated against married women.[2]

These policies generated little public outcry. Rather, working wives "were viewed as selfish, greedy women who took jobs away from male bread-winners." A 1936 poll found that 82 percent of the respondents believed that women with working husbands should not work outside the home; three fourths of the women polled agreed. There was widespread disapproval of those who "earned a 'luxury' wage in favor of those who depended on a 'necessity' wage."[3] Wages of married women came to be seen as by definition "luxury" wages.

During the Depression, police work became a desirable source of employment. Economic hardship had "the curious effect of improving the relative economic status of police work."[4] Simply put, as unemployment rose, middle-class, educated, native-born men sought police positions. Civil service job security, pensions, fringe benefits, and shorter work days and weeks made policing attractive to those who had previously scorned it as fitting only for immigrants. The relative comfort in which a policeman and his family could live in 1931 is illustrated by annual salaries in 49 small and medium-sized cities. The two largest departments had 254 and 130 officers (Atlantic City, New Jersey, and Schenectady, New York, respectively); the smallest, Rock Island, Illinois, had 11 men. Salaries ranged from about $2,500 in Atlantic City and Mount Vernon, New York, to about $1,460 in Wilmington, Delaware. More than half the families in the United States at this time had annual incomes between $500 and $1,500.[5] In addition to high salaries, all the cities paid sick-leave and vacation benefits and all but six offered pensions.

How did policewomen fare? Of the 49 cities, 25 employed policewomen or matrons (combined in the survey). The largest number of women was three in Pasadena, California, and Pontiac, Michigan. In most cities, women, whether policewomen or matrons, earned less than policemen, but this was not universal. Knoxville paid its policewoman the same salary as experienced policemen ($1,800 annually), and Lancaster, Pennsylvania, paid its policewoman $2,250 annually, $750 more than a new policeman. It is unlikely that the issue of pay equity was raised by these women. In 1937, women's average annual pay was $525, compared to

$1,027 for men.[6] Policewomen's earnings, while below those of their male colleagues, were well above national averages. Even the lowest of the women's salaries placed them near the top of the economic ladder.

In the Depression years the number of policewomen fell or remained relatively stagnant. Women's supervisory and management positions plummeted. Estimates varied, but there were probably no more than 600 policewomen in 1929. Census figures for 1930 listed 1,534 policewomen and detectives in public and private agencies. These figures, with other estimates, indicate that more than half were not paid by police agencies. A 1933 count generously estimated 800 policewomen (150 of them in New York City) in about 200 chiefly urban communities.[7] In 1940, after the Depression decade, the number of policewomen counted in the census had increased to 1,775. The figures, as in 1930, included women employed outside of police departments. According to one study, in 1940, 46 "major cities" employed only 480 policewomen.[8]

A major Progressive goal had been to professionalize the police, which meant divorcing them from political control. By the 1930s, though, professionalism had come to be defined by police themselves as managerial efficiency, technological advances, and crimefighting. By the end of the decade, not only had the policeman's image of himself changed, but so had the public's perception of the police role. Prior to the Progressive era, police departments were general-purpose agencies with an ill-defined mission, subject to the whims of local leaders. In an age of personal politics and party control, the police had performed a variety of health and welfare duties. By the 1930s they had shed many of the more obvious housekeeping roles, such as lodging the homeless and overseeing street cleaning. Agencies created specifically for these purposes became part of the urban landscape.

Professionalism hurt the cause of policewomen, who were often appointed solely in response to political pressure and who performed social service duties that were becoming less associated with police. In many cities policewomen had not achieved civil service status and were, therefore, subject to shifting political currents. There is a certain irony that professionalism did not result in appreciation for the higher education standards and social service orientation that policewomen brought to law enforcement. Other than the creation of academies for male recruits, the professionalism sought by the Progressives did not result in substantially upgrading the quality of policemen and ultimately pushed policewomen completely out of the police mainstream.

Simultaneously, interest in scientific management led reformers to view police departments not as civilian corporations, but within the military mode, leading to the creation of a highly defined rank structure. The military model was not formulated by the police—although eventually they wholeheartedly subscribed to it—but by reformers, who "probably"

viewed it as the answer to "the need for discipline within large organizations" such as urban police departments, to "enhance control up and down
the chain of command . . . lessening the influence of the political machine
and ward bosses."[9] A recurring theme in police history relates to badges,
uniforms, and even firearms being forced upon the police by those seeking
to make them more visible and accountable. An attempt to uniform New
York police prior to the Civil War led to criticism of "liveried lackeys,"
while individual officers viewed uniforms as making it difficult for them
to "melt into a crowd" to avoid their duties. The Civil War removed some
of the onus from wearing a uniform, and this, combined with demands for
greater accountability finally led to the uniforming of municipal police
officers.

The New York City Police Department in the years before the administration of Progressive Commissioner Theodore Roosevelt proves that uniforms alone did not create discipline nor adherence to the military model.
New York was not unique. Roosevelt instituted new selection procedures,
including competitive tests for entry-level positions, but Thomas A.
Reppetto, a police historian, has observed that despite Roosevelt's "dash
and vigor . . . his influence on the police, like his military career, was more
form than substance, and things soon returned to normal."[10] "Normal" by
1912 was a force of "police bureaucrats," one half of whom had served for
10 or more years and a tenth of whom had more than 20 years of service.
By the 1920s, they formed a "vast bureaucracy of long-term public ser-
vants with vested interests in their positions."[11]

Similar developments occurred around the country. By the Great Depression police officers were no longer political appointees serving for
short periods of time, but careerists, who saw the crimefighter model as
providing them with a role in municipal service that was fulfilled by no
other existing or emerging bureaucracy.

There was also an expansion of the role of the federal government in
police matters previously seen as exclusively local issues. J. Edgar Hoover,
for 48 years director of the Federal Bureau of Investigation, looked back on
the 1930s as "the Renaissance of law enforcement."[12] Actually, from
Hoover's perspective, it was not so much a rebirth, as a birth, for it was
during this era that he developed the FBI from an unimportant federal
agency into the premier power in U.S. law enforcement. Although never a
municipal police officer, he played a vital role in creating and perpetuating
the crimefighter image.

Hoover took over the Bureau of Investigation in May 1924, as acting
director, becoming director some months later. He cleaned up the scan-
dal-riddled agency and reduced its size. In the 1920s the BOI was an
unimportant agency whose agents were neither authorized to carry weapons nor to make arrests. All this changed on July 1, 1935, when the BOI

became the FBI and was given expanded law enforcement duties, particularly in interstate criminal activities.

The historian Samuel Walker attributes the FBI's rise in power to Hoover's public relations skills and his ability to exploit the fear created by a national crime wave during and just after the Depression. Although Walker does not mention it, Prohibition and efforts to circumvent it also contributed to the public's fear of crime. FBI press releases glorified the exploits of agents, described as crisscrossing the country to track down and apprehend such highly publicized criminals as John Dillinger, Pretty Boy Floyd, and the team of Bonnie and Clyde. In 1935, the FBI inaugurated its National Academy, where municipal police leaders received training. This provided a forum for the FBI to further publicize and inculcate its view of the police role and police professionalism. And what was this view? According to Walker,

professionalism had special meaning for Hoover and the FBI. Professional cops were tough, fearless crime fighters. . . were well trained and utilized the latest scientific crimefighting techniques. . . . They were expert sharpshooters. . . . The Bureau advanced this image of police professionalism. As a consequence, the crimefighting or law enforcement aspects of the police role overshadowed all others. . . . Order maintenance and service . . . sank to second-class status. Officers derided them as not being "real" police work.[13]

Even Vollmer, the advocate of college-educated police professionals working as social workers to solve societal problems, was influenced by the changing portrait of the police. Although he remained Berkeley's chief until 1932, his reputation led him into other areas. When President Herbert Hoover in 1929 established the Wickersham Commission (officially the National Commission on Law Observance and Enforcement, but commonly referred to by the name of its chairman, George W. Wickersham), Vollmer headed the task force on the police, which cast them in a negative light.

The 140-page *Report on Police* was one of two volume dealing with police. This report could have provided Vollmer with an opportunity to advocate a continued—even an expanded—role for policewomen, but nowhere in his conclusions for improving police departments did he recommend women's bureaus, stating rather that "a crime prevention unit should be established if circumstances warrant . . . and qualified women police should be engaged to handle juvenile delinquents' and women's cases."[14]

Vollmer's comments set the tone for the decade. By the 1930s policewomen were losing their claim to lead women's bureaus, which were frequently placed within juvenile or crime prevention units supervised by a male officer. Walker has noted that the progress areas Vollmer cited in his report concerned mainly internal administration and scientific crimefighting. He interprets this as a shift in Vollmer's thinking to reflect the new definition of professionalism, with the image of police-as-social-worker falling into eclipse, replaced by the cop-as-crimefighter.[15]

Vollmer was further drawn into the crimefighter orbit by Wilson, whose recognition stemmed from his concern with efficiency, particularly the use of patrol cars, which became the primary deployment method when uniformed officers abandoned foot patrol. Virtually all police historians agree that by the late 1930s Wilson had supplanted Vollmer as the foremost authority on police administration and management and that his reputation "was based largely on his concern for automobile patrol . . . increasingly the main preoccupation of efficiency-minded police administrators."[16] Marked police cars, with two-way radios that kept policemen in constant contact with a centrally located dispatcher, were a faster, more dependable way to get them to the scenes of crimes. Speed in reaching the problem had become the definition of efficiency.

Also, since officers were expected to be in their cars when not at a crime scene or other police activity, marked cars provided a way of keeping officers visible and out of taverns or political meeting places. This was the same issue that had led to badges and uniforms to make policemen more visible to an earlier generation of reformers. Technology, primarily of interest to male executives, was exciting to at least one female manager. Mary Sullivan, the NYCPD women's bureau director, called the 1932 introduction of cars in New York "the most important improvement . . . during my years in the department. . . . Now every precinct . . . is patrolled by men in constant touch with headquarters; they can reach a given address in two or three minutes after getting their orders."[17] She did not mention cars having an impact on policewomen.

When Wilson became head of the Wichita police department in 1928, he soon created a crime prevention bureau. Its functions encompassed those normally performed within women's bureaus. As expressed in the department's 1935 duty manual, this definition of crime prevention would become the basis of virtually all of Wilson's writing on the topic. The bureau's mandate was as follows:

To develop a program . . . [to] eliminate factors which induce criminal tendencies, and . . . which promote criminal activities, especially among children; to promote such a program, enlisting . . . the public, all interested agencies and other Divisions of the Police Department. . . . To actively undertake, through the press, the radio, by speeches and through personal contact, the development of a proper mental attitude on the part of the public toward all law enforcement agencies, and especially to educate the police and the public in the problems of crime prevention and suppression. To determine persons and places which contribute to delinquency, investigating and taking . . . action to correct the conditions. To supervise and inspect all places of public amusement. To promote the welfare of children, the sick, the needy and the aged; to search for lost persons. To investigate all cases involving boys and girls. To manage the women's jail and to assist in the investigation of all females.[18]

One of the first specialists Wilson hired was Pearl L'Heureux, who held a master's degree in social welfare. Wilson refused to call her a police-woman, naming her a "juvenile supervisor," and setting her salary "equiva-lent to that of her male counterparts." L'Heureux was later promoted to captain.[19]

From Wichita Wilson returned to Berkeley as dean of the School of Criminology at the University of California. There he was part of a statewide movement, much through Vollmer's efforts, to add police sci-ence and criminology to college curricula. Although Vollmer's ideas seemed visionary to many, not even he spoke of police education in the terms policewomen did. While the women envisioned fully integrated college programs with an emphasis on social work and related topics, California police education was seen as "technical training" for pre- and in-service officers. The incentives were also economic, as San Jose State Teacher's College advised chiefs that it was cheaper to train their men there than in their own departments.

The San Jose program, developed by Vollmer and the college president T.W. MacQuarrie, also involved Earl Warren, then California District Attorney, later the state's governor and Chief Justice of the U.S. Supreme Court. Women—the major advocates of an educated police force—were not involved. MacQuarrie's exhortation to chiefs to train their men at San Jose State meant just that—women were not permitted to enroll. Reflect-ing the views of police officials in the 1930s, MacQuarrie noted that although "a good many young women wished to take the work . . . they were advised to make other plans . . . [since] there may be a field someday for policewomen, but at present the demand does not seem to be great." The 1935-1936 catalogue specified: "No women were to be admitted un-less they had 'unusual qualifications' and planned to enter the police field as their life's work." Either none applied or none was found to have sufficient "unusual qualifications" or motivation; women were not admit-ted until the 1938-1939 academic year.[20]

Wilson's 1941 Public Administration Service study, *Distribution of Police Patrol Force*, cemented his reputation as the spokesman for efficiency and the application of scientific management to policing. It also served to further isolate policewomen. The introduction set the tone for his later surveys. His aim was to set forth "a method for the chronological and geographical distribution of a patrol force . . . according to the relative need for police service" because "the limited size of police forces and [their] importance to the community . . . make imperative the effective application of their energies." He stressed the need to develop "some objective measure of the need for police service . . . to permit a reasonably accurate determination of the number of officers that will afford satisfactory service to a given community."[21] Wilson made no mention at all of policewomen and their traditional functions.

When he surveyed the Hartford Police Department in 1942 police-women were not fortunate enough to be ignored. He recommended that Hartford add a third policewoman ("to provide weekly, sick and vacation relief for the matron, [and] . . . the other two policewomen"), and that the women be assigned to the juvenile division with two male detectives with social work backgrounds, but his comments pertaining to the division's leadership offer a stark commentary on the negative attitudes police-women faced. He suggested the division be headed by a man because of the need for close cooperation with other divisions within the department, the need to supervise other men officers on the staff, and because of the *tendency toward emotional instability which women display when under constant pressure.*[22]

The emergence of Vollmer, Wilson, and Hoover changed the class orientation of police leadership, representing another setback for policewomen. Early leaders, especially Theodore Roosevelt, John D. Rockefeller, Jr. (through his Bureau of Social Hygiene), and Raymond Fosdick were of at least upper-middle-class backgrounds, usually with Ivy League educations. Policewomen and their advocates were frequently of similar class and comparable educational backgrounds. In the 1930s leaders were more heterogeneous and less wealthy than earlier reformers.

Vollmer was the first of the leaders who began their careers as police-men and had middle-class backgrounds. Those who attended college had usually done so while serving as police. Even though Wilson was the son of a well-to-do Norwegian-American lawyer, he was a Californian and a police officer, rather than an Eastern, Ivy-League-educated reformer. Because of the diversity of the 1930s group, and their having served as policemen, it was "natural that they would want to convert policing into a profession akin to law or medicine, opting for the social worker, efficiency engineer, or scientific investigator role as it suited their taste or the public's."[23]

This contrasted sharply with the Progressives, who, if they served in police departments at all, held management positions. Since these Progressive police managers had entered departments laterally, without serving as police officers, they were comfortable with policewomen, and particularly women's bureau directors, following a career path similar to their own. Traditional police managers, who had moved up the ranks to achieve positions as chiefs, quite naturally were less inclined to favor outsiders.

Similar changes did not occur among policewomen. Those who spoke for policewomen in the 1930s were the same women who had spoken earlier or a small group of women, such as Mary Sullivan in New York, who came from a different background but held similar views. The women clung to their vision, even turning aside opportunities to expand their role. Eleonore L. Hutzel, director of the Detroit women's bureau, in 1929 voiced disapproval of women doing non-protective work, noting that assignment to

the detective bureau, the narcotic squad, the homicide squad and other crime detection divisions . . . [is] still very experimental. There is little doubt that in the future women . . . will be . . . in many squads of the crime detection divisions . . . but at present the few efforts . . . do not justify . . . conclusions as to their usefulness or as to the peculiar qualifications required for success in such work.[24]

Ignoring the setbacks women were facing, Hutzel in 1933 continued to paint a picture of policewomen identical to images created when they were a daring social experiment. Her book, *The Policewoman's Handbook*, reiterated her concern with recognition by other social workers, rather than by police managers. She stressed the need for a policewoman to have formal education and social work experience.[25] Hutzel's bureau reflected her concerns; it handled all cases involving girls and women. A separate juvenile division, comprised of male officers, worked with boys and young men. Police Commissioner James K. Watkins told participants in the 1933 National Conference of Social Work meeting in Detroit, that, in addition to Hutzel, the bureau's two sergeants and 33 policewomen in 1932 came into contact with more than 9,000 women and girls. He said were it not for budget restraints, he would double the number of women. The budget had already taken a toll; in March 1929 the bureau had 42 policewomen, 16 of whom had been assigned solely to "protective" patrol of areas frequented by women and girls.[26]

The bureau in Washington, D.C., also functioned in 1932 much as it had when established in 1918. The bureau, which employed 20 policewomen in 1920, was hampered by a lack of growth even before the Depression. In 1925 it still contained 20 policewomen (and four policemen); by 1926 there were 22 women and a few policemen. In 1932, Lt. Mina C. Van Winkle supervised one sergeant, 21 policewomen, and a number of civilians.[27] The women continued to work out of and administer the House of Detention, where all women over the age of 17 were detained. Following this model, in 1929 Atlanta, Baltimore, Cleveland, and Detroit policewomen were also responsible for detention quarters in their respective cities.

Leaders of the remnants of the policewomen's movement continued to advocate women's bureaus. Their sole concession to the declining numbers of policewomen was acceptance of crime prevention bureaus. Although these bureaus did provide positions for policewomen, it was only in departments that had long utilized them such as Portland, Oregon, and Seattle, or in a few large departments such as New York City and Detroit, that women were placed in charge of staffs containing both male and female personnel.

Even Chicago, which had always gone its own way in the deployment of its women, succumbed to demands for a crime prevention bureau. A reform group in 1931 suggested the creation of such a bureau, bringing together the boys' employment division and the policewomen "investigating cases of missing girls and preventing delinquency and crime through the inspection of dance halls, recreation centers, etc."[28] This resulted in an increase in the number of policewomen: from 30 in 1929, to 35 in 1933; and to 45 in 1935, the first year they were listed within the crime prevention division. Contrasting with losses in other cities, the number of policewomen in Chicago increased during the decade, rising to 52 in 1936, and 61 in 1938, but falling to 58 by 1940.[29]

New York City also continued to tread a path different from other cities. By 1930, the NYCPD, the nation's largest municipal police agency, employed the largest number of women police. Although they continued to work under two civil service titles (policewoman and patrolwoman), the number of women was usually shown as a total of the two. Between 1928 and 1937 positions for women (not all were always filled) ranged from 125 to 166. There were 125 positions from 1928 to 1930, 155 from 1932 to 1936, and 166 as of 1937, when the two titles were combined. The end of the dual career path did not bring more women into the NYCPD. The number in 1937 actually decreased, from 143 on January 1, 1937, to 137 at year's end. During the same period, the quota for patrolmen was 17,253.[30]

After experimenting with a number of ways to deploy and supervise its women officers, including the creation of a welfare bureau in 1918, a women's precinct in 1921, and a women's bureau in 1924, New York continued to try different configurations. In February 1930, pursuing recommendations of a local crime commission, the NYCPD established a crime prevention unit led by Virginia M. Murray, who kept her position as executive secretary of the Travelers' Aid Society. This was a repetition of her tenure as director of the Detroit women's division in 1921, when, already with the Travelers' Aid Society, she took the job on a temporary basis until she was succeeded by Hutzel in 1922. In Detroit, Murray had made clear her view that a women's bureau was "an additional social organization . . . for the constructive treatment of the girl who has fallen into anti-social habits." The New York bureau seemed to meet her ideal. She reported that of 1,538 complaints handled in its first four months, only 117 had resulted in arrests.[31]

IAP leaders were enthusiastic about the bureau and with Murray's selection. She assured *Policewoman's International Bulletin* readers that the new Bureau would be doing important, constructive social service . . . would aid thousands of girls living away from their parents . . . do a lot of individual case work . . . [and that] the women . . . will be social workers with police powers. . . . We want . . . to understand young people, to be their friends, and to keep them as far from jail as possible.[32]

Part of the IAP's enthusiasm was, no doubt, fostered by its rapport with Murray and her successor, Henrietta Additon. This closeness differed from the IAP's relationship with Mary E. Hamilton and Mary Sullivan, the two NYCPD women's bureau directors in the 1920s and 1930s, neither of whom were active in the IAP. Murray was succeeded in mid-1931 by Additon, who had worked with the IAP in 1924 when she was at Bryn Mawr College and taught at the New York School of Social Work training program for women's bureau directors. Prior to World War I, Additon had been the chief probation officer of the Philadelphia Municipal Court, and then assistant to the director of the Committee on Protective Work for Girls, before serving with the Philadelphia Big Sister Association in the mid-1920s, one of the groups that had lobbied unsuccessfully for police-women there. She was with the American Social Hygiene Association when she was named Sixth Deputy Police Commissioner.

Both Additon's title and her bureau echoed an earlier era, when, in January 1918, Ellen A. O'Grady had been named Fifth Deputy Police Commissioner for the welfare bureau. This time, the staff included one deputy inspector, 50 lieutenants, a number of sergeants, 60 patrolmen, 34 patrolwomen, and 25 crime prevention investigators. The latter were women hired in 1930 on a new civil service title that required they be trained social workers with at least five years' experience. Of the 5,215 cases handled in 1930, most were minors in need of "social treatment."[33]

The crime prevention bureau was separate from the women's bureau, which remained under Sullivan's command. In her autobiography, *My Double Life: The Story of a New York Policewoman,* Sullivan hints at the complexity of managing such a diverse group:

I have all types . . . in the bureau, ranging from blondes who can look very dizzy if they wish, to white-haired, motherly souls whom no one would ever dream of identifying as detectives. In apportioning the work I must bear in mind the characteristics and abilities of 150 women.

About half . . . are willing and even eager to undertake dangerous jobs; the others prefer assignments in the social welfare field that carry fewer possibilities of adventure, though no part of a policewoman's work can be called entirely safe.

Some . . . are especially apt in taking the part of a tenement housewife; some, who look young, can best investigate dance halls and fraudulent advertisements directed at young women; others, of the quiet, mousey type, can get away with dangerous jobs that a more conspicuous person could not handle. A number . . .

dislike . . . detective work but possess a degree of courage, sympathy and understanding that makes them very proficient in handling prisoners. Sometimes, as I try to give each officer the part she can manage best, I imagine myself a Hollywood casting director trying to find suitable roles for a widely assorted group of actresses.[34]

These "actresses" were involved in "investigations of every kind, involving an offense against a woman or girl." They returned to New York City female prisoners arrested elsewhere, supervised female prisoners, and secured custodial care and treatment for mentally ill or defective persons. Seven were assigned to the shoplifting squad, which arrested [more accurately, took into custody] more than 1,000 people in 1931, even though most juveniles were referred for counseling or to their parents rather than legally placed under arrest. Women also searched for missing persons and investigated fictitious or misleading advertisements, which were often a cover for houses of prostitution, fortune tellers, or fake doctors.

Sullivan mentions a "fairly new development"—the Coney Island Patrol, involving "policewomen, most . . . in uniform," assigned to beaches, primarily to care for lost children, but also to pick up runaways, to prevent people from undressing on the beach, and to catch pocketbook thieves.[35] This was a busy time for Sullivan's bureau but the crime prevention bureau, which had been set up on an experimental basis, fell victim to the NYCPD's recurring reorganizations. In 1934 it was placed under a new director and renamed the juvenile aid bureau.

An altogether different change for policewomen occurred in 1934 when pistol practice was introduced. By order of Commissioner Lewis J. Valentine, women were issued firearms. Most carried them in pocketbooks, not in holsters at their waists, as male officers did. The regulation pocketbook was an over-the-shoulder bag, with a compartment for the firearm and with space similar to a regular pocketbook for other police or personal items the policewoman chose to carry. Sullivan observed that most of the women were "surprisingly efficient marksmen."[36]

By 1938 no civil service exam had been given in almost nine years. Sullivan was hampered in filling assignments that required a young officer due to the age of her staff, with only a few under 35. Another reason she hoped for expansion harked back to Lola Baldwin's beginnings in 1905. New York City was to host the 1939 World's Fair and Sullivan was concerned about an increase in "runaway girls, as well as pickpockets and riffraff from all parts of the country." Despite her worry about having women at the fair, its public safety director spoke only of the "approximately 1,000 men" needed for the task. He favored candidates who spoke a foreign language, had military training, possessed a driver's license, and knew how to ride a motorcycle or a horse. He made no mention of the skills in handling women and children that Sullivan thought would make policewomen vital to the success of the fair.[37]

New York City officials finally gave a civil service exam for police-women in 1938. Although only 27 vacancies existed, 3,500 women applied. Requirements were a college degree or high school graduation combined with two years of full-time paid experience in a related criminal justice field or profession involving public contact, high-level clerical skills, or a combination of these.[38]

Due to size, the large number of women employed, and constantly changing politics, the NYCPD was one of few departments with both a women's and a crime prevention (later, juvenile) bureau. It was also one of few in which the head of the crime prevention bureau was a woman. This, too, was attributable to politics and size. In smaller agencies, the crime prevention bureau was headed by a sworn member of the department. The size of the New York bureau, combined with the political power of its advocates, led to the appointment of a civilian manager. This opened the position to a female social service professional, rather than a male police manager.

More typical was the crime prevention division created in Los Angeles in 1924 based on Vollmer's recommendations. This division, the model for many others, originally was staffed with 20 policewomen; by 1937 there were 39, including Alice Stebbins Wells. At first, 5 officers did policewomen's work and 15 acted as matrons. By 1937, assignments had expanded—16 women were in the crime prevention division, 10 in stations, 8 in the jail doing matron duties, 3 in the women's probation office, 1 in the city mother's bureau, and 1 in the detective division.[39]

The use of policewomen in Los Angeles contrasted sharply with the sporadic, unsuccessful efforts of another California city. In 1936, San Diego officials hired women officers for the fourth time. They did not last much longer than their predecessors. The city authorized a social worker and a matron to patrol the 1935-1936 World Exposition at Balboa Park, the same park that in the 1920s had been the scene of three shootings involving policewomen. Neither carried weapons or handcuffs, and no shootings were reported. They handled problems involving women, children, and morals—including checking burlesque and girlie shows—and illegal gambling, and looked after lost children. The department appointed permanent policewomen in September 1936, but only to supervise dance halls. The women received dismissal letters on July 15, 1939, resulting in protests from church and civic groups and from the Women Peace Officers Association of California. Despite government indecision and at least one court ruling in their favor, neither worked as policewomen again. The social worker continued to assist the department until 1943. The woman who worked throughout the controversy remained a policewoman until 1945, when she asked to return to her former matron position. San Diego was once again without policewomen, this time until 1954.[40]

Countering the declining numbers of and interest in policewomen after 1929, a few cities named their first women in the Depression years. Officials in Fort Worth, Texas, in 1930 appointed four women, who were trained by Sgt. Rhoda J. Milliken, loaned from Washington, D.C., at the request of the city manager. Milliken, who led the woman's bureau in Washington, D.C., after Van Winkle's death in 1932, prepared and graded the exams and set up the Fort Worth bureau. Officials in Richmond, Virginia, hired two women in 1930 and sent them to Washington, D.C., for two weeks of training. Officials in Williamsport, Pennsylvania, appointed the city's first policewoman the same year, while others in Shreveport, Louisiana, gave a civil service exam in anticipation of adding women to the police department. In 1933, Phoenix officials hired the city's first policewoman, who served primarily as a jail matron.[41]

Philadelphia was the last large city to employ policewomen. By 1930 all cities of any size or importance had at least one policewoman, but Philadelphia had none until 1936. The city's only prior experiences with "policewomen" had been an unpaid dance censor who in 1921 provided free dance instruction to keep youngsters out of dance halls, and seven women appointed in 1927 as special policewomen during the Sesquicentennial Exposition.

Although the date was later, the pattern of civic associations' efforts leading to policewomen was identical to that of earlier decades. A Crime Prevention Association was formed in 1932 to combat crime among older boys. Police cooperation led in March 1936 to the formation within the crime prevention division of a policewomen's unit, staffed by one senior policewoman (former City Magistrate Norma Carson) and four officers. They worked from an abandoned school building, apart from male colleagues, handling boys and girls under 16 years of age, supervising recreation, organizing a bootblacks' club, arranging for underprivileged children to attend summer camp, and taking youngsters to the circus. Two projects were a campaign against youthful scavengers and the control of male bootblacks and children of either sex engaged in street peddling. The women were also assigned to "restraining streetwalkers . . . in center city." In 1939, added duties also included investigations of cases involving morals, shoplifters, and lost children.[42]

Elsewhere, until World War II created a recovery, women's bureaus in smaller cities were left with only one or two officers who were often incorporated into other divisions. Much prevention work was assumed by social workers in other public agencies. Basing its information on a 1938 U.S. Bureau of Labor Statistics survey, *The Woman Worker*, a publication of the U.S. Department of Labor's Women's Bureau, reported that women "helped to enforce the laws and protect citizens" in 126 of 362 cities. These 126 cities employed 452 women who were engaged in law enforcement functions, as distinct from matrons and clerical workers. Salaries varied greatly; 61 cities paid at least one woman the same as a first-grade patrolman, while in four cities there was at least one woman earning more than the highest paid patrolmen. In 41 cities women earned less than any patrolman; in 11 of these the differences ranged from $500 to $99 annually below a first-grade patrolman's pay.[43]

Generally, policewomen suffered a number of setbacks during the Depression years. This period ended with fewer cities employing fewer policewomen. Factors in the declining numbers—as well as the declining importance—of policewomen included the economic downturn itself, the loss of momentum by and splintering of reformist groups that had supported the policewomen's movement, the growing lack of enthusiasm for positions as policewomen among social workers now employed in other municipal and federal agencies, and the militarization of the police, which resulted in the role of the crimefighter overshadowing all other aspects of police work. The collapse of the IAP and the stagnation of ideas among the few remaining leaders of the policewomen's movement also contributed to the decline. These factors combined to relegate women to little more than a footnote in Depression-era policing, but World War II would bring a change, as the nation again turned to the police to enforce war-related concerns about morality and delinquency.

NOTES

1. Susan Ware, *Holding Their Own: American Women in the 1930s* (Boston: Twayne Publishers, 1982), 13, 14.

2. Sheila M. Rothman, *Woman's Proper Place: A History of Changing Ideals and Practices, 1870 to the Present* (New York: Basic Books, 1978), 221-222; Alice Kessler-Harris, *A Woman's Wage: Historical Meanings and Social Consequences* (Lexington: University Press of Kentucky, 1990), 68.

3. Susan M. Hartmann, *The Home Front and Beyond: American Women in the 1940s* (Boston: Twayne Publishers, 1982), 17; Kessler-Harris, *A Woman's Wage*, 2.

4. Samuel Walker, *A Critical History of Police Reform: The Emergence of Professionalism* (Lexington, MA: Lexington Books, 1977), 139. This point is also made by James F. Richardson, *Urban Police in the United States* (Port Washington, NY: Kennikat Press, 1974), 137 and Robert M. Fogelson, *Big-City Police* (Cambridge, MA: Harvard University Press, 1977), 122.

5. Municipal Administration Service, "Policemen's Salaries, Hours, Etc., in 49 Cities," *The American City*, Apr. 1930, 108; Ware, *Holding Their Own*, 3 (for family income).

6. Municipal Administration Service, "Policemen's Salaries, Hours, Etc., in 49 Cities," 108-109; Ware, *Holding Their Own*, 27 (for women's income).

7. Lois Lundell Higgins, "The Feminine Arm of the Law: Women in Crime," paper presented at the 1st Biennial IAWP Conference, Lafayette, IN, Sept. 30-Oct.

2, 1958, 2; Albert R. Roberts, "Police Social Workers: A History," *Social Work* 21, no. 4 (July 1976), 295; Eleonore L. Hutzel, "The Policewoman," *The Annals of the American Academy of Police and Social Science* 146, (Nov. 1929), 105, 106, 112; Susan Ehrlich Martin, *Breaking and Entering: Policewomen on Patrol* (Berkeley: University of California Press, 1980), 24; Helen D. Pigeon, "Policewomen," *Social Work Yearbook 1933*, 360.

8. Martin, *Breaking and Entering*, 24; study cited in Lois Lundell Higgins, "Women in Law Enforcement: A Special Survey on Policewomen Throughout the United States," *Law and Order*, Apr. 1958, 22.

9. Thomas J. Deakin, *Police Professionalism: The Renaissance of American Law Enforcement* (Springfield, IL: Charles C Thomas, 1988), 24-25.

10. Thomas A. Reppetto, *The Blue Parade* (New York: The Free Press, 1978), 65.

11. Jerald E. Levine, "Police, Parties and Polity: The Bureaucratization, Unionization and Professionalization of the New York City Police, 1870-1910," Ph.D. diss., University of Wisconsin, 1971, 35, 48.

12. Deakin, *Police Professionalism*, xi.

13. Samuel Walker, *The Police in America: An Introduction* (New York: McGraw-Hill, 1983) 15-16; Deakin, *Police Professionalism*, 129-133, mentions New Deal military metaphors, which included the phrase "war on crime," and calls by President Roosevelt for the nation to "move as a trained and loyal army willing to sacrifice for the good of a common discipline." These exhortations to wage war against economic and social problems prepared the nation to view police as soldiers in the war against crime.

14. U.S. National Commission on Law Observance and Enforcement (The Wickersham Report) Report No. 14. *Report on Police* (Washington, DC: Government Printing Office, 1931), 40. Vollmer's text, *The Police and Modern Society* (Berkeley: University of California Press, 1936), also does not mention policewomen.

15. Walker, *A Critical History of Police Reform*, 135.

16. Ibid. 142.

17. Mary Sullivan, *My Double Life: The Story of a New York Policewoman* (New York: Farrar & Rinehart, 1938), 286-287.

18. Wichita Manual (1935), quoted in Helen D. Pigeon and Others, *Principles and Methods in Dealing with Offenders* (State College, PA: Public Service Institute, 1949), 21.

19. William J. Bopp, *"O.W.": O.W. Wilson and the Search for a Police Profession* (Port Washington, NY: Kennikat Press, 1977), 52. Bopp incorrectly calls L'Heureux the first woman captain in the United States, but Baldwin was a captain in Portland, Oregon, by 1913, and Burnside was a captain in Indianapolis in 1921.

20. Deakin, *Police Professionalism*, 200, 201; Jack. L. Kuykendall and Armand P. Hernandez, "Undergraduate Justice System Education and Training at San Jose State University: An Historical Perspective," *Journal of Criminal Justice* 3, no. 2 (Summer 1975), 112, 116.

21. O.W. Wilson, *Distribution of Police Patrol Force* (Chicago: Public Administration Service, 1941), 1.

22. O.W. Wilson, *Report of Police Department Survey, Hartford, CT* (Chicago: Public Administration Service, 1942), 49, 115-116, 117 (my emphasis). His view did not change. Through all editions of his text, *Police Administration*, Wilson advocated

limited roles for women and discouraged using them as supervisors. See O.W. Wilson, *Police Administration* (New York: McGraw-Hill, 1950), 125-126, 217; 2d ed. (New York: McGraw-Hill, 1953), 290, 334-335; O.W. Wilson and Roy C. McLaren, *Police Administration*, 3d and 4th ed. (New York: McGraw-Hill, 1972 and 1977), 374, 421-422. Wilson's views on women were not new. Nancy F. Cott, *The Grounding of Modern Feminism* (New Haven, CT: Yale University Press, 1987), 216, notes that in the late nineteenth and early twentieth centuries prejudice existed against women entering various professions because of "long-standing stereotypes" that they "were presumed to be emotional, subjective, irrational, and personal." Why Wilson so wholly accepted this view cannot be determined from his writings.

23. Reppetto, *The Blue Parade*, 244.

24. Eleonore L. Hutzel, "The Policewoman," 108.

25. Eleonore L. Hutzel, *The Policewoman's Handbook* (New York: Columbia University Press, 1933), 1, 4. Nothing in the book indicates the new emphasis on efficiency and crimefighting.

26. James K. Watkins, "The Function of a Police Department in a Community Social Welfare Program," *Proceedings* of the NCSW, 60th Annual Session, Detroit, MI, June 11-17, 1933, 109, 111; Hutzel, "The Policewoman," 107.

27. Woman's Bureau, Metropolitan PD, Washington D.C., "Policewomen Reporting a Year's Work," *The Police Journal*, Nov. 1925, 30; Edith Rockwood and Augusta J. Street, *Social Protective Work of Public Agencies: With Special Emphasis on the Policewoman* (Washington, DC: Committee on Social Hygiene-National League of Women Voters, 1932), 11.

28. The Citizens' Police Committee, *Chicago Police Problems*, 1931; reprint (Montclair, NJ: Patterson Smith), 15 (reference is to reprint edition).

29. *Chicago Police Department. Annual Report. Year Ending December 31, 1929*, 8a; *Year Ending December 31, 1933*, 10; *Year Ending December 31, 1935*, 10; *Year Ending December 31, 1936*, 10; *Year Ending December 31, 1938*, 10; *Year Ending December 31, 1940*, 10.

30. *Annual Report of the Police Department, City of New York, For the Year 1937*, 3-4.

31. "The Crime Prevention Bureau," *The Police Journal*, May 1930, 8, 25; Virginia M. Murray, "Policewomen in Detroit," *The American City*, Sept. 1921, 209-210.

32. *Policewoman's International Bulletin*, June 1930, 14, 15.

33. Henrietta Additon, "The Prevention of Crime and Delinquency," *Journal of Social Hygiene* 17, no. 4 (Apr. 1931), 200-208; Rockwood and Street, *Social Protective Work Of Public Agencies*, 20. Pigeon, "Policewomen," 361, states that staff exceeded 200 by 1933.

34. Sullivan, *My Double Life*, 280-281.

35. Mary Sullivan, The Functions of Police-Women," *The Police Journal*, Jan. 1932, 11, 17.

36. Sullivan, *My Double Life*, 287.

37. Ibid., 296-297, 298; John J. Sullivan, "Policing a World's Fair," *The Police Yearbook 1938-1939* (Proceedings of the 45th Annual Conference of the IACP, Toronto, ON, Canada, Aug. 29-Sept. 1, 1938), 58, 60.

38. Gerald Astor, *The New York Cops: An Informal History* (New York: Charles Scribners, 1971), 200. This far exceeded the percentage of male applicants, which generally ran two or three times the number of available openings. Sullivan, *My Double Life*, 298.

39. Joseph J. Woods, *The Progressives and the Police: Urban Reform and the Professionalism of the Los Angeles Police* (Ann Arbor, MI: University Microfilms, 1979 [Ph.D., diss., University of California at Los Angeles, 1973]), 197; WPOAC, *Convention Program and Yearbook*, Oakland, CA, Sept. 16-18, 1937, 6.

40. Anne Findlay Patton, "Women Officers of the San Diego Police Department, 1912-1988," M.A. thesis, University of San Diego, 1989, 59-73.

41. *Policewoman's International Bulletin*, June 1930, 10, 11; Bruce B. Drewett, letter to the author, January 15, 1989 (for Phoenix).

42. Geraldine A. Kelley, "Policewomen Play Important Role in Philadelphia, Pa.," *FBI Law Enforcement Bulletin*, Oct. 1957, 3-4; Harry G. Fox, *Philadelphia Policewomen—Established 1936* (Philadelphia: Police Department, 1972), 3.

43. "Women on Police Forces," *The Woman Worker*, May 1942, 16.

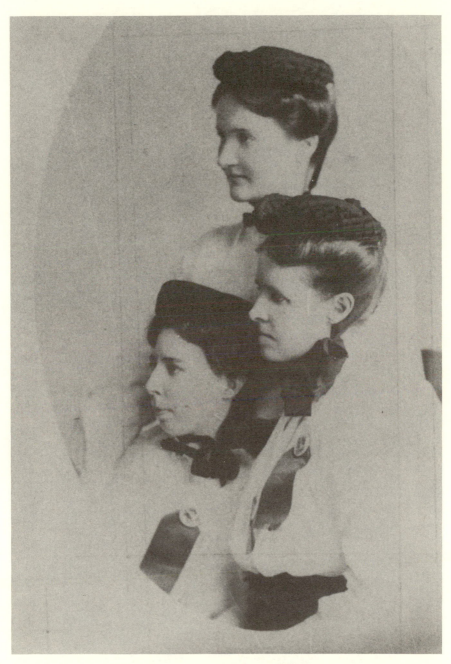

Lola Baldwin (center) with Grace E. Fix and Dagmar Riley, two of the "operatives" serving with her in Portland, Oregon, in 1908. (Courtesy of the Portland, Oregon, Police Museum)

Alice Stebbins Wells displays her Los Angeles Police Department badge; and at the end of her career in the department. (Courtesy of the Los Angeles Police Historical Society)

Georgia Robinson of the Los Angeles Police Department, the first African-American policewoman in the United States. (Courtesy of the Los Angeles Police Historical Society)

San Francisco's Three Kates (from left): Katherine O'Connor, Kathryne Eisenhart, and Kathlyn Sullivan. (Courtesy of the San Francisco Police Department)

Gathered together in 1914 were the Chicago Police Department's first policewomen, including (from left): Agnes Walsh, Anna Loucks, Theresa Johnson, Anna Sheridan, Lulu Bert, Mabell Rockwell, and Clara Olsen. (Courtesy of the Chicago Historical Society)

A New York City Police Department World War I-era reserve officer. (Courtesy of the New York City Police Department Museum)

Lt. Mina C. Van Winkle, Washington, D.C., early in her career and later, during the years she served as president of the International Association of Policewomen. (Courtesy of the Washington, D.C., Metropolitan Police Department)

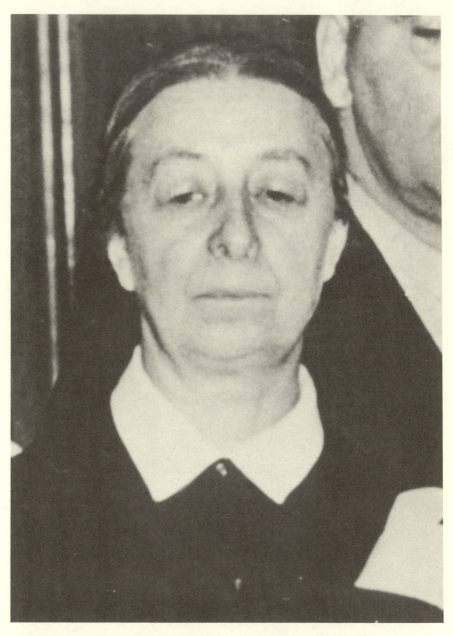

Eleanor L. Hutzel, Fourth Deputy Commissioner of the Detroit Police Department. (Courtesy of the Detroit Police Department)

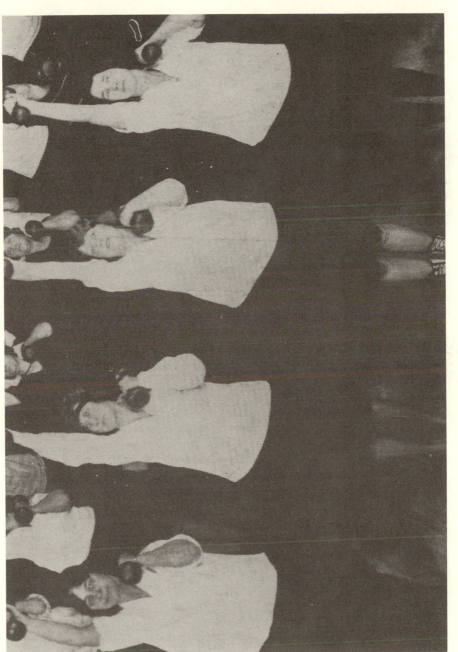

New York City Police Department policewomen in physical training at the Police Academy in 1923. (Courtesy of the New York City Police Department Museum)

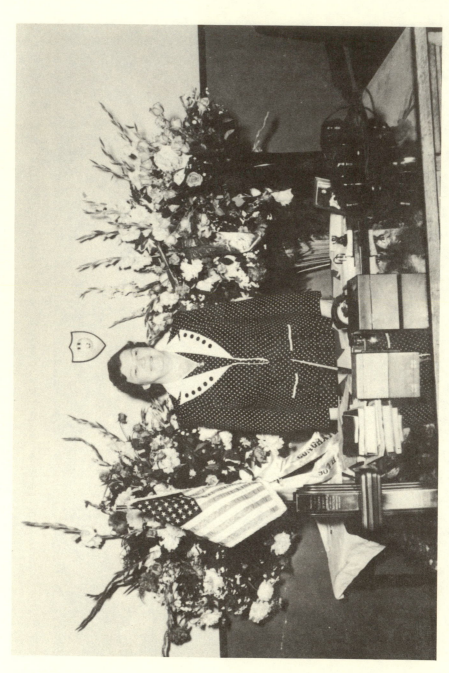

New York City Police Department women's bureau director Mary Sullivan poses at her desk on June 12, 1941, her thirtieth anniversary with the department. (Courtesy of the New York City Police Department Museum)

A New York City Police Department patrolman and a policewoman comfort a lost child at Coney Island beach in the mid-1950s. (Courtesy of the New York City Police Department Museum)

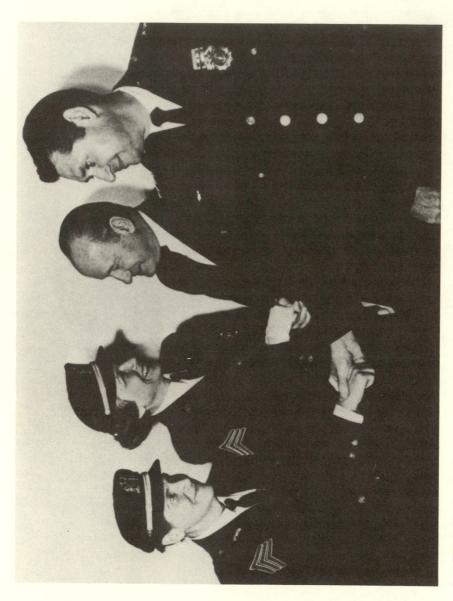

Sgts. Felicia Shpritzer (left) and Gertrude Schimmel receive congratulations from New York City Police Commissioner Howard Leary and Chief Sanford Garelick (right) at their December 1967 promotion to lieutenants. (Courtesy of the New York City Police Department Museum)

Washington, D.C., Policewoman Gail Cobb was fatally wounded on September 20, 1974 while searching for two bank robbery suspects in an underground garage. (Courtesy of the Washington, D.C., Metropolitan Police Department)

Lois Lundell Higgins in 1977 displays a souvenir .38 caliber revolver from her years in the Chicago Police Department. Her star-shaped pin closely resembles the Chicago PD's star-shaped badge. (Courtesy of Lois Lundell Higgins)

Policewomen Betty Blankenship (right) and Elizabeth Coffal at the time they were assigned to uniform patrol by the Indianapolis Police Department. (Courtesy of the Indianapolis Police Department)

Chapter 6

World War II and the 1940s

Women overcame their Depression decade losses and resurfaced in police departments during the 1940s. The pace of the increase quickened during World War II (just as it had during World War I). The 1940 census counted 1,775 policewomen and detectives, a slight increase over the 1930 figure of 1,534, but this figure is misleadingly high, since it combines public and private agencies. A 1945 government publication, basing its numbers on the census, estimated that in 1940 there were about 1,000 publicly funded policewomen and that fewer than 3 percent of the nation's law enforcement agencies employed them. By 1950, the census reported 2,610 publicly employed policewomen, comprising slightly more than 1 percent of all police and detectives.[1]

World War II brought numerical increases—but not new roles—for women, who remained social service providers at a time when non-crimefighting tasks continued to be minimized by the police establishment. Despite the creation of crime prevention bureaus and juvenile delinquency prevention programs in many departments, these efforts were a small part of the police mission. Prevention efforts involved few male officers, while women were almost universally assigned to them. Functional segregation by sex was common; male officers dealt with male juveniles and policewomen dealt with female juveniles and women, whether as offenders, victims, or witnesses.

As the decade began, police leaders were oblivious to the war that would soon embroil the nation. Most were equally unconcerned with the problems it would force upon police managers, particularly in the areas of vice and delinquency control. Chiefs were primarily concerned with scientific management and efficiency. Numerous surveys of police agencies were completed in the early 1940s by a variety of consultants and municipal management bureaus. While the surveys ceased during the war, by 1946 they reappeared, still concentrating on efficiency, but also now concerned with crime prevention and delinquency.

The surveys provide a brief history of particular departments and a review of their table of organization, staffing patterns, and salary history. These are followed by recommendations on consolidation and/or separation of specific units, shifting or adding staff (police officers or supervisors) based on population and crime data, and salary considerations based on area or comparable size departments. Virtually all mention policewomen, listing numbers and describing the officers' tasks. Suggestions almost always called for placing women in crime prevention or juvenile divisions.

As in earlier decades, virtually nowhere from within the police establishment were women's bureaus being advocated. The outside groups that in the 1920s had lobbied for women's bureaus now spoke for crime prevention bureaus containing male and female officers. Those women's bureaus that survived the Depression remained, but smaller units were placed under either crime prevention or juvenile divisions, which were themselves often part of detective divisions. The creation of crime prevention and delinquency units reflected a perception by police that delinquency was a major threat to cities. This concern escalated during the war, providing new positions for women but few new roles.

Peter Horne has stated that women's re-entry into policing during World War II to some degree supplemented "the manpower needs of police forces" and provided positions primarily as auxiliary police who were terminated at the war's end.[2] Although this view persists among police historians, it is an incomplete picture. While female auxiliary police were hired due to wartime manpower shortages, their roles were different from traditional policewomen and more limited than the roles of male auxiliaries, who were also hired to augment diminished patrol capabilities due to large numbers of policemen serving in the armed forces.

The vast majority of wartime auxiliaries were men who could not serve in the military. After being activated through legislation which stipulated they would be disbanded when officers returned from military duty, the auxiliaries generally acted as full-time officers despite their limited training. Although they performed regular police duties, these men were temporary employees whose jobs ended when police officers returned.

Women auxiliaries did not replace men in the same way men auxiliaries did. Some cities used them to inspect dance halls and night clubs, where they acted more as chaperones than as police. The vast majority served as dispatchers and as traffic control agents. Many performed duties that after the war became associated with school crossing guards. Eventually some women were also permitted to issue parking tickets. Some cities called these women "policewomen," but they very rarely had police powers and they were not police by any generally accepted definition. Although they lacked police authority, in many cities they were the first women to wear police–style uniforms.

The two largest cities to use auxiliary women in traffic enforcement were Chicago and San Francisco, although there were differences in selection, titles, and assignment. The women "service guards" recruited in the summer of 1942 by the Chicago Park District were typical. An initial group of 50 was selected by written test. After two weeks of training, the women controlled traffic at school and church crossings and guarded cars and directed traffic in municipal parking lots. They carried no firearms and had no police status. San Francisco relied more heavily on its women auxiliaries. Six women, hired temporarily to alleviate manpower shortages, were assigned to parking enforcement, although they assisted in traffic control and learned to operate three-wheeled cycles. One of the first hired, the wife of a city policeman, in December 1944, was credited with the unit's first arrest, when she pursued and arrested a merchant seaman for driving while intoxicated. Eventually, some of the 22 women patrolled the streets and bars as part of the Big Sister program. Their jobs ended in mid-1949, when the position of women protective officer was created and eight women were hired, trained at a special academy class, and assigned to the juvenile bureau.[3]

The majority of actual policewomen continued to work in civilian street clothes, but the war did bring about the first public consciousness of women in uniform, whether military or police. Most policewomen, even if issued uniforms before the 1970s (many were not), wore them only for parades or special events—rarely in carrying out their duties. While female auxiliaries actually escaped some gender stereotyping by wearing uniforms and performing traffic duties, they were not policewomen.

Police departments also resumed hiring permanent policewomen to perform their traditional duties. Rather than "graphically demonstrate how idioms of sex-typing can be flexibly applied," these new, permanent women "illustrate the resilience of job segregation by sex."[4] The gender-specific role policewomen played in law enforcement was not altered by World War II. While the war did spawn Rosie the Riveter, there was no Connie the Crimefighter.

A look behind the Rosie the Riveter myth explains why this was so. Studies of women's work experiences during World War II have confirmed that they were hired to fill positions that prior to U.S. entry into the war in December 1941 had been filled exclusively by men. As men were mobilized, women filled jobs previously seen as requiring masculine abilities and attitudes. These jobs were virtually all in heavy industry or industries producing goods for the war effort. Upon the return of the soldiers, women either voluntarily left or were terminated. Although some women had believed the jobs would continue, most understood that their employment was temporary, to last until the soldiers returned to reclaim their positions. These women were overwhelmingly working-class, nonprofessional women, rather than the middle-class, trained social workers who continued to fill most policewomen's positions. Although Rosie the Riveter remains an enduring symbol of women's war work, she represents a highly specialized form of women's entry into previously male occupations.[5]

Even though the war did result in the breakdown of some workplace gender stereotypes, the majority of women worked in traditional women's jobs. They continued to earn salaries below those earned by men in men's jobs and by women who temporarily filled some of the men's positions.[6]

To realize the impact the war had on policewomen, it is necessary only to look at the police management surveys issued in 1941 and 1942. Women were few and worthy of only cursory mention. Advocacy of crime prevention and juvenile services is less urgent than after the war. Efforts to stem sexual immorality and delinquency during the war, as well as population shifts and life-style changes that seemed to bring about an increase in juvenile crime, focused attention on these areas by both male and female officers. After the war police became involved in many programs, including athletic leagues, junior and cadet units, and other activities that encouraged policemen to befriend male juveniles in a way that previously had been reserved for female officers and female juveniles. Although the programs were similar to the efforts of policewomen, the parallel, if seen by male police executives, was rarely mentioned. The few remaining female police executives neither saw nor mentioned it, either.

It is interesting to contemplate what the reaction might have been had policewomen countered the argument of Wilson and other police chiefs that men should head crime prevention divisions due to their experience in other areas of policing and their credibility with other police officers, with an argument that, based on their experience in social casework and their credibility with other providers of similar preventive services, these positions in crime prevention should naturally fall to policewomen.

Philadelphia, the last large East Coast city to appoint women, was—surprisingly—one of the first to expand their roles during the war. In 1941 and 1942 Senior Policewoman Norma B. Carson and her staff were given jurisdiction over other units in cases involving women and girls. A series of undercover investigations in some "notorious bars" resulted in raids, closings, and favorable headlines. Carson recalled that "policewomen gathered evidence, rounded up witnesses, testified day after day in court. Places were closed; a number of prostitutes were rescued; then came the tremendous task of entertaining servicemen with the hope of keeping many of them from temptations that might well lead to disaster." The five policewomen in two and one half years had contact with more than 6,000 girls, many of whom had come to the city solely to meet servicemen.[7]

Carson's words and deeds echo those of World War I-era policewomen.

Her efforts may have been new in Philadelphia, a city that did not hire policewomen until 1936, but they were identical to efforts by policewomen in other cities during World War I. It was also the same as the work done by female protective officers of the Committee on Protective Work for Girls, established in 1918 by the Law Enforcement Division of the Commission on Training Camp Activities, to combat prostitution and venereal disease. Even then, the efforts were not new, but could be traced back to the duties Lola Baldwin had performed in Portland in 1905 during the Lewis and Clark Exposition.

In 1943, Philadelphia officials hired six additional women and assigned four to the detective bureau. An increase in servicemen resulted in an increase in street prostitutes. Just as officials in other cities had done during World War I, those in Philadelphia placed policewomen on preventive street patrol, checking theaters, luncheonettes, bars, and other "juvenile hazards." After a 1944 grand jury investigating delinquency recommended additional staff, a civil service exam was scheduled, and on February 1, 1945, after 10 women were appointed, day and night patrols were initiated. The women, according to a department pamphlet, were "performing a type of social casework—offering counsel and guidance to maladjusted and delinquent girls," investigating fortune tellers and morals cases, guarding women prisoners, filling in on matron duty, and presenting crime prevention programs throughout the city.[8]

The efforts to police sexually active girls and women were typical of a number of cities beginning in late 1942 and continuing until the end of the war in August 1945 and demobilization by year's end. Karen Anderson's study of women's sex roles, family relations, and status during World War II, *Wartime Women*, provides the background for how the work of policewomen in Philadelphia and many other cities echoed the efforts of policewomen during World War I:

Although designed to protect public health and increase military efficiency by preventing and treating venereal disease, the social protection campaign encompassed a broader effort to isolate women whose conduct indicated that they might be sexually active outside the institution of marriage and to provide them with medical treatment, if necessary, and with punishment and/or rehabilitative counseling so that they might lead more upright lives.[9]

Fulfilling the role of the World War I Committee on Protective Work for Girls was its World War II equivalent, the Community War Services Office, which shortly after its creation on April 29, 1943 as part of the expanded Federal Security Agency, established the Social Protection Division. The SPD was led by well-known crimefighter former Prohibition Special Agent Eliot Ness, who had gained fame as a participant in the prosecution of gangster Al Capone and had then served as public safety director of Cleveland.   One of a number of divisions within the FSA concerned with the health, morality, and recreation of soldiers, the SPD remained active until mid-1946.

Anderson found that the SPD expanded its mandate to run a health program "into a purity campaign dedicated to the search for 'incipient and confirmed sex delinquents' who, not coincidentally, happened always to be women." In 1943 Rhoda J. Milliken, director of the Washington, D.C., woman's bureau, also commented on this preoccupation with women's morality, noting that: "Too often both local law enforcement and health controls degenerate into a persecution of individual women. . . . At no time is this more true than during a war." She believed that the "greatest value" of policewomen in prostitution control was their emphasis that the fight is "against prostitution . . . not . . . prostitutes,"[10] but such discretion did not prevail during the war.

The SPD differed from its World War I counterpart. Rather than hire its own female protective officers, it provided local governments with legal background and justification for laws under which police could curtail sexual misconduct. New laws involved extending the definition of prostitution to include not only sex for hire but also indiscriminate or promiscuous intercourse without a commercial aspect; broadening disorderly conduct to include "endangering morals, safety, or health" and vagrancy to include lewd, wanton, or lascivious speech or conduct; as well as laws involving loitering, frequenting bars, or falsely registering in a hotel as married.[11]

Although the SPD's concern with eradicating venereal disease, primarily through the elimination of prostitution, created positions for policewomen, the SPD did not lobby for them the way the Committee on Protective Work for Girls had during World War I. When Ness addressed the National Conference of Social Work in 1944 it was not to urge hiring policewomen, but to urge cooperation between policemen and social workers. He appealed to the social workers not as one of them (as World War I protective agents and IAP leaders had), but as a law enforcement professional. Ness reminded delegates that "obviously the police have a prominent role to play by 'cracking down' on those . . . who aid and abet the corruption of minors, but the problem will not be disposed of with a nightstick." He never mentioned policewomen.[12]

While Ness's mandate may have been the same as that of Raymond Fosdick's during World War I, times had changed. Fosdick was a Progressive; Ness was a crimefighter. Notwithstanding the passage of two decades between the wars, and changes in the views of police, social workers, and feminists, societal changes did not prevent the development of an identical concern with venereal disease, prostitution, and female promiscuity. Only the means of control changed; while policewomen still had a role in curing these ills, during World War II they were not viewed as vital to enforcement, as they had been during World War I.

During World War I, policewomen, through the IAP and local women's, civic, and social purity groups, were aligned with social workers and other women professionals in the emerging "helping" fields. By World War II, policewomen had no association of their own and were too few in number to lobby effectively on an individual basis. Additionally, social workers had gained power and authority in a variety of private and government agencies and were no longer interested in police positions. They concentrated on expanding their influence by working with police, rather than by becoming policewomen. Social work had changed; no longer emerging, it was a recognized profession.

By 1940 there were some 48,000 women social workers (67 percent of the total).[13] The small number of policewomen who were social workers had little impact in a group of this size and appear to have been seen by some as competition. Imra Buwalda, a former District of Columbia policewoman who was a consultant to the wartime FSA, chastised social workers in 1945 for failing to recognize the importance of the police function and for withholding cooperation. She was critical of their failure to see that "the juvenile bureau was *not* an intruding and competing new welfare agency for treatment, but a police unit with a social welfare point of view."[14] The feeling by social workers that policewomen, if not truly competitors, at least overlapped their functions, continued through the decade and persisted to some extent until policewomen relinquished social service functions to join the ranks of police crimefighters.

The end of the Depression also brought a shift in police employment that was obvious by the onset of the war. During the Depression departments had been able to recruit native-born, middle-class men with high educational levels. Depression-era policemen were somewhat similar in class and educational levels to early policewomen, but the return to full employment during and after World War II showed how temporary these changes were. By then, departments were "reverting to their traditional role as a haven of security for working and lower-middle class youth."[15]

At the same time that the profile of policemen was returning to pre-Depression standards, the profile of policewomen was changing for the first time since the creation of the title in 1910 in Los Angeles for Alice Stebbins Wells. The few women hired in the post-Depression years and those who would follow during and after World War II differed from the first generation of policewomen, who were frequently upper-middle-class, college educated, native-born women with social service backgrounds. The second generation women, while higher in class orientation and education levels than their male colleagues, were more likely to be from the middle class. Also, due to a number of cities' having placed policewomen under civil service, not as many were college trained, since other prerequisites, usually jobs involving public contact or high-level clerical skills, were substitutes for college training. After the war, many were veterans.

Another change brought about by wartime population shifts was that social workers were no longer the only ones concerned about social protection and delinquency. International Association of Chiefs of Police meetings also provided a forum for police executives to concentrate on these issues. But whereas during World War I panels on prostitution and delinquency had featured women speakers, whether social workers or policewomen, the only prominent policewoman at the IACP during World War II was Hutzel from Detroit. Policewomen's diminished importance is obvious not only by their lack of participation, but also by the minimal mention of them. Exceptions were the 1943 discussion on New York City Police Department efforts to curtail "Victory Girls" (young girls who entered the city to follow soldiers) by assigning teams of male and female officers to patrol the Times Square area and a 1944 panel on social protection. Learning that the NYCPD had almost 200 policewomen, who were "a very definite part" of the social protection efforts, Ness, the prototypical crimefighter, voiced surprise. "At one time," he said, "I was one of those officials who thought if you sent a policewoman out to do a job you had to send a couple of men to pull her out of the difficulties she would get into. That is a very erroneous belief." His initial views were typical. The 14 delinquency and crime prevention presentations at the 1944 conference were delivered by men; only one even mentioned policewomen.[16]

An FSA manual detailing how policewomen should be used in social protection enforcement reinforced the view that policewomen should "discover young girls who are in hazardous conditions" and "take appropriate action before they become a problem to the community." The manual also echoed Ness's concerns about policewomen working alone. Chiefs were advised to assign a man to accompany a woman officer at night.[17]

The manual was indicative of the new police concerns about social protection, venereal disease, female morality, and delinquency. These concerns resulted in employment gains for policewomen, just as similar concerns had led to an increase during World War I. Investigation and enforcement of many of the local laws strengthened through SPD efforts provided renewed visibility for veteran policewomen and justified hiring new ones. In cities around the country the number of policewomen increased and everywhere duties resembled those performed during World War I.

Detroit is an excellent example of this. Due to Detroit wartime activities having been closely reviewed, and the prominence of Hutzel, data on the city's efforts to stem prostitution and delinquency are available from a variety of sources. Detroit and surrounding communities experienced population shifts (including a huge increase in its labor force) as automobile factories turned to military production. By early 1941, Michigan ranked seventh in defense contracts.[18] By 1942, Detroit employed 3,600 policemen and 54 policewomen. This was an increase over 1932, when the director and two sergeants supervised 33 women.

The American Mercury described half of the women as under 30, half with college degrees, four out of five with some college, six registered nurses and two lawyers. In 1941 the women investigated 11,900 cases. Applicants, between the ages of 22 and 28, needed two years' experience in social work, although a degree was not required. The women were described as "young, attractive, refined, thoroughly feminine and usually unarmed." The reporter joined the women on their evening tour and reported: "Our two policegirls are ready to start—flashlights tested, handbags stuffed with leather billies, patrol box keys, lipstick, violation blanks, police whistles, gold badges, dainty handkerchiefs. . . . Neither carries a revolver, although some members . . . always go armed."

He also noted that despite recurring scandals in the department, the "ladies of the law" had never been charged with graft or crime, and that even when dealing with the seamier side of life they retained their "soft, motherly, feminine touch." Able to "talk like a society matron or a Marine sergeant as occasion demanded," the women "protected boys under 10 and girls under 21 from exploiters, sex-criminals, perverts, 'white slavers,' from immoral influences and depraved surroundings, and from their own folly."[19] This was one of many articles about policewomen that appeared in general circulation and women's magazines in the 1940s and 1950s, always stressing their femininity and often telling readers how their husbands felt about their wives' unusual and potentially dangerous line of work.

Detroit policewomen were active in Social Protection Division enforcement. Women suspected of "immoral" activities were detained as disorderly persons and could be interviewed, tested for venereal disease, held until the results were obtained, and then released without court action or legal recourse. All young girls and first offenders were interviewed by a policewoman for possible referral to a social agency for casework services.[20]

In 1943, the women contacted 8,936 girls between 10 and 17 years old, resulting in fewer than 450 court complaints. Hutzel noted that 50 percent of the contacts were "adjusted" by the police. The figures indicate that the large number of girls with whom policewomen interacted were guilty of no crime. The policewomen decided either to release them with a warning, or to refer them to public or private social service agencies. In the summer of 1944, Detroit experimented with teams of policemen and policewomen patrolling from 10 P.M. to 6 A.M. in the central city and in parks. Two teams were expanded to four, according to Hutzel, "at the request of men executives" after it was found that "invariably the contacts are with boys and girls and a man and woman police team seemed better suited."[21]

By 1945, Detroit had become so concerned with restricting women's behavior that the city prohibited serving unescorted women at a bar or tavern after 8 P.M. and ruled that women who had entered a dining area unescorted had to remain so. These activities led to police staff increases; by 1945 there were 64 policewomen, all of whom earned a fairly high initial salary of $2,829. That year, the women, who measured their productivity in casework terminology, had an "intake" of approximately 1,200 cases monthly, which put them on a pace ahead of the total of 8,936 teenage girls "contacted" in 1944.[22]

Although wartime population shifts were not as extreme in other Midwestern cities as in Detroit, many responded to changing local conditions by hiring additional policewomen. Cleveland, which had formed a women's bureau with 15 officers and a woman captain in 1924 (after 14 years of lobbying by women's groups), disbanded it in 1941 and transferred the women into the crime prevention division to work with female offenders and victims. By mid-1944 there were 27 women in a force of 1,313. The number increased slightly after the war, by 1947 reaching 1 captain, 1 lieutenant, 2 sergeants, and 29 policewomen.[23]

Chicago also hired more women in the 1940s but they did not participate actively in SPD-type enforcement. By 1946 there were 60 women in the juvenile bureau; numbers continued to increase slightly throughout the late 1940s. On February 14, 1947 (more than 30 years after clubwomen and reformers raised the issue), the department established a women's bureau, placing policewomen and matrons under the supervision of Policewoman Ruth Beiderman. The bureau, part of the crime prevention division, was also responsible for the women's jail. The 1949 *Annual Report* listed the 71 policewomen within the crime prevention unit. Information and statistics do not appear for a women's division until 1951.[24]

Baltimore was one of the few Southern cities whose hiring of women was effected by the war. In 1941, the city employed a chief policewoman, three white policewomen, who worked out of headquarters under direction of a male chief inspector, and one African-American policewoman, who was assigned to the district in which the majority of African-Americans lived. The women's salaries were identical to those of male officers. A department survey suggested hiring one or more additional African-American women due to the number of cases the sole officer handled.

In December 1942, Baltimore formed a V.D. Council to which young women were referred by clinics, hospitals, policewomen, the vice squad, the courts, and social agencies. In January 1944, the department created a juvenile protective bureau to serve as a referral agency so those accused of minor offenses could be sent for casework services rather than to court. Although the police enforced a curfew for young women unescorted in public places, they were not as active as the Detroit police in pursuing vice enforcement. In 1945, an 18-year veteran of the department was promoted to policewoman-sergeant and six more women were appointed.[25]

Seattle, like Detroit and Baltimore, witnessed a large growth in women employed in traditionally male areas; between 1940 and 1945 the number skyrocketed from 6,200 to 40,800, principally in the Boeing airplane plants. Large numbers of servicemen also attracted underage girls, resulting in increased police activity. As they had during World War I, Seattle officials set a curfew. Men treated at venereal disease clinics were expected to provide the names of women with whom they had had sexual contact. The information was turned over to the police for follow-up. Reviewing the history of police morality enforcement in Seattle, it is not surprising that Karen Anderson describes it as "particularly zealous" in Social Protection Division enforcement and cites its "sex delinquents" program as one the SPD called a model for other cities.[26]

San Francisco, at the urging of the Federation of Women's Clubs and a woman municipal judge, in 1942 created a Big Sister program similar to a Big Brother program led by a male lieutenant. Kate Sullivan, who in 1914 had been one of the city's first three policewomen, was placed in charge of the program; she remained until her 1948 retirement. She convinced the chief to place 87 women with limited police authority in bars, nightclubs, and other places liquor was served to assure that minors did not enter. Twenty-eight were still serving six months after Sullivan's retirement, their salaries paid by bar owners who requested their presence.[27]

Police executives in Boston were urged by outsiders to appoint policewomen, as they had been decades earlier. A committee studying protective measures in 1942 observed that the police were not finding young women whom servicemen with venereal diseases had named as their contacts. The failure was attributed in part to the absence of trained policewomen. When Boston had reluctantly hired women in 1921, their duties were ill-defined; lobbying for a women's bureau was not successful. World War II brought renewed efforts. This time a recommendation that the department employ "policewomen adequately trained in social work" to provide "proper policing of . . . public places where servicemen and girls meet" was acted upon within a year.[28]

On June 2, 1942, Boston officials appointed "10 properly qualified" civil service policewomen. On August 9, 1943, a crime prevention bureau was established under a deputy superintendent, staffed by 2 lieutenants, 2 acting sergeants (policewomen), 19 patrolmen, and 12 policewomen. In an attempt to meet the committee's recommendations, one year later the number of women was increased to 16, each earning the same salary (from $2,300 to $2,500 over four years) as patrolmen. They devoted "full time to the welfare of female juveniles and adults" and were enrolled in social work courses. Perhaps reflecting the commissioner's view that "police should not attempt to engage in social work not consistent with their primary purpose in the community," by 1946 the number of women had fallen to 14, despite their work being described as "outstanding." By 1948, there were only 12, although 1 had been assigned as a detective.[29] Nevertheless, the number was higher than at the start of the war.

This was not so in New York City, where the number of women in the postwar years decreased from the 1939-1941 figures. The NYCPD was the largest employer of policewomen, but its actions pertaining to women continued to differ from other departments. At the end of 1941, there were 164 policewomen; by January 1, 1943, there were 183. Despite quota increases, the number of women did not increase. The 1943 figure was not matched until January 1, 1950, when there were 189 policewomen. Although Mary Sullivan was named women's bureau director in 1926 and remained until her 1946 retirement, annual reports do not mention the bureau as a separate entity until 1947. Activities were reported as part of the juvenile aid bureau, with no breakdown of the number of male and female officers. The social work orientation is apparent, with references to "cases contacted," "social treatment—minors . . . requiring intensive supervision," "community condition cases," and "other service cases."[30]

The 1947 description of the women's bureau points up two contradictory trends. Those assigned to precincts where female prisoners were detained performed work normally assigned to matrons; yet, this is the first mention of women "assigned to patrol duty in uniform to supervise . . . children at beaches and outdoor dances and concerts in city parks; to all large parades, public gatherings and demonstrations; and to piers from which excursion boats depart and return with large numbers of women and children." These assignments began in the 1930s but were ignored in department reports. Women also investigated illegal abortions, unlicensed doctors and dentists, misleading advertisements (usually to attract women for immoral or illegal purposes), "degenerates" in theaters and subways, and fortune tellers, although the majority of policewomen continued to be assigned to matron-related functions.[31]

How, then, had policewomen's roles been affected by the war? Not very much is the most appropriate answer. Some policewomen, primarily volunteers or auxiliaries, performed traffic duties and some received uniforms for the first time. Little else changed. American policing, even when faced with the loss of men during wartime, rarely permitted women to step outside their traditional roles.

Yet because few policewomen had taken men's jobs, they were not faced with the postwar loss of employment that women in war-related industries faced. In fact, the post-World War II period resulted in gains for policewomen. Cities retained the women they had hired and, amid continuing concerns with delinquency, increased their numbers in crime prevention bureaus. Many municipalities also continued to rely on civilian women, usually part-time employees, to perform traffic functions, enforce parking regulations, or control school crossings. This World War II legacy continues, although today these women are not called policewomen.

Hutzel in Detroit, Milliken in Washington, D.C., and Imra Buwalda of the FSA, three of the World War I-era women still active, believed wartime hiring would lead to a reinvigorated policewoman's movement. Milliken and Buwalda, anticipating a "rising tide of demand for policewomen," planned to revive the IAP. They based their optimism on having received over 200 inquiries in 1945 about hiring and training women. But the IAP remained dormant until the next decade.

Buwalda cited returning servicewomen as excellent candidates for policewomen's positions. She described them as "highly selected; in good physical condition; they have learned to work with men; to operate in units under direction; and many . . . have . . . specialized training in fields that would be extremely useful." She urged that schools of social work be made aware of opportunities in law enforcement for women and that women be guided into the field.[32] The assumption by Buwalda and the remaining leaders of the movement that schools of social work would provide future policewomen is indicative of their failure to recognize the changing profile of women entering policing.

In 1946, Carol M. Williams attempted a census, sending questionnaires to 417 cities with populations of over 25,000. She received 141 replies from cities with policewomen and 155 from cities without policewomen. Many did not differentiate between policewomen and matrons; of those with policewomen or matrons, 24 employed matrons only and 50 had separate women's bureaus. Eighty-nine said the rank of policewoman was equal to policeman; 75 paid policewomen the same as policemen. Only 21 permitted women to be promoted. Policies pertaining to firearms and training differed from city to city. Policewomen carried firearms in 40 cities, did not in 45, had the option but were not required to in 36, and 20 did not specify. Fifty-nine cities placed women into training, 61 had no school for women, 14 had academies but women did not attend, and 7 did not reply. Summing up, Williams noted that policewomen were "more commonly found in the heavily industrialized sections of the country," were more prevalent in the northeast, east, and midwest, and that there was no "necessary relation between the number of policewomen employed and the size of the city."[33]

In early 1948, *The American City* reported that New York employed 174 "lady police"; Chicago, 79; Detroit, 60; Indianapolis, 56; and Washington, D.C., 35. Commenting on an "Annie-Get-Your-Gun" trend, *The Police Journal* found that

the distaff part of the police force in most cities specializes in dealing with women prisoners, girl delinquents and children generally. Much of the work . . . is handling the grievances of women and girls against whom crimes have been committed.

Detective assignments also are being given women in an increasing number of cities, and women police are being used in many juvenile courts.[34]

Yet things had not changed much. In early 1948, the NYCPD employed not 174 policewomen, but 137. By the end of the year, there were still only 153.[35] New officers, all World War II military veterans, found "little equity" and numerous "signals of separatism." Mildred Shannon, one of the recruits, recalled that they

had full police powers but restricted opportunity to use them . . . were paid the same salaries as patrolmen but had no procedures for advancement. . . . Written examination was harder. . . . Physical tests were a farce. . . . Recruit training lasted only one-fourth of the time [of the men] . . . with a separate curriculum presented in separate classrooms. . . . While the men carried .38 caliber, four-inch barrel guns, we carried .32 caliber guns with two-inch barrels.[36]

That Shannon and the others were all veterans had little impact on their instructors, who, after telling them they "would be treated no differently than the men," didn't expect them to know how to march in formation. Her recollections are graphic evidence that the numerical gains police-women made during and after World War II did not change their roles. Yet their increased numbers and broader view of themselves (sometimes as a result of military service) led Shannon and those hired with her to question both these signals of separatism and their limited role within the police environment.

These women were not the social workers of an earlier era. Most did not come from upper-middle-class families. They were of middle-class origins, many the first in their families to attend college, and they entered policing as much for their own career aspirations as to act as the community's morals enforcers. These women, and those who would follow them in the 1950s, set the tone for the next generation of women, who would demand full equality with their male peers at the expense of giving up their special status within policing.

NOTES

1. Susan Ehrlich Martin, *Breaking and Entering: Policewomen on Patrol* (Berkeley: University of California Press, 1980), 24; National Advisory Police Committee on Social Protection of the Federal Security Agency, *Techniques of Law Enforcement in the Use of Policewomen with Special Reference to Social Protection* (Washington, DC: Government Printing Office, 1945), 2.

2. Peter Horne, *Women in Law Enforcement*, 2d ed. (Springfield, IL: Charles C Thomas, 1980), 31-32.

3. "Hires Women 'Service Guards'," *The Police Journal*, July-Aug. 1942, 19 (for

Chicago); San Francisco Police Museum and Archives, miscellaneous collected material.

4. Ruth Milkman, *Gender at Work: The Dynamics of Job Segregation by Sex During World War II* (Chicago: University of Illinois Press, 1987), 49, 50.

5. For analyses of women's entry into war-related industries and the phenomenon of Rosie the Riveter, see: Leila J. Rupp, *Mobilizing Women for War: German and American Propaganda, 1939-1945* (Princeton, NJ: Princeton University Press, 1978); Karen Anderson, *Wartime Women: Sex Roles, Family Relations and the Status of Women in World War II* (Westport, CT: Greenwood Press, 1981); Maureen Honey, *Creating Rosie the Riveter: Class, Gender, and Propaganda During World War II* (Amherst, MA: University of Massachusetts Press, 1984); Sherna Berger Gluck, *Rosie the Riveter Revisited: Women, the War, and Social Change* (Boston: Twayne Publishers, 1987); and Milkman, *Gender at Work*.

6. Susan M. Hartmann, *The Home Front and Beyond: American Women in the 1940s* (Boston: Twayne Publishers, 1982), 61.

7. Harry G. Fox, *Philadelphia Policewomen—Established 1936* (Philadelphia: Police Department, 1972), 3; Norma B. Carson, "Policewomen Are an Important Factor in Law Enforcement," *FBI Law Enforcement Bulletin*, Oct. 1953, 18-19.

8. Fox, *Philadelphia Policewomen*, 3-4.

9. Anderson, *Wartime Women*, 104.

10. Ibid., 104, 118; Rhoda J. Milliken, "The Role of the Policewoman's Bureau in Combatting Prostitution," *Federal Probation*, Apr.-June 1943, 20.

11. Anderson, *Wartime Women*, 104-105.

12. Eliot Ness, "Sex Delinquency As a Social Hazard," *Proceedings* of the NCSW, 71st Annual Meeting, Cleveland, OH, May 21-27, 1944, 279, 281, 283.

13. Susan Ware, *Holding Their Own: American Women in the 1930s* (Boston: Twayne Publishers, 1982), 74.

14. Imra Buwalda, "The Policewoman—Yesterday, Today and Tomorrow," *Journal of Social Hygiene* 31, no. 5, (May 1945), 291.

15. James F. Richardson, *Urban Police in the United States* (Port Washington, NY: Kennikat Press, 1972), 138.

16. John W. Sutter, "Crime Prevention and Juvenile Delinquency," *The Police Yearbook 1944* (Proceedings of the 50th Annual Conference of the IACP, Detroit, MI, Aug. 9-11, 1943), 117-118, 119; "The Social Protection Program," *The Police Yearbook 1945* (Proceedings of the 51st Annual and Third War Conference of the IACP, Cleveland, OH, Aug. 14-16, 1944), 52; "Delinquency and Crime Prevention (A Symposium on Juvenile Delinquency)," 143-200; James J. Mitchell, "The St. Louis Police Juvenile Division," 156.

17. "National Advisory Police Committee on Social Protection Formed," *Journal of Social Hygiene* 28, no. 6 (June 1942), 430; National Advisory Police Committee, *Techniques of Law Enforcement in the Use of Policewomen*, front material, 3, 5, 6.

18. Anderson, *Wartime Women*, 12, 16.

19. Karl Detzer, "Detroit's Lady Cops," *The American Mercury*, Mar. 1942, 345, 346, 348, 349, 351. For similar articles, see Rolland McCombs, "Lady Constable: 'Sis' Dickerson Polices a Tough Texas County," *Life*, Sept. 17, 1945, 19-20+, describing "probably the only female chief of police in the U.S.," sworn in 1940 to fill the term of her late father, re-elected twice, involved in many dangerous situations, who, "after a tough night on the highway . . . likes . . . to come home and busy

herself with needle and thread . . . makes all her own clothes." Also, Dan Fowler, "The Lady Is a Cop," *Look*, Mar. 6, 1956, 56-60, calls Fransis Sumner, the LAPD Policewoman of the Year, a former nurse, a "crack marksman and humanitarian, . . . she handles a man's tough job with womanly skills" and notes that she "is a housewife par excellence who likes to knit handsome wool socks for her marine-engineer husband and who can toss a fine green salad." Photos show her in uniform pointing her six-inch barrel firearm at the camera and tossing not a salad, but a 200-pound man, during judo practice. Miriam Borgenicht, "Welcome, Policewoman!" *Parent's Magazine*, Nov. 1945, 34+, complains: "Too many city officials still think of the policewoman as a broad-shouldered, heavy-handed lady-flatfoot in navy blue." The author notes that a policewoman "is not fat or funny or even dressed in navy blue. She wears neat, feminine clothes and pins her badge in her pocketbook or under her lapel", yet the accompanying photo is a woman in full uniform, with dark jacket, tie and cap, white shirt, and policewoman-style pocketbook slung over her shoulder.

20. Detzer, "Detroit's Lady Cops," 106, 107.

21. Eleonore L. Hutzel, "The Policewoman's Role in Social Protection," *The Police Journal*, July-Aug. 1945, 3, 4.

22. Anderson, *Wartime Women*, 108; Hutzel, "The Policewoman's Role in Social Protection," 3, 21.

23. J.M. Leonard, *The Cleveland Police Survey* (Cleveland: Bureau of Governmental Research, 1945), 26, 86, 98, 99-100; *Police Annual Report. Cleveland, Ohio, 1947*, 30.

24. *Chicago Police Department. Annual Report. Year Ending December 30, 1940*, 10; *Year Ending December 31, 1946*, 9, 10; *Year Ending December 31, 1949*, 6; *Year Ending December 31, 1951*, 35.

25. Bruce Smith, *The Baltimore Police Survey* (New York: Institute of Public Administration, 1941), 130-132; Mazie Rappaport, "A Protective Service for Promiscuous Girls," *Federal Probation*, Jan.-Mar. 1945, 32, 33; Anderson, *Wartime Women*, 32, 101, 105; *Report of the Police Commissioner for the City of Baltimore to His Excellency the Governor of Maryland For The Year 1945*, 16, 23; *For the Year 1947*, 16, 22.

26. Anderson, *Wartime Women*, 32, 77-78, 92, 96, 103, 106.

27. San Francisco Police Museum and Archives, miscellaneous collected material.

28. "A Study of Protective Measures in the City of Boston," *Journal of Social Hygiene* 28, no. 6 (June 1942), 412, 413, 414.

29. *Annual Report of the Police Commissioner for the City of Boston for the Year Ending November 30, 1943*, 9, 11, 12, 13; *Year Ending November 30, 1944*, 9, 11, 12; *Year Ending November 30, 1946*, 13, 45; *Year Ending November 30, 1948*, 7-8.

30. *Annual Report of the Police Department, City of New York, For the Year 1940*, 4, 38; *For the Year 1941*, 1, 19; *For the Year 1942*, 1, 22; *For the Year 1943*, 2, 22; *For the Year 1950*, 36.

31. *Annual Report of the Police Department, City of New York, For the Year 1947*, 68.

32. Buwalda, "The Policewoman," 292.

33. Carol M. Williams, *The Organization and Practices of Police Women's Divisions in the United States* (Detroit: National Training School of Public Service, 1946), 1, 4, 5, 7, 8, 13, 16.

34. "More Cities Employ Policewomen," *The American City*, Feb. 1948, 17; "More Cities Employ Policewomen," *The Police Journal*, May-June 1948, 14.

35. *Annual Report of the Police Department, City of New York, For the Year 1948*, 9.

36. Mildred Shannon, "Remarks for Panel on 'Organizing for Equality'," presented at the Women in Policing Workshop, John Jay College of Criminal Justice, CUNY, New York, NY, Feb. 5, 1980, 1-4, photocopied.

Chapter 7

Paving the Way for Patrol, 1950–1967

The 1950s, often viewed by feminists as a dormant period in women's activism and female consciousness, was a period of growth for police-women. They began to increase not only their numbers but also their responsibilities. The changes these women precipitated played a key role in the transition they and their sister officers made from social workers to crimefighters beginning in 1968.

When women first went on uniform patrol in the late 1960s and early 1970s, it was not an isolated event, although it seemed that way to most observers. The move to patrol was part of a continuum that led women out of a specialized, gender-based role in policing into genderless, general assignment policing. The idea that uniform patrol on an equal basis with male officers was a viable use of female police personnel was part of a progression toward greater integration of women into the police environment. A large measure of this integration was fostered by the diminishing importance of the concept of "women's sphere" in many areas of society.

Expansion in the number of policewomen during both world wars was attributable almost solely to morality concerns. At the end of World War I, policewomen's gains were aborted by the Depression. But after World War II, policewomen were able to maintain newly acquired positions and increase both their numbers and duties throughout the 1950s. The 1950 Census reported 2,610 publicly employed policewomen, slightly more than 1 percent of all police and detectives. The numbers of policewomen continued to increase throughout the 1950s. By 1956 policewomen were employed in more than 150 cities. The 1960 census counted 5,617 police-women, about 2 percent of publicly employed officers.[1] In the 10 years from 1950 to 1960 the number of women increased by 3,000, doubling the 1950 figure and almost equalling the total number of policewomen in the title since it had been created in 1910.

Concerns with morality and delinquency intensified after World War II and ultimately led to diversified roles for women, who were teamed with male officers on undercover assignments and for the first time investigated other than morality crimes. They were issued uniforms based on female military garb (although they rarely wore them except at special events) and were trained in the use of and expected to carry firearms.

The postwar period and the 1950s also brought a different type of woman into policing. Often military veterans, these "second generation" policewomen, were middle-class careerists. Although better educated (most had some college but not necessarily a degree) and higher in social class orientation than their male peers, these women were less different from policemen than their predecessors had been. They formed a bridge between the upper-middle-class, college educated women who had served as policewomen before them and today's women officers, most of whom are comparable to the primarily working-class, high school educated men with whom they serve.

Policewomen were not the only women to contradict the image of "the quiet '50s" as a decade of stagnation for American women. Leila J. Rupp and Verta Taylor, in *Survival in the Doldrums: The American Women's Rights Movement, 1945 to the 1960s*, asked, "Feminism in the fifties?" and answered: "Presumably these were years of domesticity and conformity for American women, not years of discontent and protest . . . we did not expect to discover many women carrying on the struggle for women's rights. . . . However, we found that a great deal was going on." Rupp and Taylor came to see 1945 to the mid-1960s "as a particular stage of the women's rights movement that survived from the suffrage struggle . . . to connect with the resurgent movement of the 1960s."[2] While the continuity may not be as direct for policewomen, there is a commonality in that 1945 to the mid-1960s were years of activity among them that paved the way for developments that would radically alter women's place in policing.

This view of female advancement and activism in the 1950s contrasts with the traditional assessment, exemplified by June Sochen, who described college women in the 1930s, 1940s, and 1950s as sharing the values of women who did not attend college, agreeing that marriage was their prime occupation and that "home remained, as always, the main center of their lives."[3]

This was certainly not the case with policewomen. Most viewed policing as a career and worked in excess of the 20 or 25 years required for retirement. Police reports that list separations show that few women left voluntarily. Women were hired when quotas were expanded or when older women retired. These second generation women sought upward mobility through rank, again resembling their male colleagues and underlining the differences between themselves and the first generation policewomen. By the end of the 1950s, women had returned to the supervisory ranks, although most were appointees. Battles in the 1960s centered on achieving civil service promotion.

In 1956 policewomen re-established the International Association of Policewomen, their professional association that had existed from 1915 to 1932. Through the newly formed International Association of Women Police, they diverged from their social service roots and developed a group consciousness distinct from social workers. This absence of contact with organized social work pushed the women to see themselves more fully as police officers, reinforcing the changes in orientation among younger policewomen that ultimately resulted in demands for equality in the 1970s. However, the IAWP came to embody many of the contradictions within the policewomen's movement. One of few single-sex organizations created in the 1950s, it sought to integrate women more fully into the police environment but still endorsed a gender-based role for women and sex segregation through women's bureaus.

It is one of the ironies of policewomen's history that when the IAP was resurrected as the IAWP, the driving force was a woman from Chicago and the site was San Diego, neither of whose departments, although employing women for decades, had been associated with the social work aspects of the movement.

In September 1949, Illinois officials created a statewide Crime Prevention Bureau headquartered in Chicago. One of those assigned was Lois Lundell Higgins, a 14-year veteran Chicago policewoman whose career had begun in the sex offense bureau, where she was the only woman amid 50 men. Prior to becoming a policewoman, Higgins had been a juvenile court probation officer, a domestic relations court counselor, and a family caseworker with the United Charities of Chicago. Named assistant director of the crime prevention unit at its 1949 inception, in 1951, she became director, serving also as crime prevention coordinator for the municipal court.

Higgins's training was similar to that of early policewomen. In 1931, she graduated cum laude from Mount Mary College in Milwaukee; in 1947, she wrote her master's of social work thesis at Loyola University's School of Social Work on women's bureaus in eight U.S. cities, and in 1949, Mount Mary College awarded her an honorary doctor of laws degree. Yet she moved beyond social work concerns. In 1951 she was the only woman to testify at drug control hearings before a House of Representatives subcommittee and a Senate committee investigating organized crime in interstate commerce, and in 1955 she became the first woman to attend the Southern Police Institute at the University of Louisville.[4]

Higgins spoke and wrote extensively in the 1950s and 1960s, initially as director of the Illinois crime prevention bureau and after 1956 as president of the IAWP. Her philosophy of women's role in law enforcement (which remained consistent throughout her career) appeared in a 1950 article. She used social work terminology to describe the work of policewomen, but she did not believe that policewomen were social workers, although she did feel that their primary duty was dealing with the causes of crime, rather than with enforcement and punishment. She believed that

while case work . . . is not within the province of the policewoman, she must . . . be conscious . . . that she is dealing with human beings and with . . . factors in society which . . . hinder their . . . adjustment to society and to its laws. From this standpoint, her work has at least one characteristic that is common to all social work; it inquires into causes.[5]

In May 1956, Higgins attended a Women Peace Officers Association of California meeting at which she and others formed the IAWP. The WPOAC met annually with the California Peace Officers Association, its male counterpart. While addressing a luncheon to which both men and women had been invited, Higgins unveiled plans for an international association of women officers that would serve as a clearinghouse for information, would adopt a code of ethics, and would be a prelude to professional status, which she felt was vital to all law enforcement officers, but particularly to women. Just as Alice Stebbins Wells, the first American woman to be officially called a policewoman, had gone before the National Conference of Charities and Correction in 1915 with a plan to form the IAP, so Higgins approached the WPOAC. Letters to 275 departments to gauge interest resulted in returned applications and dues from more than 200 women from 25 states and the District of Columbia.

When Higgins was named president, among those who watched her sworn in was Wells, who had retired from the LAPD in 1940. Wells died in 1957, a year after the IAWP's creation. A new name was selected for the association because there were questions about old debts. Board members were concerned, too, that *policewoman* referred to a specific job title which would disqualify women serving as troopers, marshals, sheriffs, or matrons. Though the organizers did not want to eliminate any sworn officers regardless of titles, there was agreement that non-sworn women, whether matrons, school crossing guards, or traffic enforcement officers, could not become members.[6] The large number of women performing such functions who were called "police" but who were civilian employees of police agencies resulted in confusion when policewomen were described. To combat this, the IAWP limited membership to women with full police authority.

Indicative of the changing orientation of both social workers and policewomen, the IAWP did not form the social work alliances that had characterized the IAP. Although many policewomen in the 1950s had social work training, it was not as universal as in earlier decades. Also, social workers no longer viewed policewomen as colleagues, as they had during the Progressive era. Higgins was not concerned with the absence of social work affiliations; she sought a much closer relationship with the IACP than had the IAP. Higgins believes she was the first woman member of the IACP. Certainly when she addressed the association in 1957, she was one of very few (if not still the only) female members and the only woman on its crime prevention committee. She appears also to have been the first woman to address the group as a full conference participant, rather than solely as a representative of policewomen. Her talk, "The Feminine Force in Crime Prevention," described policewomen as "competent, efficient, attractive and well groomed" professionals who were "selfless, educated women who can and do minister to the world's *socially* ill."[7]

Higgins's views on professionalism, rather than equality, influenced the IAWP throughout her presidency (ending in 1964) and her tenure as executive director until 1976. These views, seemingly shared by the majority of members, resulted in the endorsing by the IAWP of separate roles for policewomen even after some women began to demand equality in the 1970s. Not until 1972, four years after Indianapolis officials assigned women to general patrol, did the IAWP delete from its constitution the clause encouraging establishment of women's bureaus. In 1990, Higgins indicated that she still did not agree with women abandoning their positions as educated professionals to, in her view, lower their status to assume the generalist position of uniformed patrol officer.[8]

The IAWP continued to see itself as an educational and sororal association, rather than as an advocacy group. It used as its model the old IAP at a time when the roles of women were changing. Even if the IAWP leadership had been more forward-looking, there was no way in the early years of the 1960s that IAWP leaders or anyone else would have predicted the changes in the role of policewomen that would be set in motion before the decade ended. Certainly the women who formed the IAWP would never have predicted patrol, particularly because most of them agreed with Higgins and never accepted crimefighting as a role to be filled equally by men and women. To those who continued to see themselves as educated specialists, patrol was not something to covet, but was a step down on the career ladder.

The issue that retained its emotional appeal throughout the 1950s and 1960s continued to be women's bureaus. Despite the increasing number of cities employing women, by 1958 only 10 of the largest 100 cities reported separate bureaus: New York; Chicago; Detroit; Cleveland; Washington, D.C.; Baltimore; Grand Rapids; Rochester, New York; Portland, Oregon, and Tacoma.[9] The decline resulted from most of them having been consolidated into juvenile or crime prevention bureaus. While this ultimately aided the integration of women into areas of police work not concerned with women and children and placed them in closer proximity to men, it hampered their upward mobility, since women rarely achieved rank other than within the sex segregated women's bureaus. The major exceptions to this were in Seattle and Portland, where bureaus involved with morality violations had historically been commanded by ranking women officers who supervised male officers working within the units.

The style of policing that continued to dominate in the 1950s—O.W. Wilson's efficient, military model—was not conducive to progress by policewomen, particularly in their battles to achieve rank. His text *Police Administration* (the "bible" of law enforcement managers) went through four editions, the first published in 1950 and the last in 1977. Through all editions, Wilson advocated highly circumscribed roles for policewomen. Although he conceded that women had value in juvenile work and other, limited activities, he stated unequivocally that women were not qualified to lead. Wilson argued that male officers had wider police experience, would be better able to secure the cooperation of other supervisors, and were "less likely to become irritable and overcritical under emotional stress" than women.[10]

Wilson's influence was so strong in California that the style of policing he promoted became known as "the California style" or "California professionalism." Exemplified by the LAPD during the tenure of Chief William H. Parker from 1950 to 1966, California professionalism combined authoritative administrative practices, centralized command and control that tolerated neither corruption nor dissent, and intensive public relations. Parker, who had served during World War II under Wilson, portrayed police as the "thin blue line" between "civilization and chaos." He and his men personified on a municipal level the almost mythical crimefighter created in the 1930s by J. Edgar Hoover and agents of the Federal Bureau of Investigation.

Parker cooperated with the television show "Dragnet," which assured a generation of Americans that their police were just like Sgt. Joe Friday: relentless, efficient, and quietly professional. The fictional Friday's trademark demeanor and request for "just the facts, Ma'am" symbolized the depersonalized policing that embodied a department distant from the community.[11] California policing was the opposite of policewomen's interventionist, individual-centered concept of crime prevention, where the crime was less important than the social situation surrounding it. Despite this, even Los Angeles policewomen managed to make gains. By 1956 they exceeded 2 percent of the LAPD, including 11 sergeants selected by competitive exam and one appointed female lieutenant. In 1958, the 97 policewomen were the second largest group in the nation, exceeded only by the 249 in the New York City Police Department.[12]

Parker was not unaware of the women in his department. He reminded groups he addressed that "the young men and women" who entered policing were products of the American scene, including many military veterans.[13] He was one of the few police leaders who even mentioned women. The prevailing custom among chiefs and in department reports was to use feminine pronouns only on the pages describing policewomen's activities; otherwise, references were always to "the men," "policemen," "patrolmen," "he," or "him."

Elsewhere in California, policewomen returned to the San Diego Police Department in 1954, when Chief Elmer Jansen hired four women detectives. Concerned with a rise in rapes, female criminality, and juvenile delinquency, Jansen, who joined the department as a police officer in 1932 and served as chief from late 1947 to early 1962, believed that his department's reliance on matrons to do policewomen's work was no longer sufficient. At the time he decided to hire policewomen, Jansen was engaged to a female captain in the Los Angeles County Sheriff's Department. Seemingly influenced not only by his fiancée (whom he married in 1955), but by the ethos of California policing, Jansen "was not interested in hiring altruistic, social-worker types" but "'real' policewomen." Sylvia Bate, hired in 1957, remembered that when Jansen asked why she wanted to join the department, thinking a noble answer would enhance her chances, she said she wanted to help make the world a better place. Not pleased, Jansen thundered, "Then go work in the Welfare Department, that's not what we expect from our policewomen."

What was expected of this "elite group," who earned the same pay as starting policemen, was at least two years of college and experience dealing with people (men needed only a high school diploma), outstanding physical appearance, adherence to a strict dress code (including hats, white gloves, conservatively colored business suits and high heels), and an even higher moral code (the sole unmarried policewoman recalled being under scrutiny among her 500 male peers until she married one of them). Due to the small number of women officers in the area, throughout the 1950s and 1960s, the San Diego women, "always wearing hats and high heels," were loaned to other police agencies for narcotics raids, extradition cases, and undercover work related to prostitution, abortion, and pornography.[14] The San Diego women were representative of the second generation policewomen; while distinct from their male co-workers, they were a far cry from their social worker foremothers.

Although police historians view the 1950s as the decade of California policing, it was not as dominant in large cities that were more ethnically diverse and whose police were less military in style and in bearing. Additionally, the crimefighter image did not erase concerns about crime prevention and juvenile delinquency, where women did the majority of their work. In 1952 the IACP sought data on departments with juvenile bureaus. Of the 611 replies, 303 had at least one officer doing juvenile work. Of these, 132 assigned women to juvenile duties. All responding cities with populations over 500,000 had policewomen in their juvenile units, as did the majority of cities with populations between 100,000 and 500,000.[15]

This nationwide interest in juvenile work is what led the IACP in 1958 to act as a sponsor for the first IAWP conference, the start of what would become biannual (and eventually annual) events. Initially, the IACP urged chiefs to send officers and at least two chiefs participated, as did the IACP training director. There were nearly 70 attendees from 43 cities within 19 states and three Canadian provinces. Most were from small or medium-sized departments; fewer than 10 held ranks above policewoman. Training sessions, many taught by the ranking officers of women's bureaus, included urban and rural juvenile policing, youth and crime, interrogating juveniles and teenagers, interrogating abnormal persons, adult interviews and interrogation, investigative techniques, public relations, and professionalization issues confronting women police.

The social work origins of the policewomen's movement were not easily left behind. One speaker advised the women that their activities involved four main fields: law enforcement, crime prevention, protection of youth, and service to their own sex in trouble. Higgins addressed similar themes, calling the feminine arm of the law the one that "rocks the cradle, and sometimes shoots a wicked .38."[16] The IAWP reported 320 members, including 295 from the United States, 3 from Canada, and 22 from all other countries.

Higgins, and the IAWP during her leadership, bridged the generations of policewomen. It is unlikely an association as closely linked to social work as the IAP had been could have been created in the 1950s. Social work had changed, but so had policewomen. These women were interested in career opportunities within law enforcement, not within social work. Like their male colleagues, who had become careerists in the 1930s, policewomen in the 1950s saw their future in civil service promotion and in diversified assignments.

In November 1960, *Law and Order*, a magazine aimed at police officers, began a section on women police written by Higgins. It appeared regularly until October 1964, then, after Higgins was no longer IAWP president, sporadically until August 1965, when it disappeared. Although it covered many aspects of police work, nothing was written that challenged the views of the police hierarchy on the roles of women. Yet, no one seemed quite sure of exactly what these roles were.

By the late 1950s and early 1960s the utilization of women, even in departments where policewomen comprised 1 or 2 percent of sworn personnel (a large percentage at the time), fluctuated greatly. A review of women's activities in three departments employing a large number of them indicates that their histories within their agencies continued to affect how they were perceived years later. The ways in which cities reacted to women's demands for assignment, promotion, and, later, equality in hiring, also differed. Numbers alone rarely overcame tradition.

Chicago, the nation's second largest city, in 1958 had the fourth largest number of women (84), behind New York City (249), Los Angeles (97), and Detroit (93), and followed by Cleveland (55), Philadelphia (40), and Indianapolis (39).[17]

Although Chicago officials appointed policewomen as early as 1913, they did not organize them into a women's bureau until 1947. Even then, the women worked out of precincts rather than a central headquarters. Throughout the 1950s the number of policewomen averaged about 80. Policewomen and matrons were used interchangeably, although they were counted separately in personnel listings. Educational requirements were the same; no college or advanced training was required, nor was social work experience a prerequisite.

Chicago policewomen, far fewer in number than those in New York, made many more arrests. This appears attributable to their decentralized assignments, as well as to a less social service oriented view of their duties by both the department and the women. While the 98 members of the New York women's bureau made fewer than 150 arrests in both 1952 and 1953, Chicago policewomen in 1953 arrested 862 adults and also handled 2,063 juvenile girls. They conducted 7,674 investigations and 2,588 interviews leading either to arrest or to referral to other agencies. Matrons performed duties that in New York were the responsibility of policewomen assigned to precincts with female jail cells. In January 1956, Sgt. Marilynn Olson, women's division commanding officer, became the first female lieutenant in the city. Both her father and brother were members of the department. Later that year, a veteran policewoman was promoted to sergeant. Both women's salaries were identical to those of men in the same ranks, although their promotions were appointive, rather than civil service.[18]

Chicago introduced uniforms for policewomen in 1956. The Patrolmen's Association magazine featured the women on its cover, each wearing the regulation navy blue skirt, light blue shirt, navy blue jacket and overseas cap, a man's style tie and navy blue leather pumps and shoulder bag. It was typical of women's uniforms around the country, although most cities avoided a man's tie, favoring a small cross-tie for women. The 1956 *Annual Report* also featured the women, including a photo of one uniformed officer standing with a male in plainclothes pointing her revolver at the camera.[19]

Detroit policewomen came from a totally different background than those in Chicago. Their very strong social work tradition followed them into the 1950s, by which time the approximately 90 women made up somewhat more than 2 percent of the total police personnel. Detroit had a woman commissioner and provided promotions for women. In 1956 there were six sergeants and five lieutenants in competitive ranks and one appointed chief (Fourth Deputy Commissioner Margaret Snow, who also had the title of Chief of the Women's Division). Snow's predecessor, Eleanore L. Hutzel, had been one of the leading advocates of a purely social service role for policewomen. Hutzel also had imposed high educational standards. This legacy continued; although by 1955 women were no longer limited only to cases involving traditional social work, they were still required to have a college degree or professional training. One was attending law school.

The women worked in plainclothes, their .38 caliber revolvers (which they were now mandated to carry on duty) tucked into department issued pocketbooks with built in holsters that had become standard for police-women around the country. All were assigned to the women's division, although a number were loaned to the detective division to assist in a variety of cases, including "a number of important narcotics cases during the past few years." Women on the day shift worked alone. Those assigned between 4 P.M. and 8 A.M. worked with another woman, patrol-ling in cars and, "unless physical violence is anticipated or the arrest of adult men is involved, they perform their task satisfactorily without the aid of men officers." Twenty women assigned to the courts worked with six male detectives. Although the men were under Deputy Commissioner Snow's command, their immediate supervisor was a male detective ser-geant. The women were supervised by a female lieutenant and sergeant.[20]

In Detroit promotion policies for women contrasted starkly with those of the New York City Police Department, which opened the decade by appointing a record number of policewomen but did not provide any upward mobility for them. The 1950 *Annual Report* pictured women re-cruits in uniform, calling them "a valuable aid to many aspects of police work." That year the quota for policewomen was 190; all but three posi-tions were filled on New Year's Day and there was only one vacancy on the last day of 1950. The next year, the quota was increased; 56 women were appointed, including 45 on October 3, 1951. This was the largest group of women ever appointed at one time in New York or in the nation. By 1959 the quota was 253, approximately 1 percent of the force.[21] Because the NYCPD was so much larger than other departments, 253 women (the largest number in the country) constituted a smaller percentage than fewer women did elsewhere.

The increasing numbers did not result in greater responsibility. The major activity was "detained females," which refers to matron duty at precincts with cells for women prisoners. The next largest category was "deceased females searched." Women worked in a variety of bureaus, but the largest group was assigned to the women's bureau. In 1952, Theresa M. Melchionne, a ten-year veteran, was appointed director. Although Melchionne had planned to be a math teacher rather than a social worker, her background was similar to that of early women's bureau directors. A college graduate at 19, the Depression led her to seek the security of a civil service position. She worked as an investigator with the New York Society for the Prevention of Cruelty to Children before becoming a policewoman. She remained director of policewomen until 1963, when she was promoted to Deputy Commissioner of Youth Programs. Prior to being named director, she had been promoted twice within the detective rank. Detective rank, and promotions within it, were appointive. It was the only method of promotion open to women, since they were barred from taking promotion exams.

Melchionne "tried very hard to expand the role of women," particularly investigating "crimes and offenses directed towards women and children." Her efforts on behalf of "her girls" resulted in 1953 in 22 of the 98 women in the bureau being transferred temporarily to assist male officers in anti-gambling enforcement. Although expected primarily to assist in observation and detection, the women made 85 arrests, a considerable number (the entire women's bureau made only 131 arrests in 1952). By the end of 1953, 32 women were in the juvenile aid bureau (which required a college degree and specialized training), and 16 were assigned to narcotics. Others were scattered about, many serving as secretaries for high-ranking officers.[22]

A 1952 management survey, combined with the increasing number of women and the start of an internal "struggle for equal promotion" by the women,[23] forced the department to address the issue in 1954. According to the *Annual Report*,

consideration was given to . . . establishing within the Policewomen's Bureau a procedure for advancement to . . . captain [the highest rank that could be achieved via civil service],. . . .Now . . . a policewoman enters . . . at the level of a patrolman and is unable to advance . . . except within the Detective Division. . . . The commanding officer of . . . policewomen . . . although she receives a salary equivalent to . . . captain, has . . . no superior officer's rank . . . an archaic double standard which we hope will be corrected in the very near future, at least to the extent of having comparable, competitive ranks of policewomen with authority only over lower ranks in the Bureau.[24]

Regardless of intentions, the "near future" did not come soon and did not come voluntarily. Civil service promotion for New York City policewomen did not occur until the 1960s, after a court ruling in favor of Policewoman Felicia Shpritzer who sued to take the exam for sergeant. At the time Shpritzer began her fight, the promotion policies of the NYCPD were among the most restrictive of any large department in the nation. By 1958, 28 of the 100 largest cities provided promotions for women, although in 13 the only upward mobility was to sergeant.[25]

Shpritzer personified the changes for policewomen that began in the 1960s. A college graduate with two masters degrees, she had previously taught in public high schools. She had taken and passed the first civil service test for policewomen in New York City in 1938, although, due to the small quota for women, she was not appointed until 1942. At the time of her suit, she was assigned to the youth division, where she had worked for most of her career.

Yet, even she failed to see what the future would yield. In 1959, tackling the most vexing question pertaining to promotions for women, namely, "where could women sergeants be assigned?" she allayed men's fears in a manner reminiscent of earlier policewomen who assured policemen that women were not seeking their jobs. "Obviously," Shpritzer wrote, "it would be misuse of policewomen sergeants to assign them to a precinct to direct uniformed men on patrol duty."[26]

In 1961 Shpritzer sued New York City on behalf of all policewomen barred from taking the sergeant promotional test. Her battle was one of the first by policewomen to achieve equality through the courts. Ultimately, in many cities this would become their primary path to equal opportunity. Her suit questioned whether the use of "Patrolman" as an eligible title constituted a denial of opportunity solely because of sex. "Nothing in the broad definition of the duties of Sergeant . . . are clearly impossible of performance by policewomen because of sex," declared the Appellate Division of the New York State Supreme Court on January 4, 1962. The court said the women could not "be arbitrarily denied the right to take the examination for Sergeant because of their sex, and no reasonable grounds have been shown to warrant the 'sex selection' evidenced."[27] New York City officials appealed the decision, but the State Court of Appeals unanimously upheld the lower court.

Based on this decision, the NYCPD in April 1964 gave a make-up exam to 126 women denied access to the earlier test. On March 12, 1965, Shpritzer and Gertrude Schimmel, who led the civil service list, became the first two women sergeants. In December 1967, after passing another exam, both were promoted again, becoming the first female lieutenants. Shpritzer was on the list for promotion to captain but never attained the rank before she retired. Schimmel's career continued its upward spiral; subsequently she was promoted to captain in 1971; deputy inspector in 1972; inspector in 1974, and deputy chief in 1978, when she was named commanding officer of the Office of the Deputy Commissioner, Community Affairs. Schimmel remained the only woman in a rank above captain (the highest civil service rank; others are appointive). After Schimmel retired, on June 29, 1979, Vittoria Renzullo, the only female captain, was promoted to deputy inspector. In December 1976, Renzullo had become the first woman in the NYCPD to command a precinct.[28]

Obviously, the promotions of Shpritzer and Schimmel did not result in overnight changes, although glimpses of the increasing involvement of New York policewomen with crimefighter roles can be seen in department reports. In 1960 the women's bureau was credited with 568 arrests; by 1961 the number had increased to 903. In 1963 the number of policewomen for the first time exceeded 300. By 1966 the department expanded to a record size of 27,806, which included a quota for 351 policewomen.

Beginning in 1967 categories listed as women's activities disappeared from annual reports. After a six-month pilot program, the approximately 180 women in the women's bureau were sent to precincts, resulting in the bureau's performing only limited staff functions from 1967 until it was disbanded in 1973, a move that had been recommended in 1952.[29] The 1967 assignments "to stationhouses . . . in clerical assignments, to replace policemen . . . reassigned to street patrol"[30] meant that women who might have spent their entire careers in the women's bureau took their first tentative steps into precincts, although most rarely left their precincts except to search female corpses.

Yet by the start of the 1960s, the more than 5,500 policewomen in municipal departments around the nation no longer held a monolithic view of themselves in the police environment. Higgins and many of her generation continued to view women within the context of their separate sphere, while others, often younger, rarely supervisors, and usually more involved in direct "hands-on" police activities, sought an even wider, less gender-based set of roles and responsibilities than had been achieved in the 1950s. These younger women, products of an activist, rather than a quiet 1950s, would not prevail for another decade. The views of Melchionne, Higgins, and supporters of the expanded role of women within a gender context summarized the 1950s but unwittingly set the tone of the coming debate for greater equality. Indicative of how attitudes and individuals changed, 15 years after she had assured men that women supervisors did not want their jobs, Shpritzer was serving as a tour lieutenant, supervising men and women on patrol.

Despite their own portrayal of themselves in a gender context, as women gained numerically in the postwar decade, and as a changing society led to altered definitions of women's sphere, policewomen moved further away from their original role of dealing solely with women and children and societal housekeeping functions. Assignment to a greater range of police activities was still rooted in concepts of gender and women's sphere; women were assigned to vice or narcotics with a male partner because a male/female team would not be suspected of being police officers and could enter or explain their presence in areas that two men could not. In such instances, there was no consideration of whether the assignment was too dangerous or outside women's sphere; the decision to use the female officer was made solely on investigative requirements. This eventually provided an opening for women to expand their roles further and for police departments to use their services in yet untapped areas.

What was unique about the 1950s and the 1960s was that a combination of factors inside and outside police departments led many of the women hired during and after World War II to become dissatisfied with the limitations imposed by the women's sphere. Their increased numbers and greater range of assignments, combined with differences in their social class, made change inevitable. Additionally, younger policewomen became convinced that segregation was hampering their chances for career mobility.

New assignments also brought them into closer contact with policemen. They saw that even men who were not in traditional uniform patrol had greater career opportunities. Men were eligible for transfer to any bureau. More importantly, men were eligible for civil service promotions that could greatly enhance their status and their incomes. Women would soon expand their own sphere to include uniform patrol.

NOTES

1. Susan Ehrlich Martin, *Breaking and Entering: Policewomen on Patrol* (Berkeley: University of California Press, 1980), 24; Lois Lundell Higgins, "Women and Crime—Cherchez La Femme." Speech at the 29th WPOAC Conference, San Diego, CA, May 22, 1956, photocopied. In 1957, Lois Lundell Higgins, "The Feminine Force in Crime Prevention," *The Police Yearbook 1958* (Proceedings of the 64th Annual Cionference of the IACP, Honolulu, HI, Sept. 29-Oct. 3, 1957), 106, stated that in addition to 2,500 policewomen in at least 150 U.S. cities, there were more than 2,000 serving as deputy sheriffs and performing police functions in federal agencies. She estimated that women made up about 1 percent of all police.

2. Lelia J. Rupp and Verta Taylor, *Survival in the Doldrums: The American Women's Rights Movement, 1945 to the 1960s* (New York: Oxford University Press, 1987), vii.

3. June Sochen, *Movers and Shakers: American Women Thinkers and Activists, 1900-1970* (New York: Quandrangle, 1973), 174-175. For a reiteration of the 1950s as a time when marriage, children, and a stylish home epitomized women's goals, see Wini Breines, *Young, White, and Miserable: Growing Up Female in the Fifties* (Boston: Beacon, 1992).

4. Lois Lundell Higgins, *Dope-ology: Articles and Lectures* (Chicago: Police Department, 1953), 40; Lois Lundell Higgins, "The Policewoman," *Police*, Nov.-Dec. 1958, 66; *Who's Who in American Law Enforcement*, 3d ed. (North Miami, FL: American Law Enforcement Officers Association, 1980), ix; Lois Lundell Higgins, interview with author, Jan. 22, 1990 and Dec. 2, 1994.

5. Lois Lundell Higgins, "Women Police Service," *Journal of Criminal Law, Criminology and Police Science* 41, no. 1 (June 1950), 104-105.

6. IAWP, miscellaneous collected material; Higgins, interview with author, Jan. 22, 1990.

Concern over confusion between themselves and non-sworn women was well founded. Newspapers, magazines, and even some police departments labelled matrons, crossing guards, and parking enforcement agents "policewomen." In 1952, according to "New Orleans Has Women Traffic Cops," *The Police Journal*, June 1952, 24, the city hired 32 "lady traffic 'cops'" to work 15 hours weekly, hoping to expand use of these "patrolwomen" to school zones. Pasadena, according to Varreece Berry, "Pasadena (Texas) Policewomen Protect School Crossings," *Law and Order*, Dec. 1955, 6, 16, also called its part-time crossing guards "policewomen." In "Women Tough Traffic Police," *The Police Journal*, Jan.-Feb.-Mar. 1955, 24, the terms *traffic guards*, *parking checkers*, and *female police* are used interchangeably in a five paragraph story.

7. Lois Lundell Higgins, "The Feminine Force in Crime Prevention," *The Police Yearbook 1958* (Proceedings of the 64th Annual Conference of the IACP, Honolulu, HI, Sept. 29-Oct. 3, 1957), 102, 108-109; Higgins, interview with author, Dec. 2, 1994.

8. Higgins, interview with author, Jan. 22, 1990.

9. Lois Lundell Higgins, "Women in Law Enforcement: A Special Survey on Policewomen Throughout the United States," *Law and Order*, Apr. 1958, 22.

10. Wilson, *Report of Police Department Survey, Hartford, CT* (Chicago: Public Administration Service, 1942), 49, 115-116, 117.

11. Thomas J. Deakin, *Police Professionalism: The Renaissance of American Law Enforcement* (Springfield, IL: Charles C Thomas, 1988), 22, 225; Samuel Walker, *The Police in America: An Introduction* (New York: McGraw-Hill, 1983), 16-17.

12. Felicia Shpritzer, "A Case for the Promotion of Policewomen in the City of New York," *Journal of Criminal Law, Criminology and Police Science* 50, no. 4 (Nov.-Dec. 1959), 417; Higgins, "Women in Law Enforcement: A Special Survey on Policewomen Throughout the United States," 22. African-American officers were unhappy with Parker over promotions; yet in 1950 he appointed African-American policewoman Vivian Strange, an officer since 1943, to the rank of sergeant, making her the first African-American female sergeant in the LAPD. See Joseph J. Woods, *The Progressives and the Police: Urban Reform and the Professionalism of the Los Angeles Police* (Ann Arbor, MI: University Microfilms, 1979 [Ph.D. diss., University of California at Los Angeles, 1973]), 460 and Homer F. Broome, Jr., *LAPD's Black History 1886-1976* (Norwalk, CA: Stockton Trade Press, 1977), 215, 216.

13. O.W. Wilson, ed., *Parker on Police* (Springfield, IL: Charles C Thomas, 1957), 27. His awareness may have come from the fact that one year after joining the LAPD he married a policewoman. See Woods, *The Progressives and the Police*, 419.

14. Anne Findlay Patton, "Women Officers of the San Diego Police Department, 1912-1988," M.A. thesis, University of San Diego, 1989, 85, 94, 104, 107-109, 111, 125, 127-128, 150. Whether due to Jansen's disdain for social workers or whether the women's recollections were influenced by the modern role of women in policing, none mentioned social service or youth assignments during interviews with Patton.

15. U.S. Department of Health, Education and Welfare, *Police Service for Juveniles* (Washington, DC: Government Printing Office, 1954), 70, 71.

16. Lois Lundell Higgins, "The Feminine Arm of the Law: Women in Crime." Paper presented at the 1st Biennial IAWP Conference, Lafayette, IN, Sept. 30-Oct. 2, 1958. Microfiched. IAWP, miscellaneous collected material; IAWP, *Official Program*. 1st Biennial Conference and Seminar, Lafayette, IN, Sept. 30-Oct. 2, 1958.

17. Higgins, "Women in Law Enforcement: A Special Survey on Policewomen Throughout the United States," 22. Although Higgins indicates her numbers came from departments, they are higher than those in annual reports and other references but the differences are insignificant in determining policies toward women.

18. *Annual Report of the Police Department, City of New York, For the Year 1953*, 76-77; *Chicago Police Department. Annual Report. Year Ending December 31, 1953*, 54; *Official Magazine. Chicago Patrolmen's Association*, Dec.-Jan. 1956, 33; June-July

1956, 49; *Chicago Police Department. Annual Report. Year Ending December 31, 1955,* 71; *Year Ending December 31, 1956,* 71; Shpritzer, "A Case for the Promotion of Policewomen in the City of New York," 417. Indicative of the crazy-quilt pattern of upward mobility, Cleveland, whose 25 women were about 2 percent of the force, had sergeants, lieutenants, and one captain, all of whom earned their positions by civil service exam.

19. *Official Magazine. Chicago Patrolmen's Association,* Apr.-May 1956, 39; June-July 1956, cover, 3; *Chicago Police Department. Annual Report. Year Ending 1956,* 67. By 1959 Cleveland (*Police Annual Report, 1959),* 31, too, joined the cities that had succumbed to picturing female officers in firearms training when five, in street clothes and high heels, were photographed at the firing range.

20. Margaret Snow, "Women's Role in Crime Control," *The Police Yearbook 1956* (Proceedings of the 62nd Annual Conference of the IACP, Philadelphia, PA, Oct. 2-6, 1955), 71-79; Shpritzer, "A Case for the Promotion of Policewomen in the City of New York," 417; Higgins, "Women in Law Enforcement," 22.

21. *Annual Report of the Police Department, City of New York, For the Year 1950,* 35, 26, 83; *For the Year 1951,* 7; Shpritzer, "A Case for the Promotion of Policewomen in the City of New York," 416, 417.

22. "From Police Officer to Professor (via Deputy Commissioner)," *Spring 3100,* Nov.-Dec. 1989, 32; *Annual Report of the Police Department, City of New York, For the Year 1953,* 76-77; *For the Year 1952,* 76, 79; S.E. Rink, " 'Arresting Females': The Policewoman's Story," *Law and Order,* Nov. 1953, 7.

23. Lucy Acerra, "From Matron to Commanding Officer: Women's Changing Role in Law Enforcement," in *Law Enforcement Bible,* ed. Robert A. Scanlan (South Hackensack, NJ: Stoeger Publishing, 1978), 133.

24. *Annual Report of the Police Department, City of New York, For the Year 1954,* 16.

25. Higgins, "Women in Law Enforcement: A Special Survey on Policewomen Throughout the United States," 24, notes that Chicago, Philadelphia, Cleveland, Pittsburgh, Minneapolis, New Haven, and Washington, D.C., had female lieutenants. Women captains worked in Cleveland, Pittsburgh, Washington, D.C., Seattle, Portland, and Tacoma. Women in Denver could take the sergeant exam for salary advancement only, not for rank.

26. Shpritzer, "A Case for the Promotion of Policewomen in the City of New York," 418.

27. *Shpritzer v Lang,* 32 Misc. 2d 693, 1961, modified and affirmed, 234 NYS 2d 285, 1962, 286-287, 290.

28. Lois Decker O'Neill, ed., *The Women's Book of World Records and Achievements* (Garden City, NY: Anchor Press/Doubleday, 1979), 373; Leonard Buder, "Precinct's Female Commander Promoted," *The New York Times,* June 30, 1979, 22:2-4. Renzullo, who held bachelors and masters degrees, was a precinct commander when promoted. She had been in the NYCPD for almost 20 years, 9 as a captain.

29. *Annual Report of the Police Department, City of New York, For the Year 1962,* 20; *For the Year 1963,* 15; *For the Year 1966,* 3, 4, 15; Acerra, "From Matron to Commanding Officer: Women's Changing Role in Law Enforcement," 134; Bruce Smith, *The New York Police Survey: A Report for the Mayor's Committee on Management Survey* (New York: Institute of Public Administration, 1952), 53-54.

30. *Annual Report of the Police Department, City of New York, For the Year 1967,* 6.

Chapter 8

Women Become Crimefighters, 1968–The Present

In September 1968, Indianapolis policewomen Betty Blankenship and Elizabeth Coffal donned uniforms, strapped gunbelts to their waists, and got into their marked police car to answer general calls for service. Riding together as "Car 47," they forever changed the role of women in policing, causing them to leave behind their history as police social workers to assume the role of crimefighters along with their male colleagues

Blankenship and Coffal had sought patrol assignments almost from the day they joined the police department. As recruits they had suggested the idea to Sgt. Winston Churchill, an academy instructor. When Churchill became chief in 1968, the women reminded him that he had said that if he were ever in charge he would permit women to do patrol work. True to his word, Churchill, after providing the women with one day's notice and no extra training, sent them out on patrol. Male dispatchers for some time continued to call on Car 47 only when no other units were available; women dispatchers, though, sent them on as many assignments as they could. Male officers worried they would spend more time protecting the women than answering their own calls. When the women arrested a man who had beaten a woman to death, they received acceptance by their male peers. After this "experiment," two more women were assigned to patrol in 1970, joined two years later by four additional female officers. In late 1971 and early 1972, a survey on the roles of women in policing found eight women working as patrol partners. Catherine Milton's study said of the women:

They ride into high-crime areas as easily as any man. Like most male officers, the[y] . . . call for assistance when they suspect trouble. . . . Their calls . . . are no higher than . . . male teams. The public seems to accept them. Female complainants often express relief that a policewoman instead of a policeman was sent to talk with them. Other women respect them.[1]

But change is a slow process. At the time of Milton's study, the 74 women in the department comprised 6.89 percent of the force, one of the highest in the nation. Yet even though 20 of the women had been hired after Car 47 took to the streets, the majority of the women were serving as secretaries; the next largest group were juvenile officers. Not one of the five female sergeants performed supervisory functions. By 1979, even Blankenship and Coffal were back in traditional roles; each was an administrative aide to a sector commander.[2]

Neither Blankenship nor Coffal sought patrol assignments with any idea of the affect it would ultimately have on policewomen around the United States. They were looking for personal fulfillment—"to be police officers, rather than secretaries." Their immediate goal beyond their own assignment to patrol was to see at least one additional female patrol team on the streets—a goal that was met and exceeded. Blankenship, promoted to Sergeant in December 1983 while in the communications branch, was supervising that unit in December 1994. Coffal, with whom she remains friendly "even though today we have little in common except the past and remembering how much fun we had," retired in 1989.[3] Today they fully realize their pioneer status, although it was not a role they neither sought nor anticipated.

Although the two women did not intend to revolutionize policing and despite what initially appeared to have been a return to the status quo, Car 47 was the most visible of a series of long-term changes that had occurred in some departments and were just around the corner in others. Changes affecting policewomen were only a part of the upheaval in U.S. law enforcement in the late 1960s and the 1970s. Policewomen, because they were isolated from patrol, were initially untouched by these controversies. But, as the 1970s ended, their new role as crimefighters and the changing nature of police work drew them into the larger picture, particularly after rising crime rates, urban riots, and anti-war violence led many political leaders—and a few police executives—to question the primacy of the role of police as crimefighters.

In 1967, the President's Commission on Law Enforcement and Administration of Justice (termed the Crime Commission) concluded that police ability to prevent, reduce, deter, or solve crime was limited. The commission's report, *The Challenge of Crime in a Free Society*, helped set in motion philosophical changes and task analyses that ultimately questioned whether uniform patrol actually deterred crime. Noting that "the heart of the police law enforcement effort is patrol" and noting also that in almost every city at least half the police officers performed duties in uniform on the street, the commission found that research had been unable to discover "the relationship between police patrol and deterrence."[4] Among its recommendations on many facets of policing, the largest number covered personnel issues, encouraging lateral entry, higher education for supervisors, and recruiting on college campuses and in ghetto areas.

In addition to a final report, the commission issued nine reports. The one on the police devoted more space to civilians than to policewomen. A mere five paragraphs of the 239-page report pertain to women. The task force observed that the role of policewomen was "essentially what it always has been." It concluded:

Policewomen can be an invaluable asset to modern law enforcement, and their present role should be broadened. Qualified women should be utilized in . . . planning and research, training, intelligence, inspection, public information, community relations, and as legal advisors. Women could also serve in . . . computer programming and laboratory analysis and communication. Their value should not be considered as limited to staff functions or police work with juveniles; women should also serve regularly in patrol, vice, and investigative divisions. Finally, as more and more well-qualified women enter the service, they could assume administrative responsibilities.[5]

Despite devoting three pages to educational standards, the task force did not mention the higher qualifications required of women in most cities. Nor was there mention of policewomen in the recommendations pertaining to police in the overall report.

The next year the Kerner Commission *Report of the National Advisory Commission on Civil Disorders*, found "aggressive patrol" counterproductive, determining that it created "tension and hostility." The commission urged police managers to "take vigorous action to improve law enforcement and to decrease the potential for disorder." This 11-person commission was highly critical of the police, calling them at least partially responsible for 23 disorders in 24 cities during the first nine months of 1967.[6] The commission totally ignored policewomen. The term *policeman* is used throughout; comments on recruitment pertain only to increasing the numbers and percentages of African-American officers, with a presumption that they would all be male.

Studies undertaken in the wake of these reports indicated that despite police reliance on patrol as the primary crime deterrence strategy, little of a police officer's time was spent fighting crime. Maintaining order and assisting the public were the most time-consuming functions of the police. These studies, many funded by the Police Foundation, a Ford Foundation-funded research group, ultimately played a part in women's demands for patrol assignments, for if patrol officers were not fighting crime, but were helping people and providing social intervention, there was no reason women could not provide the same police service as men. It is not coincidental that the Police Foundation provided support for later studies of women on patrol.

Forces outside policing were also causing departments to alter their traditional assignment patterns. In 1963 Congress passed the Equal Pay

Act, prohibiting unequal pay between the sexes for equal work. In 1969 President Richard M. Nixon issued Executive Order 11478, which decreed that the federal government could not use sex as a qualification for hiring. The effect was felt in federal policing by 1971, when both the Executive Protective Service and the Secret Service hired female agents. When, in July 1972, the FBI assigned two women to its academy for training as special agents, the handwriting was on the wall that municipal police departments would also have to assign women to training and tasks identical to those of men.

In 1972 Title VII of the 1964 Civil Rights Act, which prohibited discrimination on the basis of race, color, religion, sex, or national origin in such employment activities as recruitment, hiring, working conditions, promotion, and benefits by private employers of 25 or more people or whose business involved interstate commerce, was extended to public agencies—including police departments. In the same year, Congress passed the Revenue Sharing Act, which prohibited discriminatory use of revenue-sharing funds and allowed the Treasury Department to withhold funds from jurisdictions engaged in unlawful employment practices.

Yet another impetus to equal employment was the Law Enforcement Assistance Administration, a Justice Department agency created under the Omnibus Crime Control and Safe Streets Act of 1968. Forty percent of the funds for law enforcement dispensed by LEAA went to local governments. When the act was amended in 1973, the new Crime Control Act specified that grantees be prohibited from discriminating in employment practices. Departments that discriminated against women jeopardized federal grants that many used to upgrade training, equipment, and facilities.

Collectively these laws meant that police departments faced not only political pressure and lawsuits, but loss of funds if their hiring and promotion policies were deemed unlawful. This expansion of civil rights activity coalesced at a time when the women who had entered policing in the 1950s and 1960s were slowly moving up the ranks and changing the nature of women's participation in policing. When women went on uniform patrol in the late 1960s and early 1970s, it was not an isolated event. It was part of a continuum that led them out of a specialized, gender-based role into genderless, general assignment policing. By the time anti-discrimination laws had become commonplace, policewomen were already dismantling their traditional roles in policing.

Despite action by women to alter their status in policing, the early years of the 1960s gave few clues to the changes that would be set in motion before the decade ended. In the 1960s, battles for promotion and diversified assignment were led by policewomen themselves, rather than by outsiders lobbying on their behalf. The larger numbers of policewomen, their continuity of police service, the rising expectations of women in all fields, and the belief that this was a "pocketbook" rather than a philosophic issue, coalesced to create demands for advancement in traditional areas such as women's and juvenile bureaus (still viewed as "women's sphere"), and later, within other units where women were assigned. By the 1970s the women were aided by new allies—federal legislation and the courts.

A 1969 International Association of Chiefs of Police survey of 1,330 law enforcement agencies (a small sample of the approximately 18,000 police agencies in the nation) found that 34 percent employed women full time, a large increase over earlier years, even though women remained less than 2 percent of U.S. police personnel. By 1975 female police officers still constituted only 2.1 percent of sworn officers, but only three years later, they had increased to more than 9,000, constituting about 3 percent of all municipal, state, and federal law enforcement personnel. By 1980, when the women on patrol era had taken root, women had further increased their presence; approximately 11,200 officers represented 3.8 percent of the sworn officers in municipal departments.[7] Between 1960 and 1980 the number of municipal women police officers had more than doubled (just as it had from 1950 to 1960).

No one—not the International Association of Chiefs of Police, the International Association of Women Police or women officers themselves—predicted such increases, although in 1966 the IACP held its first and only workshop for policewomen, an event attended by approximately 30 people, the majority of whom were policewomen in various ranks.[8]

Yet, the IACP continued to show the same lack of interest in policewomen that it had historically displayed. Conference proceedings from 1961 to 1972 show that only one policewoman addressed the group. There was no comment about the assignment of Blankenship and Coffal to patrol in Indianapolis. Not surprising, it took a woman to notice the absence of women at IACP and other police gatherings. In 1972 Milton, a Police Foundation assistant director and author of its report *Women in Policing*, found that after four years of attending police conferences she had observed a total lack of women in responsible positions and that she had not seen even a single policewoman or met another professional woman involved in policing.

These thoughts occurred to Milton after the foundation's receipt of a 1971 proposal from Berkeley, California, Chief Bruce Baker to put women on patrol to achieve "a wider selection of . . . minority officers . . . since we have . . . difficulty in attracting qualified blacks. . . . With the changing nature of police work,. . . there is no reason why we shouldn't broaden the base of recruitment to include women."[9] The recruitment problem was a nationwide dilemma. In the 1960s and 1970s departments were unable to find qualified applicants to fill vacancies due to the poor image of the police, the low salaries, and the "deplorable working conditions" officers faced.[10]

While qualified men may have disdained policing for its relatively low wages, women, even those with education beyond that of their male colleagues, found the salaries higher than in other positions open to them. This resulted in police work's becoming highly desirable to African-American female high school graduates after the 1970s when education requirements for men and women were equalized. The number of African-American women increased substantially, and their percentage in practically all departments far exceeded the percentage of African-American men. Thus, by hiring women and men on an equal basis, departments were able to increase the numbers and percentages of African-American officers in their ranks. The hiring of men and women on an equal basis also opened policing to women whose social class and education levels were similar to those of their male colleagues. These women, who differed greatly from the upper-middle-class and middle-class women who preceded them, sought police positions for the same reasons men did, namely, salary, benefits, and job security.

IAWP leaders were no more able to predict these radical changes than was the IACP leadership. In many ways their views paralleled those of male chiefs, for most of the women who spoke for the IAWP never accepted crimefighting as a role to be filled equally by men and women. For them patrol assignments meant a loss of prestige associated with specialist positions. Uniform patrol was at the bottom of the organizational power structure. It was not something to covet, but was a step down on the career ladder. The IAWP continued to see itself as an educational and sororal association, rather than as an advocacy group for women in policing. Much of the momentum the IAWP generated in its early years was not sustained. Leadership changes, financial problems, and a small membership combined to place it on the fringes of activity by and on behalf of policewomen. In 1966 there were 133 paid members, a large increase over the 54 in 1964, but by 1968, the year women went on patrol, the number had fallen to under 110.

In the early patrol years, IAWP conference programs, similar to those of the IACP, continued to stress traditional areas concerning juveniles and women. It was not until 1972 that members deleted from the constitution the clause "[to encourage] the establishment of women's bureaus in police departments."[11] IAWP leadership was out of touch with the crimefighter ideology that had entered the consciousness of large numbers of women police. Throughout the 1960s and 1970s the IAWP was not in the forefront of policewomen's demands for equality, although by the 1980s the leadership had changed—and with it the group's focus—to encouraging women's full participation in policing.

As the 1970s began, officials in Indianapolis had placed women on patrol; officials in Washington, D.C., were hiring women for patrol; and officials in other cities were considering doing the same.   Additional women were demanding patrol assignments, although some specifically fought against the change, resigning or retiring rather than becoming uniform patrol officers.   Demands for total sexual equality in hiring, training, and assignment did not gain currency until later in the 1970s. Although the change appeared to take place overnight, this was far from the case. As in all the generational changes policewomen had made, the seeds had been planted at least one decade earlier.

By this time, most policewomen, regardless of department histories, were moving along similar paths even though New York City (which employed the largest number of policewomen in the United States) and other large cities lagged behind smaller cities, many of which entered the policewoman-as-crimefighter era prior to metropolitan departments. Indicative of change coming more rapidly to smaller departments than to large ones, in 1971 Indianapolis (6.89 percent) and Peoria, Illinois (4.31 percent) had the largest and third largest percentages of female officers among the seven departments surveyed by the Police Foundation.   The city with the second largest percentage of female officers was Miami (4.85).   Percentages in larger cities were Philadelphia (.88), New York (1.09), Dallas (1.63), and Washington, D.C. (2.11).[12]

A review of activities by and pertaining to women in a number of these departments illustrates the upheaval caused by the breaking down by younger women of the remaining gender stereotypes. Washington, D.C., which in 1957 had curtailed the independence of its woman's bureau by placing it under the youth aid division, in 1967 disbanded it totally. Although not intended as such, this set in motion changes that would make Washington, D.C., policewomen the first big-city women to enter patrol in sizable numbers.

As late as 1964, Washington, D.C., women did more social work than officers in other cities, although one area in which they were technically equal to men was promotion. The highest rank that could be attained via civil service was captain, first achieved by a woman in 1930. Theoretically, an unlimited number of female captains was possible, but there was never more than one. That women whose educations far exceeded their male colleagues were unable to achieve additional promotions was attributed to poor ratings by male supervisors "simply to prevent them from being promoted." Thus, while the department permitted women to compete for promotion and did promote a few to sergeant and lieutenant, the only captaincy open to women was director of the woman's bureau.

The President's Commission on Crime in the District of Columbia did not look favorably on the women's activities in 1966, noting that they were too involved in social welfare and that they possessed "special education, training and abilities which can be utilized to a greater extent in achieving police objectives."[13] Following this assessment, the bureau was disbanded and women began to work more closely with male juvenile officers, but far greater changes awaited them.

When Jerry V. Wilson became chief in July 1969, he announced the end of different entry requirements for male and female officers. Less than a year later, he issued guidelines for the interchangeable assignment of men and women. In December 1971, women received uniforms for the first time and were sent out on uniform patrol. To assist them in making the transition from social workers to crimefighters, Sgt. Earnestine Johnson, a 15-year veteran African-American officer, was named policewomen's co-ordinator. Her job was not an easy one; by 1971 all but 8 of the 25 women who had been in the bureau in 1967 had resigned rather than accept their new role.[14]

The resignations in Washington and other cities that placed women on patrol were indicative of the discord among policewomen, some of whom eagerly sought sexual equality and some of whom were content to remain in roles based on earlier definitions of women's sphere. Although age was often a factor in the conflicting views, with younger women seeking crimefighter roles and older women seeking to remain in their traditional role, this was not universal.

In 1967 when the chief of the Miami Police Department proposed as-signing women to uniform patrol, half of the 14 officers opposed the plan and questioned its legality. Chief Bernard L. Garmire cited civil service rules to support his view that female officers were not limited to plainclothes assignments. His position was upheld; by 1972 all 37 women except 2 were assigned to work identical to that of male officers. Twenty women, including 10 recruits, patrolled with either male or female partners. The sole female patrol sergeant, a ten-year veteran who had made numerous arrests, had been awarded a "Policeman of the Month" citation, and was attending law school, supervised eight male officers.[15]

Washington, D.C., and Miami are among the few departments whose women have been studied over time by outside assessors. When Cynthia G. Sulton and Roi D. Townsey in 1981 completed another Police Founda-tion report, *A Progress Report on Women in Policing*, of their case studies, only Washington, D.C., and Miami had been studied by Milton.

Reviewing the status of women in Miami (with changes occurring as a result of law suits and subsequent consent decrees between 1973 and 1977), Sulton and Townsey found a steady increase in both the numbers and percentages of female officers. In 1967, 14 policewomen comprised 2.9 percent of the department; in 1974, 34 women, 4.2 percent; and in 1979, 49 women made up 7.2 percent of the force. Much of the upsurge between 1974 and 1976 was attributed to a "marked increase" in minority women (both African-American and Hispanic). By 1976 the number and percent-age of minority women officers had more than doubled from 1974. By 1979, after seven years of equal assignment with male officers, Miami women (including one female sergeant) reflected the changing demographics of the department; 69.3 percent of them were white, 24.5 percent were African-American, and 6.1 percent were Hispanic. By May 1980 there were 150 women, representing 10 percent of the force.[16]

Events in Washington, D.C., despite resignations by most of the women serving before 1971, followed a similar pattern, although 100 women were hired before the city could assign women identically to male officers. Uniforms—"conservative blue suits" designed specifically for the women—arrived in December 1971. By then the number of women had increased to 210.[17]

At the time they decided to assign women to patrol, officials in Washington, D.C., were among those of many cities who spent an inordinate amount of time designing uniforms for their women. Department officials seemed to have forgotten that they had issued uniforms to policewomen (though rarely worn), crossing guards, and meter maids. The Delta Uniform Division of the Highway Outfitting Company had begun producing women's uniforms as early as 1946. By the late 1950s the industry had grown sufficiently for *Law and Order* to spotlight the firm and describe the problems facing women wearing a uniform adapted from a man's pattern without feeling "fat and frumpy" while appearing tidy and official. Highway Outfitting and Best Uniforms were soon advertising women's uniforms on a regular basis.[18]

Despite this, in 1974 the IACP issued a memorandum on women's uniforms. It covered the issue literally from head to toe, commenting on hats, hair, coats, blouses, ties, pants, skirts, pocketbooks, and shoes. Hosiery and undergarments were the only items not discussed. Nowhere was there a recommendation that women's uniforms be identical to men's garments, which is what ultimately occurred by the 1980s. The military-style uniform issued to women up to that time was dismissed as "inadequate [to] fulfill the needs of today's policewoman, particularly one on patrol," despite the fact that male uniforms drew heavily on military design.[19]

Prior to settling on uniforms identical to those of male officers, city officials sent women on patrol in outfits similar to those worn by airline stewardesses or trade show models. These early "cute" female uniforms, featuring short skirts, high-heeled shoes, and hats that needed to be pinned to the wearer's hair, may have been an attempt to help the women retain, at least in departments' members' eyes, some femininity. Valerie Steele, a clothing historian who has studied the symbolism of the police uniform, believes that women's first patrol uniforms "mixed symbols of authority (like the badge and gun) with those of femininity and gentility (like the pocketbook, high heels, and white gloves)." She concluded that the early "feminized uniforms indicated ambivalence about the woman's role as an authority figure, especially since the standard police uniform has always carried quasi-military associations."[20] A more realistic, but less emotion-ally charged issue rarely addressed was inadequate toilet and locker facilities for women. The 1980s and 1990s would witness considerable litigation over these matters.

The Washington, D.C., police department achieved an unwanted first on September 20, 1974, when Gail Cobb, patrolling on foot, received a call to assist in searching for two bank robbers who fled their car after an exchange of shots with police. Cobb, spotting a man dashing into an underground garage, followed him. Moments later, she was shot in the chest, her weapon never having been unholstered. Within an hour she was pronounced dead; the first United States policewoman to die of gunshot wounds.[21]

The 24-year-old Cobb, who had joined the department less than a year earlier, had been on patrol for five months at the time of her death. More than two thousand police officers (many of them women) from around the nation attended her funeral. Although police officials wondered if the shooting would result in a public outcry against placing women on patrol, nothing of the sort happened. It appeared that the police and the public viewed the shooting as an incident that could have happened to any officer. Male officers "felt that women had finally paid their dues" and agreed that if Cobb had erred in confronting the suspect, it was a rookie's, rather than a woman's, mistake.[22]

The women on patrol in Washington, D.C., became the first of many to be studied by government agencies and criminal justice theoreticians. Shortly after Wilson announced that he would hire women specifically to place them on patrol, the Police Foundation agreed to sponsor an evalua-tion of their performance. Eighty-six newly hired women were matched with an equal number of men hired at the same time. They were similar in education (average of 12.8 years for women, 12.9 for men), their civil service test scores were similar, they had held the same number of previ-ous jobs, and their pre-employment interview ratings had been similar. Sixty-eight percent of the women were African-American; as were 42 percent of the men. Fifty-four percent were mothers; 31 percent were fathers.

The study sought to answer three questions: Is it appropriate, from a performance viewpoint, to hire women for patrol assignments on the same basis as men? What advantages or disadvantages arise from hiring women on an equal basis for patrol work? What effect would the use of a substantial number of policewomen have on police operations? Findings were released in a multi-volume assessment that described the study in greater detail than the subject studied.

Policewomen on Patrol: Final Report answered each question separately. Question one: "The men and women . . . performed patrol work in a generally similar manner. They responded to similar types of calls . . .

encountered similar proportions of citizens who were dangerous, angry, upset, drunk or violent. . . . There were no reported incidents which cast serious doubt on the ability of women to perform patrol work satisfactorily." Women made fewer arrests and issued fewer traffic citations.

Question two: Hiring women "enlarges the supply of personnel resources, may reduce the cost of recruiting and may assure that police personnel will be more representative of both the racial and sexual composition of the city," but "attitudes of male officers and . . . supervisors impose a burden on a police management which wants to treat men and women equally." Men's tendency to overprotect women could make it difficult to weed out incompetent women. Women were effective in avoiding violence by defusing potentially violent situations, were less likely to engage in serious unbecoming conduct, but were more likely to be assigned to light duty as a result of injuries.

Question three: "A department with a substantial number of policewomen may be less aggressive. . . . Women may stimulate increased attention to ways of avoiding violence and cooling violent situations without the resort to the use of force."

The report concluded:

Many police departments will assign women to patrol only because of legal requirements. However, the introduction of women will create an incentive . . . to examine many management practices which are less acceptable now that they must be applied to men and women alike. This may result in the development of improved selection criteria, performance standards, and supervision for all officers.[23]

Women on patrol were also studied in the suburban St. Louis County, Missouri, Police Department. There, psychologist Louis J. Sherman reviewed the performance of 16 women and men, each assigned to one-person motor patrol. He found, as the foundation had, that women's patrol style was less aggressive, resulting in fewer arrests and less preventive activity such as car and pedestrian stops. Women, he said, were better at handling service calls and domestic quarrels. He felt the question of performance was primarily political and represented a diversion from the more important question of what kind of person, regardless of sex, made a good police officer.[24]

As Sherman suggested, most of the studies were a diversionary tactic, but each city that assigned women to patrol wanted its own. Agencies dispensing funds complied. Women, invisible first as matrons and then as policewomen for almost a century, now became the topic of numerous studies—each one similar to those before it with little except the number of women and the geography changing.[25]

After the evaluation in Washington, D.C., the next large-city study was in New York City. In 1972 there were about 350 women, including 64 detectives, 10 sergeants, 3 lieutenants, and 1 deputy inspector (Gertrude Schimmel). Despite this large number of women, they comprised fewer than 1 percent of the force; more than a third were performing clerical or matron duties. Only one woman was assigned as a patrol supervisor, and she worked in an area that was part of a "Model Precinct" program. It was not her first "model" assignment—she had previously been a coat and dress model.

Just as in Washington, D.C., and Miami, many women, particularly the older ones, did not favor change. Some of their indecision is described by Alice Fleming in *New on the Beat: Women Power in the Police Force*, which reports that planning for women on patrol had begun with a questionnaire to 180 women, asking who would be willing to participate in an experiment that might include patrol. Only 30 expressed interest. When it became apparent that patrol was the experiment's "most essential ingredient," only 15 continued to indicate a willingness to be considered. On June 26, 1972, the first New York women went on patrol.[26]

Although Fleming does not enumerate reasons for the women's lack of interest in patrol assignments, the causes were similar to those in Washington, D.C., and Miami. Having "grown accustomed to the regular hours in office work or the predictable routine of matron duty," they did not want their lives disrupted. In others "the spark that might once have attracted them to street work or responsible administrative positions" had died. A lieutenant went on sick leave rather than accept a supervisory position; "considerable friction" and "a marked difference" in motivation and goals existed between women content with their roles and those seeking exposure to all facets of police work, including patrol.[27]

Social class distinctions among the women may also have played a part; for while the older women were of primarily middle-class backgrounds; the younger women were more likely to be of working-class origins. As in other cities, these younger women, who were more comfortable with unisex roles and who viewed patrol assignments as crucial to career advancement, were willing—sometimes even eager—to forsake traditional duties for an opportunity to patrol on an equal basis with male officers.

A study of 165 women and 165 men on patrol lasted from October 1973 to March 1974. Although no effort was made to match those studied, the results indicated no statistical differences in arrests, summonses, responses to calls, sick time, or performance evaluations. A larger study was planned for 1974 and 1975, but layoffs due to the city's fiscal crisis resulted in more than half the female officers losing their jobs due to requirements that the last hired be the first fired. Many of those laid off were women who had taken the December 15, 1973, test—the first administered to both men and women for the new title of police officer, which replaced the previous titles of patrolman and policewoman. Only 41 female and 41 male officers, matched by patrol experience and type of precinct, could be observed.

After 3,625 hours of patrol and 2,400 police-civilian encounters, researchers determined that women were generally as effective as men and that their patrol style was virtually identical to male officers, although women were more restrained in using force and displaying their weapons.[28]

But not all cities were convinced of women's ability to function as crimefighters. Philadelphia, the last large city to employ policewomen, was also the last to place them on patrol. The decade began benignly; Lt. Alice E. Clifford, director of women and one of few female IACP members, was honored in 1960 by the City Council for 15 years of "exemplary service." Pictured in uniform with local IACP members, including her commissioner, Clifford, who had lectured at FBI and other police schools, was recognized as a trainer and for her work "involving juveniles, routine investigations, undercover work, and the general duties of a policewoman." Accepting her award, she noted that the city's 60 women were "engaged in every phase of law enforcement," stressing they were not "baby sitters, social workers, [or] matrons."[29]

By 1967 relations between the department and its women had soured. A challenge to the regulation requiring both an oral and a written exam for women who sought promotion to sergeant, while men required only a written exam, was unsuccessful. The court ruled that since men and women did not compete against one another and since their duties were different, it was not a denial of equal protection under the Fourteenth Amendment to the U.S. Constitution for the tests to be different. Although the suit did not question the assignment of male and female sergeants to different work, the court addressed the issue in a way that did not bode well for women:

Many of the tasks performed by the police force are of such a nature, physiologically speaking, that they cannot and should not be assigned to women; using firearms, patrolling the highways, maintaining road-blocks, conducting raids, ferreting out dangerous criminals, quelling gang warfare and riots are just a few examples.[30]

In 1971 Philadelphia officials had taken the fewest steps of any surveyed city to change the role of its policewomen, who were 1 percent of the 7,500-member force. Women trained apart from men and took different courses, although the entire teaching staff was male. Women's promotion exams emphasized youth work and social problems; the quota for female supervisors was four sergeants and two lieutenants.

Most women were assigned to the juvenile aid division; one worked in community relations and two were in the civil disobedience unit, which had included women since its 1960 creation. In 1968 one of them, after passing the exam for policewoman/sergeant, was permitted to remain, supervising male officers. However, upon her promotion to lieutenant, she was returned to juvenile work. Two women were assigned as plainclothes decoys, and the only women on uniform patrol were two in the downtown area.

Although Commissioner Joseph O'Neill submitted a 1973 budget that provided for the first woman captain in department history, as well as an additional lieutenant, 3 new sergeants, and 39 new policewomen, he was vocal in his belief in male superiority. He had no desire to use women innovatively, and he believed that they should remain in juvenile aid, detailed temporarily to other units as needed. His views were an echo of O.W. Wilson, whose opinions continued to carry weight through the various editions of *Police Administration*, the primary police administration text of the era.

The observation that O'Neill "seemed intent on maintaining the status quo as far as women were concerned" proved prophetic.[31] In 1974 Police-woman Penelope Brace filed a discrimination suit. She sought promotion to the rank of detective, which no women held. The department promoted her after being ordered to do so by a federal court. O'Neill told the court that women were unfit to become regular police officers because "God in His wisdom made them different."[32]

In 1976 the city entered into a consent decree ending two lawsuits. The decree, which pledged that 20 percent of new officers would be women, was not fulfilled. The city placed 100 women on patrol so that a study of their effectiveness could be undertaken. The study's purpose was actually to defend the department against litigation by the women; it was the only one during the decade that found that women were not competent patrol officers, concluding they did not perform as "safely or as efficiently" as men.[33]

In March 1979, the Justice Department, which had intervened on behalf of the women, did not accept this conclusion and requested that the judge hearing the case order the department to hire one woman for each man until 40 percent of the department was female, equal to the percentage of women in the population. Six months later, the judge, noting that women comprised 1.6 percent of the 7,936-member force, ruled that 25 percent of all officers hired had to be women. He also blocked the hiring of 225 recruits, all men despite the previous decree. Little changed until 1980, when a new mayor replaced O'Neill. The new commissioner permitted women, who numbered 225, to leave the juvenile aid division. Philadel-phia officials also agreed to pay damages to 96 women whose careers were held back or who had been denied positions; to fill 30 percent of the next 2,670 positions with women, and to promote women to 16 detective and 17 sergeant positions. On December 22, 1980, the department joined others that had previously appointed female commanders, placing 50-year-old Capt. Dorothy Cousins, a 25-year-veteran, in charge of a 200-officer pre-cinct.[34]

Despite the reluctance of officials in Philadelphia and other cities,[35] in the 20 years from 1968 to 1988 women had been transformed from social workers within the police world to crimefighters. The transition began in 1968, when Betty Blankenship and Elizabeth Coffal convinced their chief to put them on uniform patrol. But this historic event was not without a long history. Legislative requirements to treat men and women equally invigorated the agitation and changed its direction—no longer were women seeking merely greater opportunity; now they sought equality with their male peers.

In 1971, three years after Blankenship and Coffal went on patrol in Indianapolis, there were fewer than a dozen women officers on routine patrol. In 1974 the IACP found that over 1,000 women were patrolling city streets. Recognizing this growing role of women on patrol, the IACP in 1976 scheduled a workshop panel on the topic.[36] On October 31, 1976, the largest number of women in any of the major cities were 353 in Detroit and 319 in Washington, D.C. The largest number in a Southern city was 121 in Atlanta. In contrast, cities that had historically been inhospitable to women continued to have lower numbers: the 179 women in Philadelphia were the result of court order; a year earlier there had been only 73; Cleveland had only 45, and Boston, 26.[37]

The national figures told a story that superseded the individual battles being fought by women in large and small cities. When the 1960 census reported 5,617 policewomen, comprising 2.3 percent of all public employed officers, this represented a doubling of the 1950 figures and was the largest increase (both numerically and percentage) since the creation of the concept and title policewoman. By 1980, the number of policewomen (a title that in many jurisdictions was replaced with the unisex rank of police officer) had again doubled, although, due to increased hiring by many police agencies, the percentage growth was nowhere near as impressive.

The 1980s saw a continuation of the increases. By 1981 women comprised 5.5 percent of sworn personnel. By 1982 women in five of the ten largest departments (in order of department size) had increased to 1,405 (5.7 percent) in New York City, 457 (5.9 percent) in Philadelphia, 477 (11.3 percent) in Detroit, 323 (8.8 percent) in Washington, DC and 62 (3.7 percent) in Boston.)[38]

Many issues remained to be litigated in the 1980s and 1990s. The hostilities of male police executives and rank-and-file officers continued to frustrate many women police officers. But despite these obstacles, change, once initiated, could not be reversed. Although the roles of policewomen had remained virtually the same from 1910 until after World War II, a changing society and a changing type of policewoman resulted in women officers' having the opportunity to participate in a greater range of police activity in the postwar years. These assignments resulted in an expanding definition of women's sphere at the same time that the concept was losing its importance in determining women's roles in society generally. Even by clinging to these somewhat outmoded views of women, policewomen were able to expand their horizons. For instance, in the initial fight to take promotion exams they did not need to address the issue of competing with men in the patrol function; their housekeeping role had been so expanded that there were enough bureaus in which they could achieve rank without challenging the patrol proscription.

Uniform patrol became a viable assignment for women not only because legislation compelled departments to create gender-neutral workplaces, but also because of a shortage of qualified male candidates at a time when police employment opportunities were expanding; demands, particularly in urban areas, to increase the numbers and percentages of minorities in policing; the questioning of the patrol function and how much of it was fighting crime or providing service, and, of course, younger women's perception that their "sphere" was anything they defined it to be.

Although many of these crosscurrents were felt prior to 1968, when Indianapolis put Car 47 on its streets, the changes that occurred subsequent to that represent nothing short of a revolution in women's transition from social workers within the police environment to full-fledged crimefighters and equal participants with men as new roles emerge for police in the coming years.

NOTES

1. Catherine Milton, *Women in Policing* (Washington, DC: Police Foundation, 1972), 62, Lois Decker O'Neill, ed., *The Women's Book of World Records and Achievements* (Garden City, NY: Anchor Press/Doubleday, 1979), 373. Although the first two women worked as a team, many departments refused to allow this, ordering that patrol units be comprised of either two males or a male and a female. Officials in Des Moines, Iowa, did not permit its 24 female officers to choose a woman as a partner until 1988, when female officers were 7 percent of the 331-member force. See "Update: Order Dropped That Prohibits Female Patrol Teams," *Iowa Association of Women Police Newsletter*, Apr. 1988, 3.

2. Milton, *Women in Policing*, 65-66. Eleven years after Car 47 patrolled the streets, the city signed a consent decree requiring it to hire women for at least 20 percent of police positions. See Peter Horne, *Women in Law Enforcement* 2d ed. (Springfield, IL: Charles C Thomas, 1980), 40.

3. Betty Blankenship, interview with author, Nov. 23, 1994.

4. President's Commission on Law Enforcement and Administration of Justice, *The Challenge of Crime in a Free Society* (Washington, DC: Government Printing Office, 1967), 1, 95, 96.

5. President's Commission on Law Enforcement and Administration of Justice, *Task Force Report: The Police* (Washington, DC: Government Printing Office, 1967), 125.

6. National Advisory Commission on Civil Disorders, *The Report of the National*

Advisory Commission on Civil Disorders (New York: Bantam Books, 1968) 17, 11.

7. Cited in Clarice Feinman, *Women in the Criminal Justice System*, 3d ed. (Westport, CT: Praeger Publishers, 1994), 103. The number of agencies responsible "for enforcing laws on the federal, state, and local levels" is from the President's Commission on Law Enforcement and Administration of Justice, *Task Force Report: The Police*, 7. See also *Sourcebook of Criminal Justice Statistics—1977* (Washington, DC: Government Printing Office, 1978), 113; Cynthia G. Sulton and Roi D. Townsey, *A Progress Report on Women in Policing* (Washington, DC: Police Foundation, 1981), 12; *Sourcebook of Criminal Justice Statistics—1982* (Washington, DC: Government Printing Office, 1983), 42-43.

8. Nelson Watson and Robert N. Walker, eds. *IACP Proceedings of Workshop for Policewomen. Indiana University 1966* (Paramus, NJ: National Council on Crime and Delinquency, 1966), i, iii; 144-145.

9. Milton, *Women in Policing*, 4.

10. President's Commission on Law Enforcement and Admininstration of Justice, *Task Force Report: The Police*, 133-136.

11. IAWP, miscellaneous collected material; IAWP, *Official Program*, 7th Annual Training Conference, Madison, WI, Oct. 26-29, 1969; *Official Program*, 8th Annual Training Conference, Sault Ste. Marie, ON, Canada, Oct. 11-17, 1970; *Official Program*, 9th Annual Training Conference, Kansas City, MO, Oct. 24-27, 1971. After another constitutional change in 1976, male police personnel, who had been limited to associate membership, were permitted to join as active, voting members.

12. Milton, *Women in Policing*, 79.

13. Quoted in Ibid., 91.

14. Ibid., 90-91.

15. Ibid., 67, 68; Sulton and Townsey, *A Progress Report on Women in Policing*, 67; Horne,*Women in Law Enforcement*, 41.

16. Sulton and Townsey, *A Progress Report on Women in Policing*, 69, 70; Jane Gross, "A Police Officer in Riot- Scarred Miami Who Loves Her Job," *The New York Times*, May 23, 1980, 18:1-4.

17. Michael Kiernan and Judith Cusick, "Women on Patrol: The Nation's Capital Gives Them High Marks," *Police Magazine*, Summer 1977, 48.

18. Dorothy Fagerstrom, "Designed For the Women in Blue." *Law and Order*, Aug. 1958, 60. For examples of advertisements, see *Law and Order*, Oct. 1957, 17 and Mar. 1958, 57.

19. "IACP Memorandum on Uniforms," issued April 9, 1974. Reprinted in *A Symposium About Women in Policing*, Draft Manual of Symposium, May 28-30, 1974 (Washington, DC: Police Foundation, 1974), 56-58.

20. Valerie Steele, "Dressing for Work," in *Men and Women: Dressing the Part*, eds. Claudia Brush Kidwell and Valerie Steele (Washington, DC: Smithsonian Institution Press, 1989), 71.

21. Linda Charlton, "Capital Policewoman Is Slain on Duty," *The New York Times*, Sept. 21, 1974, 60:2-5; Kiernan and Cusick, Women on Patrol," 50. Although Charlton (quoting FBI files maintained since 1960), Kiernan and Cusick, and others termed Cobb the first U.S. policewoman killed in the line of duty, Ronald C. Van Raalte, president of the Law Enforcement Memorial Association, who is compiling a record of all law enforcement officers to die in the line of duty states that while Cobb may have been the first woman shot dead, she is not the first to

have died in the line of duty. According to his research, the first known death of a woman law enforcement officer was before 1900, when a female deputy sheriff was struck on the head with an iron bar by an escaping male prisoner. Similar to Cobb, she died the same day as the attack.

22. Shawn G. Kennedy, "Slain Policewoman Honored in Capital by 2,000 Officers," *The New York Times*, Sept. 25, 1974, 75:3-6; Kiernan and Cusick, "Women on Patrol," 50; "Slain Policewman Seen Aid to Hiring of Female Officers," *The New York Times*, Dec. 15, 1974, 83:5.

23. Peter B. Block and Deborah Anderson, *Policewomen on Patrol: Final Report* (Washington, DC: Police Foundation, 1974)), 1-4; 63.

24. Lewis J. Sherman, "An Evaluation of Policewomen on Patrol in a Suburban Police Department," *Journal of Police Science and Administration*, Dec. 1975, 434-448.

25. *Topical Bibliography—Policewomen* (Washington, DC: National Institute of Justice/National Criminal Justice Reference Service, n.d.) lists 119 studies, papers, dissertations, and articles between 1969 and 1981, with most after 1974. Sulton and Townsey, *A Progress Report on Women in Policing*, 13, found that eight "major evaluations of the patrol performance of women officers" were completed after 1973. They were Pennsylvania State Police (1973); Washington, D.C. (1974); St. Louis County, MO (1975); California Highway Patrol (1976); New York City (1977); Denver (1977); Newton, MA (1977); and Philadelphia (1978).

26. Alice Fleming, *New on the Beat: Women Power in the Police Force* (New York: Coward, McCann & Geoghegan, 1975), 205-206.

27. Milton, *Women in Policing*, 73, 74.

28. Anthony V. Bouza, "Women in Policing," *FBI Law Enforcement Bulletin*, Sept. 1975, 4, quoted in Edith Linn and Barbara Raffel Price, "The Evolving Role of Women in American Policing," in *The Ambivalent Force: Perspectives on the Police*, 3d ed. eds. Abraham S. Blumberg and Elaine Niederhoffer (New York: Holt, Rinehart & Winston, 1985), 74 (for 1973-1974 study). Lucy Acerra, "From Matron to Commanding Officer: Women's Changing Role in Law Enforcement," in *Law Enforcement Bible*, ed. Robert A. Scanlon (South Hackensack, NJ: Stoeger Publishing, 1978), 135, 137 and Sulton and Townsey, *A Progress Report on Women in Policing*, 14 (for 1974-1975 study).

29. Thomas J. Gibbons, "Policewoman Awards," *The Police Chief*, Apr. 1960, 35.

30. *Wells v Civil Service Commission* (423 Pa. 608, 225 A. 2nd 554), cited in Milton, *Women in Policing*, 54.

31. Milton, *Women in Policing*, 82-84, 88-90.

32. "U.S. Asks Quota on Women for Philadelphia Police," *The New York Times*, Mar. 28, 1979, A18:5; Horne, *Women in Law Enforcement*, 104; "Police Force in Philadelphia Gets First Female District Commander," *The New York Times*, Dec. 24, 1980, 10:5-6.

33. "Philadelphia Police Ordered To Give Women Twenty-Five Percent of Jobs," *The New York Times*, Sept. 6, 1979, 16:5; *The Study of Police Women Competency in the Performance of Sector Police Work in the City of Philadelphia* (State College, PA, 1978), quoted in Horne, *Women in Law Enforcement*, 104.

34. "U.S. Asks Quota on Women For Philadelphia Police," A18:5; "Philadelphia Police Ordered To Give Women Twenty-Five Percent of Jobs," 16:5; "Police Force in Philadelphia Gets First Female District Commander," 10:5-6.

35. Kiernan and Cusick, "Women on Patrol," 53, reported Cleveland had "more

than a dozen suits . . . from the refusal of mandatory maternity leave to the right to wear pants on the job." Sulton and Townsey, *A Progress Report on Women in Policing*, 17-21, mention: *Smith v City of East Cleveland* (363 F. Supp. 1131, 1973), veteran's preference; *Officers for Justice v Civil Service Commission, City of San Francisco* (395 F. Supp. 378, N.D. Cal. 1975), height and weight; and *Blake v City of Los Angeles* (15 FEP 76, D. Cal. 1977), selection criteria. For legal issues and LEAA money impacting police departments, see Margaret J. Gates, "Women in Policing—A Legal Analysis," *A Symposium About Women in Policing*, 95-132.

36. Kiernan and Cusick, "Women on Patrol," 45-46; "Women Police: The Patrol Function," *The Police Yearbook 1977* (Proceedings of the 83rd Annual Conference of the IACP, Miami Beach, FL, Sept. 25-30, 1976), 113-120.

37. Susan Ehrlich Martin, *Breaking and Entering: Policewomen on Patrol* (Berkeley: University of California Press, 1980), 28-29.

38. Edith Linn and Barbara Raffel Price, "The Evolving Role of Women in American Policing," in *The Ambivalent Force*, eds. Blumberg and Niederhoffer, 77.

Bibliography

BOOKS

Allen, Mary S. *The Pioneer Policewoman*. 1925; reprint, Foundations of Criminal
    Justice. New York: AMS Press, 1973.

Anderson, Karen. *Wartime Women: Sex Roles, Family Relation and the Status of
    Women in World War II*. Contributions in Women's Studies, No. 20.
    Westport, CT: Greenwood Press, 1981.

Banner, Lois W. *Women in Modern America: A Brief History*. New York: Harcourt
    Brace Jovanovich, 1974.

Berman, Jay S. *Police Administration and Progressive Reform: Theodore Roosevelt as
    Police Commissioner of New York*. Contributions in Criminology and Penol-
    ogy, No. 19. Westport, CT: Greenwood Press, 1987.

Blair, Karen J. *The Clubwoman as Feminist: True Womanhood Redefined, 1868-1914*.
    New York: Holmes & Meier, 1980

Block, Peter B. and Deborah Anderson. *Policewomen on Patrol: Final Report*. Wash-
    ington, DC: Police Foundation, 1974.

Blocker Jr., Jack S. *American Temperance Movements: Cycles of Reform*. Boston:
    Twayne Publishers, 1989.

Bopp, William J. *"O.W.": O.W. Wilson and the Search for a Police Profession*. National
    University Publications. Port Washington, NY: Kennikat Press, 1977.

Bordin, Ruth. *Woman and Temperance: The Quest for Power and Liberty, 1873-1900*.
    1981; reprint, New Brunswick, NJ: Rutgers University Press, 1990.

Breckinridge, Sophonisba P. *Women in the Twentieth Century: A Study of Their
    Political, Social and Economic Activities*. New York: McGraw-Hill, 1933.

Broome, Jr., Homer F. *LAPD's Black History 1886-1976*. Norwalk, CA: Stockton
    Trade Press, 1977.

Carte, Gene E. and Elaine H. Carte. *Police Reform in the United States: The Era of
    August Vollmer, 1905-1932*. Berkeley: University of California Press, 1975.

Chafe, William H. *The American Woman: Her Changing Social, Economic, and Political
    Roles, 1920-1970*. New York: Oxford University Press, 1972.

Chambers, Clarke A. *Seedtime of Reform: American Social Service and Social Action
    1918-1933*. Minneapolis: University of Minnesota Press, 1963.

Connelly, Mark T. *The Response to Prostitution in the Progressive Era*. Chapel Hill:

University of North Carolina Press, 1980.

Cott, Nancy F. *The Grounding of Modern Feminism*. New Haven, CT: Yale University Press, 1987.

Deakin, Thomas J. *Police Professionalism: The Renaissance of American Law Enforcement*. Springfield, IL: Charles C Thomas, 1988.

Epstein, Barbara L. *The Politics of Domesticity: Women, Evangelism and Temperance in Nineteenth-Century America*. Middletown, CT: Wesleyan University Press, 1981.

Ewing, Elizabeth. *Women in Uniform: Through the Centuries*. Totowa, NJ: Rowman & Littfield, 1975.

Feinman, Clarice. *Women In the Criminal Justice System*. 3d ed. Westport, CT: Praeger Publishers, 1994.

Fleming, Alice. *New on the Beat: Women Power in the Police Force*. New York: Coward, McCann & Geoghegan, 1975.

Fogelson, Robert M. *Big-City Police*. An Urban Institute Study. Cambridge, MA: Harvard University Press, 1977.

Fosdick, Raymond B. *American Police Systems*. 1920; Patterson Smith Reprint in Criminology, Law Enforcement, and Social Problems, No. 53. Montclair, NJ: Patterson Smith, 1969.

Frankfort, Roberta. *Collegiate Women: Domesticity and Career in Turn-of-the-Century America*. New York: New York University Press, 1977.

Freedman, Estelle B. *Their Sisters' Keepers: Women Prison Reform in America, 1830-1930*. Ann Arbor: University of Michigan Press, 1981.

Ginzberg, Lori D. *Women and the World of Benevolence: Morality, Politics, and Class in the Nineteenth-Century United States*. New Haven, CT: Yale University Press, 1990.

Hamilton, Mary E. *The Policewoman: Her Service and Ideals*. 1924; reprint, Police in America Series. New York: Arno Press, 1971.

Harrison, Cynthia. *On Account of Sex: The Politics of Women's Issues, 1945-1968*. Berkeley: University of California Press, 1988.

Hartmann, Susan M. *The Home Front and Beyond: American Women in the 1940s*. American Women in the Twentieth Century Series. Boston: Twayne Publishers, 1982.

Higgins, Lois Lundell. *Policewoman's Manual*. 2d ed. Springfield, IL: Charles C Thomas, 1961.

Hobson, Barbara Meil. *Uneasy Virtue: The Politics of Prostitution in the American Reform Tradition*. New York: Basic Books, 1987.

Horne, Peter. *Women in Law Enforcement*. 2d ed. Springfield, IL: Charles C Thomas, 1980.

Hutzel, Eleonore L. *The Policewoman's Handbook*. New York: Columbia University Press, 1933.

Kaledin, Eugenia. *Mothers and More: American Women in the 1950s*. AmericanWomen in the Twentieth Century Series. Boston: Twayne Publishers, 1984.

Kessler-Harris, Alice. *A Woman's Wage: Historical Meanings and Social Consequences*. Lexington: University Press of Kentucky, 1990.

Lemons, J. Stanley. *The Woman Citizen: Social Feminism in the 1920s*. Urbana: University of Illinois Press, 1971.

Levine, Murray and Adeline Levine. *A Social History of Helping Services: Clinic,*

Court, School, and Community. The Century Psychology Series. New York: Appleton-Century-Crofts, 1970.

Lubove, Roy. *The Professional Altruist: The Emergence of Social Work as a Career, 1880-1930.* New York: Antheneum, 1975.

McKelvey, Blake. *American Prisons: A History of Good Intentions.* Montclair, NJ: Patterson Smith, 1977.

Martin, Susan Ehrlich. *Breaking and Entering: Policewomen on Patrol.* Berkeley: University of California Press, 1980.

_____. *Women on the Move? A Report on the Status of Women in Policing.* Washington, DC: Police Foundation, 1989.

Mennel, Robert M. *Thorns and Thistles: Juvenile Delinquents in the United States 1825-1940.* Hanover, NH: University Press of New England, 1973.

Milkman, Ruth. *Gender at Work: The Dynamics of Job Segregation by Sex DuringWorld War II.* Chicago: University of Illinois Press, 1987.

Miller, Wilbur. *Cops and Bobbies: Police Authority in New York and London, 1830-1870.* Chicago: University of Chicago Press, 1977.

Milton, Catherine. *Women in Policing.* Washington, DC: Police Foundation, 1972.

Monkkonen, Eric H. *Police in Urban America, 1860-1920.* Interdisciplinary Perspectives on Modern History. Cambridge, England: Cambridge University Press, 1981.

O'Neill, William L. *Everyone Was Brave: The Rise and Fall of Feminism in America.* Chicago: Quadrangle Books, 1969.

Owings, Chloe. *Women Police: A Study of theDevelopment and Status of the Women Police Movement.* Publication of the Bureau of Social Hygiene. New York: Frederick H. Hitchcock, 1925.

Parker, Alfred E. *The Berkeley Police Story.* Springfield, IL: Charles C Thomas, 1972.

Pivar, David J. *Purity Crusade: Sexual Morality and Social Control, 1868-1900.* Contributions in American History, No. 23. Westport, CT: Greenwood Press, 1973.

Platt, Anthony M. *The Child Savers: The Invention of Delinquency.* 2d ed. Chicago: University of Chicago Press, 1977.

Rafter, Nicole Hahn. *Partial Justice: Women in State Prisons, 1800-1935.* Boston: Northeastern University Press, 1985.

Remmington, Patricia W. *Policing: The Occupation and the Introduction of Female Officers.* Washington, DC: University Press of America, 1981.

Richardson, James F. *Urban Police in the United States.* National University Publications. Port Washington, NY: Kennikat Press, 1974.

Rupp, Leila J. and Verta Taylor. *Survival in The Doldrums: The American Women's Rights Movement, 1945 to the 1960s.* New York: Oxford University Press, 1987.

Scharf, Lois and Joan M. Jensen, eds. *Decades of Discontent:The Women's Movement, 1920-1940.* Contributions in Women's Studies, No. 28. Westport, CT: Greenwood Press, 1983.

Scott, Anne Firor. *Southern Lady: From Pedestal to Politics, 1830-1930.* Chicago: University of Chicago Press, 1970.

Shane, Paul G. *Police and People: A Comparison of Five Countries.* St. Louis, MO: C.V. Mosby Co., 1980.

Sochen, June. *Movers and Shakers: American Women Thinkers and Activists 1900-*

1970. New York: Quadrangle/The New York Times Book Co., 1973.

Sullivan, Mary. *My Double Life: The Story of a New York Policewoman*. New York: Farrar & Rinehart, 1938.

Sulton, Cynthia G. and Roi D. Townsey. *A Progress Report on Women in Policing*. Washington, DC: Police Foundation, 1981.

Symposium About Women in Policing, A., Draft Manual of Symposium, May 28-30, 1974. Washington, DC: Police Foundation, 1974.

Walker, Samuel. *A Critical History of Police Reform: The Emergence of Professionalism*. Lexington, MA: Lexington Books, 1977.

————. *The Police in America: An Introduction*. McGraw-Hill Series in Criminology and Criminal Justice. New York: McGraw-Hill, 1983.

Ware, Susan. *Holding Their Own: American Women in the 1930s*. American Women in the Twentieth Century Series. Boston: Twayne Publishers, 1982.

Wiebe, Robert H. *The Search for Order: 1870-1920*. The Making of America Series. New York: Hill & Wang, 1967.

COLLECTED MATERIALS

International Association of Women Police. Miscellaneous articles, letters, documents, and minutes of board of directors' meetings covering the years 1956-1984. Received from Higgins, Lois Lundell, IAWP president, 1956-1964, and Ostrander, Mary Rita, IAWP president, 1966-1970.

San Francisco Police Museum and Archives. Miscellaneous articles pertaining to women in the Police Department. Received from Fitzer, Robert A., Department Historian.

INTERVIEWS

Blankenship, Betty. Interview with author, Nov. 23, 1994.

Bugajsky, Charles. Interview with author, Mar. 15, 1990.

Higgins, Lois Lundell. Interview with author, Jan. 20, 1990 and Dec. 2, 1994.

Shpritzer, Felicia. Interview with author, Nov. 22, 1991.

DOCUMENTS

Numerous police department annual reports from many cities were reviewed, as were consultant surveys of specific cities, particularly those by Bruce Smith and O.W. Wilson. Those from which material is quoted appear in the notes.

Researchers wanting information on policewomen in a specific city should begin by searching police annual reports and vice or citizen's commission reports, all of which will provide information on when policewomen were hired and at whose urging. Many police annual reports, particularly in smaller cities, may list the names of early policewomen, providing an opportunity to research local directories of prominent women. Once hiring dates are known, newspapers may provide additional information. Also useful would be reports or surveys by local municipal research agencies, institutes of public administration, the Public Administration Service (Chicago), or the Institute of Public Administration (New York).

Citizens' Police Committee, The. *A Reorganization Plan for the Chicago Police Department*. Report No. 4. Chicago: Citizens' Police Committee, 1930.

_____. *Chicago Police Problems*. 1931; Patterson Smith Reprint Series in Criminology, Law Enforcement and Social Problems, No. 89. Montclair, NJ: Patterson Smith, 1969.

Committee on Schools, Fire, Police and Civil Service. *Report to the Chicago City Council on the Question of a Reorganization of the Department of Police*. (Deferred and Published Nov. 25, 1919, pages 2416-2433 of the Journal of the Proceedings of the City Council.) Chicago: Municipal Reference Library, 1912.

Flynn, Edward J.; Holl, W.K., and Earl P. Hartman. *Survey Report of the Metropolitan Police Department Prepared for the Board of Commissioners of the District of Columbia*. Washington, DC: Committee on the District of Columbia, 1955.

Fox, Harry G. *Philadelphia Policewomen—Established 1936*. Philadelphia: Police Department, 1972.

National Advisory Police Committee on Social Protection of the Federal Security Agency. *Techniques of Law Enforcement in the Use of Policewomen with Special Reference to Social Protection*. Washington, DC: Government Printing Office, 1945.

National Commission on the Causes and Prevention of Violence. *Rights in Conflict: The Violent Confrontation of Demonstrators and Police in the Parks and Streets of Chicago during the week of the Democratic National Convention of 1968*. (The Walker Report—A Special Investigative Report) New York: New American Library, 1968.

_____. *To Establish Justice, To Insure Domestic Tranquility*. (Final Report) Washington, DC: Government Printing Office, 1969.

President's Commission on Law Enforcement and Administration of Justice. *Task Force Report: The Police*. Washington, DC: Government Printing Office, 1967.

Rockwood, Edith and Augusta J. Street. *Social Protective Work of Public Agencies: With Special Emphasis on the Policewoman*. Washington, DC: Committee on Social Hygiene-National League of Women Voters, 1932.

Smith, Bruce.   *The New York Police Survey: A Report for the Mayor's Committee on Management Survey*. New York: Institute of Public Administration, 1952.

U.S. Congress. Senate. Committee on the District of Columbia. *Hearing before the Committee on the District of Columbia, U.S. Senate, 69th Congress, First Session on S. 1750: A Bill to Establish a Woman's Bureau in the Metropolitan Police Department of the District of Columbia and for Other Purposes (June 8, 1926)*. Washington, DC: Government Printing Office, 1926.

U.S. Department of Health, Education and Welfare. *Police Service for Juveniles*. Children's Bureau Publication, No. 344. Washington, DC: Government Printing Office, 1954.

U.S. National Commission on Law Observance and Enforcement. (The Wickersham Report) Report No. 14. *Report on Police*. Washington, DC: Government Printing Office, 1931.

Wilson, O.W. *Distribution of Police Patrol Force*. Chicago: Public Administration Service, 1941.

_____. *Report of Police Department Survey, Hartford, Connecticut.* Chicago: Public
Administration Service, 1942.

COURT CASE

Shpritzer v Lang, 32 Misc. 2d 693, 1961, modified and affirmed, 234 NYS 2d 285,
1962.

PROCEEDINGS AND PROGRAMS

Annual proceedings of the International Association of Chiefs of Police (IACP),
the National Conference of Charities and Correction (NCCC), and the National
Conference of Social Work (NCSW) are available in bound volumes. All were
reviewed to gauge interest in policewomen, crime prevention, and juvenile delinquency and related matters. Those from which material is quoted appear in the
notes.

Proceedings of neither the International Association of Policewomen (IAP) nor
the International Association of Women Police (IAWP) are available either in
bound volumes or loose. Material on IAP conference sessions comes from NCCC
or NCSW proceedings, from IAP publications, and from articles in various women's
or police magazines for the 1915-1932 period.

IAWP training conference programs and proceedings are not readily available,
although many are in the possession of the author. Articles in police magazines
may describe conference events. The dates and locations of conferences are
provided in the event local newspaper coverage occurred.

Some of the programs and proceedings of the Women Peace Officers Association of California (WPOAC) are in magazine format and may be available in some
research libraries, particularly within California.

International Association of Women Police. *Official Program*, 1st Biennial Confer-
ence and Seminar, Lafayette, IN, Sept. 30-Oct. 2, 1958; 2d Biennial Semi-
nar, Springfield, MA, Sept. 12-14, 1960; 3d Biennial Seminar, Honolulu,
HA, Aug. 18-22, 1962; 4th Biennial Seminar, Hollywood by the Sea, FL,
Aug. 30-Sept. 4, 1964; 5th Biennial Seminar, Portland, OR, Aug. 21-26,
1966; "Policewomen and the Now Generation," 7th Annual Training
Conference, Madison, WI, Oct. 26-29, 1969; "Women Police Officers in
Modern Law Enforcement," 8th Annual Training Conference, Sault Ste.
Marie, ON, Canada, Oct. 11-17, 1970; 9th Annual Training Conference,
Kansas City, MO, Oct. 24-27, 1971; "New Horizons," 11th Annual Train-
ing Conference, Westbury, NY, Oct. 14-19, 1973; "Sixty Years of Progress,"
13th Annual Training Conference, Baltimore, MD, Oct. 12-17,1975; 14th
Annual Training Conference, Seattle, WA, Oct. 11-14, 1976; 15th Annual
Training Conference, Tucson, AZ, Oct. 17-20, 1977; 16th Annual Training
Conference, Minneapolis, MN, Oct. 8-13, 1978, 17th Annual Training
Conference, South Bend, IN, Oct. 8-12, 1979; 18th Annual Training Con
ference, Albuquerque, NM, Oct. 6-10, 1980; "Women in Law Enforce-
ment: A Turning Point, A New Dimension," 19th Annual
Training Conference, Portland, OR, Sept. 28-Oct. 2, 1981; 20th Annual

Training Conference, Chattanooga, TN, Oct. 3-8, 1982; 21st Annual Training Conference, Vancouver, BC, Canada, Oct. 3-7, 1983; "Polishing the Skills Behind the Badge," 22nd Annual Training Conference, Dearborn, MI, Sept. 17-22, 1984; "Frontier Spirit," 23rd Annual Training Conference, Anchorage, AK, Sept. 16-20, 1985; 24th Annual Training Conference, Denver, CO, Sept. 5-11, 1986; "New Roles, New Responsibilities," 25th Annual Training Conference, New York, NY, Sept. 10- 15, 1987; "Rise to the Challenge!" 26th Annual Training Conference, Atlanta, GA, Sept. 25-30, 1988; "Communicating Beyond Words," 27th Annual Training Conference, San Jose, CA, Sept. 26-30, 1989; "To the Future," 28th Annual Training Conference, St. Paul, MN, Sept. 17-21, 1990; "Evolution of Authority," 29th Annual Training Conference, San Antonio, TX, Sept. 9-13, 1991; "On the Move . . . Meeting the Challenge," 30th Annual Training Conference, Miami, FL, Sept. 20-25, 1992; "Global Policing: A Spirit of Unity," 31st Annual Training Conference, Vancouver, BC, Canada, Oct. 31-Nov. 5, 1993, and "Building Bridges Through New Partnerships," 32nd Annual Training Conference, Pittsburgh, PA, Sept. 10-17, 1994.

Watson, Nelson and Robert N. Walker, eds. *IACP Proceedings of the Workshop for Policewomen. Indiana University, 1966.* Paramus, NJ: National Council on Crime and Delinquency, 1966.

Women Peace Officers Association of California. *Yearbook, 1928-1929; Yearbook and Official Program,* Long Beach, CA, Sept. 22-24, 1930; *Legal Links,* 1931-1932; *Yearbook and Official Program,* Long Beach, CA, Sept. 24-26, 1931; *Convention Program,* Tahoe, CA, Aug. 24-26, 1933; *Convention Program,* Marysville, CA, Oct. 3-5, 1935; *Yearbook and Official Program,* Santa Monica, CA, Oct. 15-17, 1936; *Yearbook and Official Program,* Oakland, CA, Sept. 16-18, 1937; and *Conference Program,* San Diego, CA, May 21-23, 1956.

ARTICLES

Abbott, Edith. "Training for the Policewoman's Job." *The Woman Citizen,* Apr. 1926, 30.

Acerra, Lucy. "From Matron to Commanding Officer: Women's Changing Role in Law Enforcement." In *Law Enforcement Bible,* ed. Robert A. Scanlon, 131-140. South Hackensack, NJ: Stoeger Publishing, 1978.

Additon, Henrietta. "The Prevention of Crime and Delinquency." *Journal of Social Hygiene* 17, no. 4 (Apr.1931): 200-208.

Appier, Janis. "Preventive Justice: The Campaign for Women Police, 1910-1940." *Women & Criminal Justice* 4, no. 1 (1992): 3-36.

Barney, J.K. "Police Matrons." *Lend A Hand,* Aug. 1887, 471-475.

Becke, S.C. "Law Enforcement—The Feminine Angle." *International Journal of Offender Therapy and Comparative Criminology,* 17, no. 2 (1973): 196-201.

Bellairs, K.G. and Norman S. Childs. "The Hundred Per Cent. Police Force of St. Louis, Mo." *The National Police Journal,* Oct. 1919, 3-10+.

Binford, Jessie F. "Policewomen and Women Offenders." *The Police Journal,* Dec. 1927, 14.

"Black Woman Is Named Police Chief in Atlanta." *The New York Times,* Oct. 28, 1994, A28: 4-5.

Blakeslee, Harvey T. "How Portland, Oregon, Is Policed." *The National Police Journal*, Feb. 1920, 3-8+.

Bland, Lucy. "In the Name of Protection: The Policing of Women in the First World War." In *Women in Law: Explorations in Law, Family and Sexuality*, eds. Julia Brophy and Carol Smart, 23-49. Boston: Routledge and Kegan Paul, 1985.

Bowen, Louise de Koven. "Women Police." *The Survey*, Apr.12, 1913, 64-65.

Bowen, Mrs. Joseph T. [Louise de Koven] "The Policeman with a Wink: His Menace to Youth as Shown in the Present Chicago Administration." *The Survey*, Jan. 24, 1920, 458-460.

Bracey, Dorothy. "Women in Criminal Justice: The Decade after the Equal Employment Opportunity Legislation." In *Criminal Justice Administration: Linking Practice and Research*, ed. William A. Jones, Jr., 57-78. Annals of Public Administration Series. New York: Marcel Dekker, 1983.

Breece, Constance M. and Gerald R. Garrett. "Women in Policing: Changing Perspectives on the Role." In *Criminal Justice Planning*, eds. Joseph E. Scott and Simon Dinitz, 3-20. New York: Praeger Publishers, 1977.

Bromley, Dorothy D. "Chloe Owings. The Story of a Girl Who Exchanged her Sunbonnet for the 'Bonnet de Sorbonne'." *The Woman Citizen*, Apr. 1927, 12-13+.

Brown, William P. "Philadelphia's Bureau of Police." *The National Police Journal*, May 1919, 3-10+.

Brownlow, Louis. "The City Manager and the Policewoman." *The Woman Citizen*, Nov. 1925, 30.

————. "The Effectiveness of the Policewoman." *The Police Journal*, Dec. 1928, 19.

Bruere, Henry. "Police as Welfare Workers." *The American City*, Mar. 1914, 282.

Burnham, David. "More Women Joining Police Forces in U.S." *The New York Times*, June 6, 1972, 1:2-5+.

Buwalda, Imra. "Policewomen on the Pacific Coast." *The Police Journal*, Apr. 1927, 5.

————. "The Policewoman—Yesterday, Today and Tomorrow." *Journal of Social Hygiene* 31, no. 5 (May 1945): 290-293.

Cannon, Lucius H. "A Survey of the Salaries of Police and Police Departments." *The American City*, Dec. 1921, 459-462.

Carson, Norma B. "Policewomen Are an Important Factor in Law Enforcement." *FBI Law Enforcement Bulletin*, Oct. 1953, 17-24.

Charles, Michael T. and Kevin Parsons. "Female Performance in the Law Enforcement Function: A Review of Past Research, Current Issues and Future Potential." *Law and Order*, Jan. 1978, 18-22+.

Charlton, Linda. "Capital Policewoman Is Slain on Duty." *The New York Times*, Sept. 21, 1974, 60:2-5.

Chasan, Will. "New York's Finest: Female Division." *The New York Times*, Nov. 20, 1955, Sec. 6, 26+.

Conway, Jill. "Women Reformers and American Culture, 1870-1930." *Journal of Social History* 5, no. 2 (Winter 1971-1972): 164-178.

Cott, Nancy J. "What's in a Name? The Limits of 'Social Feminism'; or, Expanding the Vocabulary of Women's History." *Journal of American History* 76, no. 5 (Dec. 1989): 809-829.

"Courses for Policewomen Executives." *Journal of Social Hygiene* 10, no. 2 (Feb. 1924): 108-109.

Crook, Barbara Hustedt. "Cosmo Talks to Elizabeth Watson: Houston's Pioneering Police Chief." *Cosmopolitan*, Oct. 1990, 116+.

Daly, Kathleen and Meda Chesney-Lind. "Feminism and Criminology." *Justice Quarterly* 5, no. 4 (Dec. 1988):497-535.

Darwin, Maud. "Policewomen: Their Work in America." *The Nineteenth Century*, June 1914, 1371-1377.

Davenport, John C. "Policewomen Serve with Success in LawEnforcement." *FBI Law Enforcement Bulletin*, Aug. 1958, 3-6+.

Davis, J.C. "Woman's Work in a Police Department." *Policewoman's International Bulletin*, June 1929, 9.

Davis, Katharine B. "The Police Woman." *The Woman Citizen*, May 30, 1925, 14.

DePetit, George M. "Policing Youngstown, Ohio." *The National Police Journal*, Feb. 1923, 3-7+.

"Designers Get Down to Work." *Time Magazine*, Jan. 16, 1984, 64-65.

Detzer, Karl. "Detroit's Lady Cops." *The American Mercury*, Mar. 1942, 345-351.

Dilucchio, John A. "In Miami, Females on the Department." *The Police Chief*, Apr. 1975, 56-57.

Dunlap, Nellie H. "Report on Dance Hall Inspection." *The Police Journal*, Oct. 1927, 5+.

Eliot, Thomas D. "Policewomen—A Preventive Agency." *The Woman Citizen*, May 1926, 34.

Evans, G.G. "The Police Force of Seattle, Queen City of the Northwest." *The National Police Journal*, Dec. 1919, 3-9+.

Fagerstrom, Dorothy. "Designed for the Women in Blue." *Law and Order*, Aug. 1958, 60-61.

"First Woman Judge of Juvenile Court." *The Survey*, July 12, 1918, 433.

Flanagan, Maureen A. "Gender and Urban Political Reform: The City Club and the Woman's City Club of Chicago in the Progressive Era." *The American Historical Review* 95, no. 4 (Oct. 1990): 1032-1050.

Freedman, Estelle B. "Separatism as Strategy: Female Institution Building and American Feminism, 1870-1930." *Feminist Studies* 5, no. 3 (Fall 1979): 512-529.

————. "The New Woman: Changing Views of Women in the 1920s." In *Decades of Discontent: The Women's Movement, 1920-1940*, eds. Lois Scharf and Joan M. Jensen, 21-42. Contributions in Women's Studies, No. 28. Westport, CT: Greenwood Press, 1983.

Gainey, Mary C. "The Policewoman and the Moving Picture Manager." *The Police Journal*, July 1926, 24-25.

Garmire, Bernard L. "Female Officers in the Department." In *Police-Community Relations—Selected Readings*, 2d ed., eds. Paul F. Cromwell, Jr. and George Keefer, 393-396. St. Paul, MN: West Publishing, 1978.

Gibbons, Thomas J. "Policewomen Under Cover." *Law and Order*, Sept. 1956, 18-19.

————. Policewoman Awards." *The Police Chief*, Apr. 1960, 35-36.

Gifford, M.A. "Women and the New Order." *The Woman Citizen*, July 1926, 33.

Gilbert, Aletha. "The Duties of a 'City Mother'." *The American City*, Mar. 1922, 239-240.

"Glimpses of LAPD History Reflect The Past . . ." *The Police Chief*, Aug. 1977, 16-17.

Griffin, Harold M. "Madison, Wis., Police Department." *The Police Journal*, Nov. 1927, 6-7+.

Hamilton, Mary E. "The Policewoman's Point of View." *The Police Journal*, Jan. 1924, 8.

_____. "The Policewoman's Point of View." *The Police Journal*, Feb. 1924, 12.

_____. "Woman's Place in the Police Department." *The American City*, Feb. 1925, 194-195.

Harris, Mary B. "The Socialized Policewoman." *The Woman Citizen*, June 27, 1925, 15.

_____. "Policewoman's Organization." *The Police Journal*, Sept. 1925, 14-16.

_____. "Backwaters." *The Woman Citizen*, Nov. 1926, 35.

Hemenway, Raymond B. "The Boston Police Department." *The Police Journal*, Oct. 1926, 3-5+.

Henry, Dorothy D. "Woman's Bureau of Cleveland Department Gives Encouraging Report." *The Police Journal*, Jan. 1926, 5+.

Higgins, Lois Lundell. "Women Police Service." *Journal of Criminal Law, Criminology and Police Science* 41, no. 1 (June 1950): 101-106.

_____. "Historical Background of Policewomen's Service." *Journal of Criminal Law and Criminology* 41, no. 6 (Mar.-Apr. 1951): 822-834.

_____. "Women in Law Enforcement: A Special Survey on Policewomen Throughout the United States." *Law and Order*, Apr. 1958, 22+.

_____. "The Policewoman." *Law and Order*, Nov. 1958, 4.

_____. "The Policewoman." *Police*, Nov.-Dec. 1958, 66-69.

_____. "Golden Anniversary of Women in Police Service." *Law and Order*, Aug. 1960, 4-16.

_____. "Women in Law Enforcement: A Summary of the Functions and Duties of the Policewoman." *Law and Order*, Aug. 1962, 18-22+.

_____. "More About Women in Law Enforcement." IAWP, The Policewomen's Bulletin, *Law and Order*, Sept. 1962, 40-41.

_____. "Pornography and Our Moral Climate." IAWP, The Policewomen's Bulletin, *Law and Order*, Mar. 1964, 30+.

_____. "The Public and Liquor Law Enforcement." IAWP, The Policewomen's Bulletin, *Law and Order*, Apr. 1964, 42+.

"Highlights of the Boston Conference." *The Police Journal*, Feb. 1931, 11+.

"Hire Women as School Guards." *The Police Journal*, Sept.-Oct. 1951, 24.

"Hires Women 'Service Guards'." *The Police Journal*, July-Aug. 1942, 19.

Hodder, Jessie D. "Police—Before or After?" *The Woman Citizen*, Jan. 1926, 30.

Horn, Margo. " 'Gee, Officer Krupke, What Are We To Do?': The Politics of Professions and the Prevention of Delinquency, 1909-1940." In *Research in Law, Deviance and Social Control*, vol. 8, eds. Steven Spitzer and Andrew T. Scull, 57-81. Greenwich, CT: JAI Press, 1986.

"Humanity on the March. Will You March with It?" *The Woman Citizen*, Mar. 27, 1920, 1047.

Humiston, Grace. "The Value of Women as Police Officials." *The National Police Journal*, Jan. 1918, 17-18+.

Hutzel, Eleonore L. "The Policewoman." *The Annals of the American Academy of Police and Social Science* 146 (Nov. 1929): 104-114.

_____. "The Policewoman's Role in Social Protection." *Journal of Social Hygiene* 30, no. 9 (Dec. 1944): 538-544.

_____. "The Policewoman's Role in Social Protection." *The Police Journal*, July-Aug. 1945, 3-4+.

International Association of Policewomen. *Bulletin*, Jan. 1925; Feb. 1925; Mar. 15, 1925; Apr. 1925; May 15, 1925; June 30, 1925; July 31, 1925; Aug. 31, 1925; Sept. 30, 1925; Oct.31, 1925; Nov. 1925; Dec. 1925; Jan. 1926; Feb. 1926.

_____. *Policewoman's International Bulletin*, Aug.-Sept. 1927; Oct. 1927; Nov.-Dec. 1927; Jan. 1928; Feb. 1928; Mar. 1928; July 1928; Aug. 1928; Sept. 1928; Oct. 1928; Jan. 1929; Feb. 1929; Mar. 1929; Apr. 1929; May 1929; June 1929; June 1930; Sept. 1930.

_____. The Policewomen's Bulletin, *Law and Order*, Nov.1960, 25-26; Feb. 1961, 37-38; Mar. 1961, 33-34+; Apr.1961, 35-36; May 1961, 23; June 1961, 71-72+; July 1961, 27-28; Oct. 1961, 21; Jan. 1963, 22; June 1963, 23; July 1963, 62; Oct. 1963, 86; Jan. 1964, 26; Feb. 1964, 62; Sept. 1964, 46; Aug. 1965, 72.

"International Association of Policewomen Meets in Milwaukee." *The National Police Journal*, June 1921, 26+.

Janus, Samuel S., Janus, Cynthia, Lord, Lesli K., and Thomas Power. "Women in Police Work—Annie Oakley or Little Orphan Annie?" *Police Studies* 11, no. 3 (Fall 1988):124-127.

Jensen, Joan M. "All Pink Sisters: The War Department and the Feminist Movement in the 1920s." In *Decades of Discontent: The Women's Movement, 1920-1940*, eds. Lois Scharf and Joan M. Jensen, 199-222. Contributions in Women's Studies, No. 28. Westport, CT: Greenwood Press,1983.

Kegley, Howard C. "The Police Department of Los Angeles." *National Police Magazine*, Jan. 1913, 38-44.

Kelley, Geraldine A. "Policewomen Play Important Role in Philadelphia, Pa." *FBI Law Enforcement Bulletin*, Oct. 1957, 3-7.

Kennard, Caroline A. "Progress in Employment of Police Matrons." *Lend a Hand*, Sept. 1892, 180-184.

Kennedy, Shawn G. "Slain Policewoman Honored in Capital by 2,000 Officers." *The New York Times*, Sept. 25, 1974, 75:3-6.

Kiernan, Michael and Judith Cusick. "Women on Patrol: The Nation's Capital Gives Them High Marks." *Police Magazine*, Prototype Issue (Summer 1977): 45-53.

Klann, Fred. "Police Protection in Moline, Ill." *The National Police Journal*, Nov. 1919, 13+.

Kluchesky, Joseph. "Policewomen." *The American City*, July 1937, 17.

Koelker, E.S. "Policewomen." *The Municipality*, Jan. 1916, 31-34.

Koenig, Esther J. "An Overview of Attitudes Toward Women in Law Enforcement." *Public Administration Review* 38, no.3 (May/June 1978): 267-275.

Kuykendall, Jack L. and Armand P. Hernandez. "Undergraduate Justice System Education and Training at San Jose State University: An Historical Perspective." *Journal of Criminal Justice* 3, no. 2 (Summer 1975): 111-130.

Lane, Winthrop D. "Girls and Khaki: Some Practical Measures of Protection for Young Women in Time of War." *The Survey*, Dec. 1, 1917, 236-240.

Law and Order, Oct. 1957, 17; Mar. 1958, 57; Mar. 1966, 80; June 1968, 108.

Lawder, Lee E. "Women School Crossing Guards." *Law and Order,* Oct. 1957, 8-9.

Leevy, J. Roy. "The Role of the Police Matron." *Journal of Criminal Law and Criminology* 39, no. 4 (Nov.-Dec. 1948):538-540.

Leuck, Miriam Simon. "Women in Odd and Unusual Fields of Work." *The Annals of the American Academy of Political and Social Science* 143 (May 1929): 166-179.

Lewis, Barbara. "Women Behind the Badge." *Police Product News*, Sept. 1983, 32-34.

Linn, Edith and Barbara Raffel Price. "The Evolving Role of Women in American Policing." In *The Ambivalent Force: Perspectives on the Police*, 3d ed., eds. Abraham S. Blumberg and Elaine Niederhoffer, 69-80. New York: Holt, Rinehart & Winston, 1985.

Lossing, Elizabeth. "First Kindred Group Meeting of Policewomen of the Pacific Coast: Pacific States Conference of Social Work, Yosemite Valley, May 21-26, 1928." *Policewoman's International Bulletin*, Aug. 1928, 2, 7.

_____. "Juvenile Delinquency." *The Police Journal*, (Part I) July-Aug. 1946, 7-8+; (Part II) Sept.-Oct. 1946, 5-6+.

MacGill, Helen Gregory. "A Woman Delinquent." *The Police Journal*, Jan. 1931, 25.

McBride, S. Lee. "Pittsburgh's Efficient Police Organization." *The Police Journal*, Mar. 1923, 3-11+.

Madden, Lillian. "The Modern Policewoman's Work." *The Police Journal*, Apr. 1924, 14-15+.

Marden, Leo W. "Policewomen and Policemen as Co-Workers." *The Police Journal*, Oct. 1926, 12.

Marshall, Sabina. "Development of the Policewomen's Movement in Cleveland." *Journal of Social Hygiene* 11, no. 4 (Apr. 1925): 193-210.

Melchionne, Theresa M. "Where Policewomen are Better Than Men." *The American City*, Apr. 1960, 161.

_____. "The Role of the Policewoman in Working With Youth '. . . The Bridge Between . . .'." *Law and Order*, July 1961, 61-64+.

_____. "The Current Status and Problems of Women Police." *Journal of Criminal Law, Criminology and Police Science* 58, no. 2 (June 1967): 257-260.

_____. "The Changing Role of Policewomen." In *The Ambivalent Force: Perspectives on the Police*, 2d ed., eds. Arthur Niederhoffer and Abraham S. Blumberg, 366-377. Hinsdale, IL: Dryden Press, 1976.

"Memphis and Her New Judge." *The Survey*, May 22, 1920, 285-286.

Milliken, Rhoda J. "The Role of the Policewoman's Bureau in Combatting Prostitution." *Federal Probation*, Apr.-June 1943, 20-22.

"More Cities Employ Policewomen." *The American City*, Feb. 1948, 17.

"More Cities Employ Policewomen." *The Police Journal*, May-June 1948, 14.

"More Cities Hire Negro Policemen." *The Police Journal*, July-Aug. 1947, 13.

More, Ellen S. "'A Certain Restless Ambition': Women Physicians and World War I." *American Quarterly* 41, no. 4 (Dec. 1989): 636-660.

Moss, Margaret. "If I Were a Policewoman." *The Woman Citizen*, Oct. 1925, 30.

Munger, Elizabeth. "Policewomen for Smaller Cities." *The Woman Citizen*, July 11, 1925, 15.

Municipal Administration Service. "Policemen's Salaries, Hours, Etc., in 49 Cities." *The American City*, Apr. 1930, 108-109.

Murray, Virginia M. "Policewomen in Detroit." *The American City*, Sept. 1921, 209-210.

"National Advisory Police Committee on Social Protection Formed." *Journal of Social Hygiene* 28, no. 6 (June 1942): 430-431.

Naughton, William B. "Policing the Second City of the United States." *The National Police Journal*, Aug. 1920, 3-8.

"New Orleans Has Women Traffic Cops." *The Police Journal*, May-June 1952, 24.

O'Block, Robert L. and Vicki L. Abele. "The Emerging Role of the Female Detective." *The Police Chief*, May 1980, 54-55.

Official Magazine. Chicago Patrolmen's Association, Dec.-Jan. 1956, 33; Apr.-May 1956, 39; June-July 1956, cover, 3, 49; Feb.-Mar. 1957, 37.

O'Grady, Ellen A. "Policewomen and Their Work." *The American City*, Jan. 1919, 59-60.

O'Hara, Ralph. "History of Portland, Oregon, Law Enforcemen Functions." *The Police Chief*, Oct. 1988, 134-13

Owens, James M. "Women in Law Enforcement: A Special Survey on Policewomen Throughout the United States." *Law and Order*, Apr. 1958, 22-24+.

_____. "Policewoman in the Line." *Police*, Sept.-Oct. 1958, 21-22.

Parker, Valeria H. "A Policewoman's Life." *The Woman Citizen*, June 28, 1924, 16-17.

Payne, Dorothy E. "A New Dimension in Police Science." IAWP, The Policewomen's Bulletin, *Law and Order*, May 1963, 42-43.

"Peace Through Law: Theme of Fourth Biennial Seminar Conference," IAWP, The Policewomen's Bulletin, *Law and Order*, June 1964, 52.

Perlstein, Gary R. "Female Police: The Need for Research." *Police*, Sept.-Oct. 1970, 62-63.

"Philadelphia Consents to Placing of Women in Thirty Percent of Police Jobs." *The New York Times*, July 16, 1980, 19:1-2.

"Philadelphia Police Ordered to Give Women Twenty-five Percent of Jobs." *The New York Times*, Sept. 6, 1979, 16:5.

Phillips, Wayne. "Detective Story, Female Department." *The New York Times Magazine* (sec. 6), Feb. 28, 1960, 48-59

Pigeon, Helen D. "From the Diary of a Policewoman." *The Woman Citizen*, Dec. 1925, 32.

_____. "Senate Bill 1750." *The Woman Citizen*, Feb. 1926, 30.

_____. "From the Diary of a Policewoman—II." *The Woman Citizen*, June 1926, 32.

_____. "The Policewomen in Conference." *The Police Journal*, Aug. 1926, 17-18.

_____. "The Policewoman's Due." *The Woman Citizen*, Aug. 1926, 33.

_____. "The Policewoman's Councilors." *The Woman Citizen*, Dec. 1926, 34.

_____. "Annual Conference of Policewomen." *The Police Journal*, Mar. 1927, 5.

_____. "How Berkeley Helps Its Policewoman." *The Police Journal*, May 1927, 5.

_____. "One Thousand Sponsors." *The Woman Citizen*, May 1927, 34.

_____. "The Policewomen Meet in Conference." *The Police Journal*, June 1927, 14-15.

_____. "Policewomen in the United States." *Journal of Criminal Law and Criminology* 18, no. 3 (Nov. 1927): 372-377.

_____. "Crime Prevention by Policewomen." *Policewoman's International Bulletin*, Jan. 1929, 2-3+.

_____. "Woman's Era in the Police Department." *The Annals of the American Academy of Political and Social Science* 143 (May 1929): 249-254.

_____. "Policewomen." *Social Work Yearbook 1933*, 360-362.

"Pittsburgh Trains Women as Auxiliary Police Aides." *Federal Probation*, Apr.-June 1943, 54.

Platt, Anthony M. "The Triumph of Benevolence: The Origins of the Juvenile Justice System in the United States." In *Law and Order in American History*, ed. Joseph M. Hawes, 53-76. Port Washington, NY: Kennikat Press, 1979.

Pogrebin, Mark. "The Changing Role of Women: Female Police Officers' Occupational Problems." *Police Journal*, Apr. 1986, 127-133.

"Police Force in Philadelphia Gets First Female District Commander." *The New York Times*, Dec. 24, 1980, 10:5-6.

"Police Functions Best Performed by Men and by Women Police Officers." *The Police Journal*, Apr. 1929, 20+.

"Police Matron." *The Chief*. (New York: Chief Publishing Co., 1908), 1-7.

"Police Matrons." *Harper's Weekly*, Aug. 30, 1890, 675.

"Police Promotions Anger Black Group in Philadelphia." *The New York Times*, Dec. 16, 1980, 16:5-6.

"Police-Woman's Record in Topeka, A." *The Survey*, Sept. 25, 1915, 571.

"Policewomen and Firearms." (Editorial) *Law and Order*, Sept. 1965, 80.

"Policewomen in Chicago." *The Literary Digest*, Aug. 23, 1913, 271.

"Policewomen Ranks Grow as Men Leave." *The Police Journal*, July-Aug. 1943, 16.

"Policewomen's Bureau Is Functioning Most Satisfactorily." *Police Journal* (St. Louis, MO), Jan. 24, 1923, 1+.

Potts, Lee. "Equal Employment Opportunity and Female Criminal Justice Employment." *Police Studies* 4, no. 3 (Fall 1981): 9-19.

Powers, Matthew T. "Employment Motivations for Women in Policing." *The Police Chief*, Nov. 1983, 60-63.

Price, Barbara Raffel. "A Study of Leadership Strength of Female Police Executives." *Journal of Police Science and Administration* 2, no. 2 (June 1974): 219-226.

Price, Barbara Raffel and Susan Gavin. "A Century of Women in Policing." In *Modern Police Administration*, ed. Donald O. Schultz, 109-122. Houston: Gulf Publishing, 1979.

"Program of Vocational Training for Directors of Policewomen Units, A." *Journal of Social Hygiene* 10, no. 3 (Mar. 1924): 178-184.

Pullman, Raymond W. "Police and the Public Health." *Social Hygiene* 5, no. 3 (July 1919): 311-316.

Racine, R.P. "The Norfolk (Va.) Police Division Youth Bureau." *Law and Order*, Sept. 1959, 53-54+.

Randall, Martha. "The Curfew in Portland." *The Woman Citizen*, Jan. 1927, 34.

Rappaport, Mazie. "A Protective Service for Promiscuous Girls." *Federal Probation*, Jan.-Mar. 1945, 33-36

Reavis, J.E. "The Police Department of Portland, Oregon." *National Police Maga-*

zine, Apr. 1913, 87-95.

"Records Are Essential in Policewomen's Work." *The American City*, July 1946, 17.

"Report of the Eleventh Annual Conference of the International Association of Policewomen, Denver, Col." *The Police Journal*, Aug. 1925, 23+.

"Report on the Fourth Biennial Seminar Conference, A." IAWP, The Policewomen's Bulletin, *Law and Order*, Nov. 1964, 54.

"Rights fight takes cop to top." *USA Today*, Jan. 24, 1984, n.p.

Rink, S.E. "'Arresting Females': The Policewoman's Story." *Law and Order*, Nov. 1953, 6-7.

Rippin, Jane Deeter. "Social Hygiene and the War—Work with Women and Girls." *Social Hygiene* 5, no. 1 (Jan. 1919):125-136.

Roberts, Albert R. "Police Social Workers: A History." *Social Work* 21, no. 4 (July 1976): 294-299.

Rocco, Therese L. "Service with Compassion." *FBI Law Enforcement Bulletin*, Jan. 1969, 12-15+.

Roszelle, Mabel. "Why the Curfew Ordinance." *The Police Journal*, Feb. 1927, 62, 64.

Sawyer, Ruth. "Policewomen for University Towns." *The Woman Citizen*, Mar. 22, 1924, 15+.

Schlossman, Steven and Stephanie Wallach. "The Crime of Precocious Sexuality: Female Juvenile Delinquency and the Progressive Era." *Harvard Education Review* 48, no. 1 (Feb. 1978): 65-94.

Schweir, Mabel Bray. "Supervising Public Dances." *The Police Journal*, Dec. 1926, 9+.

Seligson, Tom. "Can Women Cut It as Cops?" *Parade*, Mar. 31, 1989, 4-7.

Sherman, Lewis J. "A Psychological View of Women in Policing." *Journal of Police Science and Administration* 1, no. 4 (Dec. 1973): 383-394.

_____. "An Evaluation of Policewomen on Patrol in a Suburban Police Department." *Journal of Police Science and Administration* 13, no. 4 (Dec. 1975): 434-448.

Shpritzer, Felicia. "A Case for the Promotion of Policewomen in the City of New York." *Journal of Criminal Law, Criminology and Police Science* 50, no. 4 (Nov.-Dec. 1959): 415-419.

"Sixteen Policewomen Called Indispensable." *Police Journal* (St. Louis, MO), July 11, 1923, 8-9.

"Slain Policewoman Seen Aid to Hiring of Female Officers." *The New York Times*, Dec. 15, 1974, 83:5.

Smith, Allen W. "The Police of Passaic, New Jersey." *The Police Journal*, May-June 1924, 2-4.

Smith, Clarence B.J. "The True Sphere of Policewomen." *The Police Journal*, Apr. 1922, 19+.

Smith, Geddes. "Petersburg, Plus." *The Survey*, July 1, 1924, 406-409+.

Sorahgan, Joseph P. "St. Louis Police Department Now One of the Most Efficient in the U.S." *The Police Journal*, Mar.-Apr. 1949, 5-6+.

Steele, Valerie. "Dressing for Work." In *Men and Women: Dressing the Part*, eds. Claudia Brush Kidwell and Valerie Steele, 69-91, 165-167. Washington, DC: Smithsonian Institution Press, 1989.

Stricker, Frank. "Cookbooks and Law Books: The Hidden History of Career Women in Twentieth-Century America." In *A Heritage of Her Own: Toward A New Social History of American Women*, eds. Nancy F. Cott and Elizabeth H. Plack, 476-498. New York: Simon & Schuster, 1979.

Stuart, Cynthia Gould. "Changing Status of Women in Police Professions." *The Police Chief*, Apr. 1975, 61-62.

Stuart, Reginald. "690 Police Officers Laid Off by Detroit." *The New York Times*, Sept. 7, 1980, 1:2.

"Study of Protective Measures in the City of Boston, A." *Journal of Social Hygiene* 28, no. 6 (June 1942): 403-418.

Sullivan, Mary. "Activities of the New York Policewoman." *The Police Journal*, Jan. 1927, 33+.

_____. "The Functions of Police-Women." *The Police Journal*, Jan. 1932, 11+.

Suro, Roberto. "Houston Mayor Removes Female Police Chief." *The New York Times*, Feb. 18, 1992, A20:1-6.

Tenney, Evabel. "Women's Work in Law Enforcement." *Journal of Criminal Law, Criminology and Police Science* 44, no.2 (July-Aug. 1953): 239-246.

"The Crime Prevention Bureau." (Interview with Virginia Murray) *The Police Journal*, May 1930, 8+.

"The Houston Police Department: A Look at the Past, A Glimpse of the Future." *The Police Chief*, Sept. 1985, 18-19.

The National Police Journal, Jan. 1918, 16; June 1918, 10-11+; Aug. 1918, 16; Sept. 1918, 12; Nov. 1918, 12; Jan. 1919, 13; Jan. 1919, 12; Feb. 1919, 16; Apr. 1919, 19; July 1919, 22, 35; Sept. 1919, 24; Oct. 1919, 3-10+, 30; Nov. 1919, 3-5+; Jan. 1920, 47; Feb. 1920, 17; June 1920, 32; July 1920, 17; Aug. 1920, 14-16+; Sept. 1920, 24, 25; Oct.-Nov. 1920, 23+, 28; Dec. 1920, 3-8; Apr. 1921, 3-5+, 10-11+; May 1921, 30; May 1921, 8; June 1921, 28; Aug. 1921, 3-9+; Nov. 1921, 27.

The Police Journal, Apr. 1925, 35; Feb. 1926, 24; Apr. 1928,19; Apr. 1929, 20+; June 1931, 4; July 1931, 17+; June 1932, 1.

"The Police-Woman Is Marching On." *The American City*, Nov. 1913, 403.

"The Policewomen of Indianapolis and Their New Methods." *Literary Digest* 69 (Apr. 23, 1921): 41-43.

"The 'Sesqui' Policewomen." *The Woman Citizen*, Feb. 1927, 34.

The Survey, Apr. 24, 1915, 95; July 10, 1915, 346; June 30, 1917, 298; Jan. 26, 1918, 474; June 15, 1918, 306; Mar. 22, 1919, 911; Apr. 26, 1919, 160.

Topping, Ruth. "Counselors-at-Large." *The Woman Citizen*, Apr. 1927, 34.

Townsey, Roi D. "Female Patrol Officers: A Review of the Physical Capability Issue." In *The Criminal Justice System and Women: Offenders-Victims-Workers*, eds. Barbara R. Price and Natalie J. Sokoloff, 413-425. New York: Clark Boardman & Co., 1982.

"Trail blazer." *Law Enforcement News*, Nov. 30, 1994.

Turner, Wallace. "Under Fire, Woman Quit as Portland Police Chief," *The New York Times*, June 3, 1986, A16:1-5.

Valz, Fred M. "Policewomen Fill Long Felt Need in Jacksonville, Fla." *The Police Journal*, Aug. 1927, 14+.

_____. "Jacksonville Women's Bureau Latest in Field Reports Progress." *Policewoman's International Bulletin*, Aug.-Sept. 1927, 3.

Van Waters, Miriam. "Your Town and the Delinquent Child: A Program for the

Adjustment of Delinquency in the Average Community." *The Survey*, Sept. 15, 1924, 609-611.

Van Winkle, Mina C. "Policewomen—Their Duties and Opportunities." *The National Police Journal*, Aug. 1921, 14-15+.

————. "The Policewoman." *The Survey*, Sept. 15, 1924, 629-631.

————. "Socializing the Police." *The Woman Citizen*, June 13, 1925, 14.

————. "Policewomen in Conference." *The Woman Citizen*, Aug. 8, 1925, 15.

Vollmer, August. "The Policewoman and Pre-Delinquency." *The Woman Citizen*, Mar. 1926, 30.

————. "Meet the Lady Cop." *The Survey*, Mar. 15, 1930, 702-703.

————. "Police Progress in the Past Twenty-five Years." *Journal of Criminal Law, Criminology and Police Science* 24, no. 1 (May-June 1933): 161-175.

Walbrook, H.M. "Women Police and Their Work." *The Nineteenth Century*, Feb. 1919, 377-382.

Walker, Samuel. "The Rise and Fall of the Policewomen's Movement, 1905-1975." In *Law and Order in American History*, ed. Joseph M. Hawes, 101-111. Port Washington, NY: Kennikat Press, 1979.

Walkowitz, Daniel J. "The Making of a Feminine Professional Identity: Social Workers in the 1920s." *American Historical Review* 95, no. 4 (Oct. 1990): 1051-1075.

Walz, Marguerite. "Police Woman Talks on Dancing." *The Police Journal*, Dec. 1923, 29+.

Weatherly, Eugene T. "Local Control of Prostitution in Wartime." *Journal of Social Hygiene* 28, no. 6 (June 1942): 383-388.

Wells, Alice Stebbins. "Women on the Police Force." *The American City*, Apr. 1913, 401.

————. "Policewomen." (Letter to the Editor) *The Survey*, May 16, 1914, 207-208.

————. "Policewoman Badge Number One." IAWP, The Policewomen's Bulletin, *Law and Order*, Jan. 1961, 75-76. Reprint, Los Angles Police Association *Bulletin*, Oct.-Nov. 1940.

Wills, Dorothy E. "Pittsburgh Women Traffic Officers Safeguard School Children." *The American City*, Aug. 1947, 19.

Wilson, Nanci Koser. "Feminist Pedagogy in Criminology." *Journal of Criminal Justice Education* 2, no. 1 (Spring 1991): 81-93.

Winter, Alice Ames. "The Policewoman of Policewomen." *Ladies Home Journal*, July 1927, 27, 62.

Wheeler, Harry M. "Decatur, Illinois, Efficient Police Department." *The Police Journal*, Aug. 1927, 10-11+.

The Woman Citizen, Aug. 4, 1917, 166; Sept. 22, 1917, 309; Nov. 3, 1917, 439; Feb. 23, 1918, 248, 257; June 22, 1918, 77; Nov. 9, 1918, 496; Dec. 14, 1918, 598; Dec. 21, 1918; 611; Apr. 26, 1919, 1015; May 3, 1919, 1055; Sept. 13, 1919, 381; Jan. 3, 1920, 664; Apr. 23, 1921 1197; July 2, 1921, 25.

"Woman to Be Police Chief." *The New York Times*, Oct. 27,1994: A24:1.

Woman's Bureau, Metropolitan PD, Washington, DC. "Policewomen Reporting a Year's Work." *The Police Journal*, Nov. 1925, 30-33.

"Woman's Police Bureau, A." *The Woman Citizen*, Sept. 6, 1919, 336.

"Women on Police Forces." *The Woman Worker*, May 1942, 16.

"Women Tough Traffic Police." *The Police Journal*, Jan.-Feb.-Mar. 1955, 24.

Index

About the Author

DOROTHY MOSES SCHULZ is currently an Assistant Professor at John Jay College of Criminal Justice. Formerly a captain with the Metro-North Police Department, she received her Ph.D. in American Civilization from New York University.

ISBN 0-275-94996-6

HARDCOVER BAR CODE